How to rebu̶i̶l̶d̶
SMALL-BLOC̶K̶

By David Vizard

INTRODUCTION 2
1 INSPECTION 3
2 SMALL-BLOCK FACTS & FIGURES 12
3 TOOLS & MACHINISTS 22
4 ENGINE REMOVAL PROCEDURE 24
5 DISASSEMBLY 31
6 RECONDITIONING PARTS 45
7 THE REBUILD 76
8 REPLACING THE ENGINE 160
9 BREAKING IN 164

Library of Congress Cataloging-in-Publication Data
Vizard, David.
    How to rebuild your small-block Chevy; how to find out what needs fixing, how to remove engine, strip & inspect for wear, repair and recondition, assemble, install, and tune up / by David Vizard.
    p. cm.
    Includes index.
    ISBN 1-55788-029-8
1. Automobiles Motors Maintenance and repair. 2. Chevrolet automobile. I. Title.
TL210.V57   629.2'50I'028   78-52775
                                                                MARC
Library of Congress   79

This book is printed on acid-free paper.
Cover photos by Michael Lutfy. Interior photos by David Vizard unless otherwise noted.

NOTICE: The information contained in this book is true and complete to the best of our knowledge. All recommendations on parts and procedures are made without any guarantees on the part of the author or the publisher. Author and publisher disclaim all liability incurred in connection with use of this information. Parts and procedures, especially those that affect emission control devices, may not be legal for sales or use.

The cooperation of the Chevrolet Division of General Motors is gratefully acknowledged. However, this publication is a wholly independent production of HPBooks.

HPBooks
are published by The Berkley Publishing Group,
200 Madison Avenue, New York, New York 10016.
© 1991, 1978 Price Stern Sloan, Inc.
Printed in U.S.A.   Revised Edition

15   14   13   12   11

INTRODUCTION

After many years these two fine Chevys are still going strong. The '57 Nomad station wagon is fuel-injected, which makes it a rare example of its type. Photos courtesy Bob Wingate Chevrolet.

When Chevrolet introduced their small-block V-8 engine in 1955, it set new standards of performance. It quickly brought about the demise of ohv sixes and the side-valve V-8s.

That was only part of the story. Although the small-block Chevy design was not revolutionary in itself, it had one strong point. It made the very best use of all the previously tried and tested techniques of engine production. From the point of view of power, economy and reliability, there's no question that the small-block Chevy is one of the best production engines in automotive history.

As a result of its successful application in a wide range of vehicles, there are a large number of these engines available today. There have been literally millions of small-block Chevy engines produced since its introduction. In fact, more small-block Chevy engines have been built than any other type of engine. But like any power-

plant, it will eventually wear out. This doesn't mean it is scrap—far from it! With some new engines costing close to $4000, an overhaul of a used engine, which can cost less than $1000 if done right, makes good dollars and *sense*!

Throughout the years, the engine has seen many changes—both major and minor. Though the engine itself is simple in design, the number of differences and combinations which have appeared cloud the issue. The endless variations can confuse even the most astute Chevy enthusiast. However, once you determine which parts can be interchanged for others among the various sized engines available, the cost of doing a rebuild becomes less. You also need to become adept with basic mechanical procedures. These factors will help you decide the best course to take on your rebuild to suit your driving and financial needs.

Another influencing factor is in the spare parts situation. Should you use

only genuine GM parts, or will any of the independent parts manufacturers give as good, or better, value? If you're doing a Concourse-quality restoration, then you will need to stay with factory parts. However, if you're just rebuilding, then you have the option of shopping around.

The information in this book is based on my decades of engine-building experience, plus that of many true experts in the field. This book should give you the ability to restore your engine to "as good as new" for a fraction of the cost of a new engine. Even if you've never rebuilt an engine before, the simple steps that follow should lead you through the process without getting you into trouble. Basically, the only rule you need to follow is; "When in doubt, play it safe." Remember, it is better to do the job a little too well than not well enough. With that little bit of advice in mind, let's proceed.

1955 265 CID Chevy is easily distinguished by the tall oil-bath air filter. In the late '50s lower hood lines forced the adoption of flatter filters.

At some point, you will have to decide whether or not your engine needs to be overhauled. Sometimes it is plainly obvious; other times it isn't. Don't make the mistake of thinking your engine needs an extensive overhaul just because it has run a great many miles. At the same time, don't assume that a low-mileage engine can't possibly need an overhaul. A number of factors dictate the condition the engine can be in. The first one is the frequency at which the engine was serviced. Secondly, like the chain whose strength is only that of the weakest link, engine reliability is only as good as its least reliable part. On an engine which has been in production as long as the small-block Chevy, most parts-breakage problems have been eliminated by Chevrolet — unless the motor has been over-revved. This leaves *wear* as the major enemy. The fastest wearing part is the weakest link.

HOW MUCH OIL IS IT BURNING?

I will assume you have an engine you are not sure needs rebuilding. I have already stated that wear is an engine's worst enemy. As certain parts wear, oil consumption increases. Your first task is to determine the amount of oil consumed, excluding any lost due to leakage. If the engine is consuming one quart of oil for every 500 miles, then something is not right. Generally speaking, the oil is used because it gets past rings and down valve guides and ends up either in the combustion chamber or exhaust port where it is burned. If nothing is broken then usually about 40-50 percent of the oil consumed is going past worn valve guides. The rest is going past the piston rings. With some engines other things occur and you could have a curable complaint without resorting to a complete rebuild.

HOW IS IT PERFORMING?

Apart from the oil-consumption factor, many use the car's performance as an indication of whether or not the car needs to be fixed. This is not as good a guide as you might think. If the engine is performing badly and it is not using oil, chances are it needs a tune-up and/or decarbonizing job (internal carbon build-up removed). There are exceptions. The compression rings may be worn, or the oil-control rings may be worn to the point of losing control. That's the first possibility. The second one involves one of the few weak points of the small-block Chevy; the camshaft lobes and lifters (tappets) have a tendency to wear drastically, leading to reduced valve lift. As a result, performance falls off and valve train noise may drastically increase.

Having discussed possibilities, let's look at ways to check what needs to be done. To do so you will need a compression gauge, a dial indicator gauge and a few wrenches.

I'll first discuss the case where you have the toughest decision to make. Oil consumption is average — around 1000 miles to the quart — but performance is bad. First remove all the spark plugs and inspect them. Chances are they are long overdue for replacement. Few people remember to replace plugs at the correct

An oil-fouled plug indicates piston ring or valve guide wear or combination of both. Photo courtesy Champion Spark Plugs.

intervals but at this point that's not the principal thing you are looking for.

It's possible to have one or two cylinders starting to burn oil so the oil-burning situation isn't bad *yet* but it could be in the near future. When a cylinder starts burning oil, it will inevitably affect the condition of the spark plug by giving it an oily appearance around the edge. As the situation deteriorates, the center electrode begins to look oily too. Unless the engine has an electronic ignition, the oily center electrode usually means a misfire which rarely clears itself. If one or two cylinders are oiling, the rest may be about to do the same. Or, the rings in the oily cylinders may be stuck or broken. If none of the plugs are oily, then your engine

A compression test gives a good indication of a cylinder's sealing ability. Low pressures can be due to worn rings or valves not seating (sealing).

may just need a tune-up or decarbonizing.

Check the Compression—At this point you need a compression gauge to determine the engine's condition. Doing a compression check requires a helper.

Warm up the engine so the automatic choke is in the open position, then remove all the spark plugs and central coil wire. Insert the compression gauge into the spark-plug hole of the cylinder you want to check. Have your helper *depress the throttle pedal and hold it to the floor,* then have him crank the motor over. Note the gauge reading and write down the figure. Do this for each cylinder as you will need these figures for comparison purposes. If your piston rings and valves are doing their job, you should see cylinder pressures in the region of 105–120 psi for 8/1 compression-ratio (CR) engines. 120–135 for 9/1 and 140 or so for engines with around 10/1 CR. Engines with high-performance cams will usually show 10 to 15 psi *less* than engines with ordinary cams. Pressure readings more than 30–35 psi below these figures mean your rings or valves—or both—may be tired or sick.

There are a few things you should know about compression tests before you make a decision based on any readings you may have. Although I have quoted compression readings to give you a guide, this is sticking my neck out. Let me explain: so many things influence the compression readings, that at best you should use these figures as a rough guide. There are numerous variables not only within the engine, but also externally affecting any compression readings you may take. For instance: due to manufacturing tolerances, compression ratios may vary. You may think you have an 8/1 engine but in fact it could easily be 7.5, which is often the case. Or, on more rare occasions, it could be 8.5. That's a whole ratio between the two extremes. Such a difference could make 12–15 psi difference on two

otherwise identical engines.

At the other end of the scale, I have seen stock, high-performance, small-block Chevys run cylinder pressures of 185–190 on a supposed 10.5/1 compression ratio, and a high-performance cam. A virtually identical engine checked sometime later barely made 140 psi. Incidentally, both engines appeared to be in perfect order. What could cause such a big discrepancy? Apart from internal differences caused through production tolerances, the external variables include:
1. Engine temperature at time of test.
2. Ambient (prevailing) temperature at time of test.
3. Atmospheric pressure, due to altitude above sea level or normal barometric changes due to weather.
4. Humidity.
5. Cranking speed of starter motor, also affected by battery voltage.

Analyzing these variables, the first two are the most important. The bigger the difference between the ambient air temperature and the engine temperature, the more cylinder pressure you will see during a test. This may lead you to question the sense of warming the engine prior to performing the test. The reason for having the engine warm and for having the plugs removed is to achieve a higher cranking speed. This leads to more consistent results so far as the readings are concerned. Because the cranking speed of the engine is a factor, battery condition is also important. Don't perform any tests with a battery which is run down. Unless it cranks the motor over at a speed well above the normal cranking speed you'd see with the plugs installed, you may find your tests won't tell you much.

Lastly let's look at the atmospheric conditions. Humidity is a small factor which can be neglected. Barometric pressure and altitude cannot. For every 0.3 of an inch of mercury pressure (barometric pressure) above 30 inches, subtract 1% from your readings, and for every 0.3 of an inch below, add 1%.

How to remove the heads for decarbonizing (which ordinarily includes a valve job):

1. Open hood. If coolant includes antifreeze, drain it into a suitable container for re-use.

2. Disconnect cable from battery negative (−) terminal. Use a puller if terminal is corroded. Cover battery with a cloth to prevent accidentally shorting out the terminals.

3. Note the connections of all emission vacuum lines and other emission equipment you may find necessary to remove. Tag these lines so you will know where to reinstall them. This is important, so don't skip it.

4. Remove fan belt by loosening the belt tensioning bolt on the alternator and lifting the belt out of its pulley groove. Undo the alternator mounting bolts and remove the alternator. Don't disconnect the alternator wires, just lay alternator out of the way to one side.

5. If you have a head or manifold-mounted air-conditioning pump, loosen and remove the belt. Undo bolts securing pump and lay pump to one side. *Do not* disconnect pump lines.

6. Remove top hose from thermostat housing on intake manifold.

7. Remove distributor cap and spark-plug leads from the engine. On some installations it is difficult to remove the plug wires so take off the distributor cap and tie it back to the firewall out of the way.

8. Undo exhaust-manifold securing bolts and lever manifolds free from heads.

9. Disconnect any distributor wires and remove distributor after undoing clamp under distributor body.

10. Remove any heater hoses from intake manifold.

11. Remove fuel lines from carburetor.

12. Disconnect carburetor linkage. Sometimes it is easier to remove carburetor linkage bracket from manifold.

13. Disconnect temperature-sender wires from intake manifold. Undo intake-manifold securing bolts and remove manifold.

14. Remove rocker covers.

15. Undo 17 head bolts from each head. With the exception of a short bolt at each end of the head, remove the head bolts. Leave the two remaining bolts with only 2 or 3 threads engaged in the block.

16. Place a bar into an intake port and lift to break the gasket seal. With the head levered up, turn the rockers 45° to disengage them from the pushrods.

17. Remove pushrods and push them through a piece of cardboard. Number each pushrod so it can be returned to its original place when assembly time comes.

18. Remove two short bolts from each head and lift heads off their block-locating dowels.

19. To strip and rebuild heads, refer to Chapter 6 headings Cylinder Heads through to Pushrods and Chapter 7 Cylinder Head Assembly.

20. Decarbonize the heads as you clean and overhaul them. The piston crowns must also be decarbonized. To prevent particles of carbon going into lifter valley, cover this area with a cloth.

21. Turn crankshaft to bring each piston in turn to top dead center. Scrape the piston crown to remove the carbon build-up. A blunt screwdriver is fine for the job. Rather than trying to blow or brush the carbon particles from the piston crown, use a vacuum cleaner to suck them up. This method means a minimum of carbon will find its way down the sides of the piston to the top ring.

22. Use a screwdriver or scraper, a wire brush and a vacuum cleaner to remove any old gasket material from the gasket faces of the block and intake manifold. Take care to keep this debris out of the lifter valley.

ASSEMBLY PROCEDURE

Install *cleaned* or overhauled parts in the reverse order of stripdown. Use composition-type head gaskets, not the steel-shim type. You will get all the gaskets required in a *valve grind gasket set.* Correct cylinder-head-installation technique and bolt-tightening sequence and torque settings are in Cylinder Head Installation, pages 122-124. Correct method of adjustment with sequnce and lash settings for either mechanical or hydraulic cams is in Setting the Valve Clearances With Mechanical Lifters, page 128 or Setting the Clearance With Hydraulic Lifters, page 127. Before attempting distributor and plug cable installation, read the sections entitled Distributor Installation through Timing HEI Ignitions, starting at page 146. All these sections will be found in Chapter 7.

Next to engine temperature, altitude is the biggest variable. For every 1000 feet above sea level, add 3-1/2% to your readings. This approximation will hold good up to about 10,000 feet.

At this point you are probably thinking the compression test is not such a good deal. That isn't necessarily true. If you consider exactly what the compression test can reveal, you will discover a great deal more about your engine than without the test. How you interpret the test, though, is important.

First of all, it is uncommon for all cylinders to wear the same. This means readings will vary, due to wear differences between cylinders. Those with substantially lower readings are worn more than the high reading ones. The highest reading cylinder will be the one by which you should judge the performance of the others. If any cylinders are down by more than 25% of the highest reading one, you can bet something is wrong.

It is possible to have a "rogue" high compression reading. Cam lobes which have worn enough to remove 20°–30° of valve-open period from the opening and closing sides of the cam profile will show a high compression reading because of the reduced cam duration. Don't compare the other cylinders against a suspect high-reading cylinder. If one or two cylinders are reading high, check their valve lifts to determine cam wear as detailed a little later.

Here's another check which gives you a clue to the state of a cylinder, regardless of the actual pressure it attains. When you crank the engine, note how many compression strokes are needed to reach maximum pressure. If it comes up to pressure in two compression strokes, leakage is probably low. If it takes five or more compression strokes, that cylinder is leaking more than it should.

Having just discussed the rate at which cylinders achieve their peak pressure, I should say something about compression gauges. There are two types. One has a tapered rubber cone which is merely pressed into the spark plug hole to take the readings. Other more expensive ones have a screw-in adapter which allows you to securely screw the adapter and gauge into the plug hole.

With the first type you will find, as soon as the compression starts to achieve any notable value, that the pressure has a tendency to push the gauge out of the hole, and it takes considerable effort to keep it in there. This makes your test somewhat lengthy and also prevents you from accurately determining how quickly the engine reaches its maximum pressure. For the little extra they cost, compression gauges with a screw-in adapter are easier to use than push-in ones. The screw-in adapter allows you to take accurate readings of how long it takes to come up to pressure and, as I have said, this can be a good guide as to

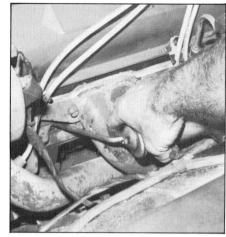

The next thing is to establish where the leak is occuring. Squirt the four shots of oil into the cylinder toward the piston. Do not squirt it toward the valve seats. The object is to get oil around the rings to make them seal better for the next test.

the leakage of that particular cylinder.

So far, all your tests have been aimed at deciding whether or not the cylinder is leaking badly enough to warrant some sort of repair. Assume repairs are needed. This will take you on to the next stage of your tests with a compression gauge, a test commonly known as the *wet test*. This will help determine where the leak may be occurring.

LEAKING RINGS OR VALVES?

Now you must go one step further to determine the real source of the suspected sealing problem. Squirt heavy engine oil—about four shots from a typical oil can—through the plug hole into the cylinder so it will oil the rings but not the valve seats. To do this, have the piston about 1/2 inch down the bore, squirt the oil to the far side and give it time to run around to the plug side. Usually about a minute is long enough.

Using the compression gauge, retest the cylinder pressure. If it stays about the same as the previous reading, this indicates the rings are in reasonable shape. If you see an increase of 10 per cent or more in pressure, then the oil is sealing and not the rings, so the rings are worn out. If the pressure was low before and after the injection of oil into

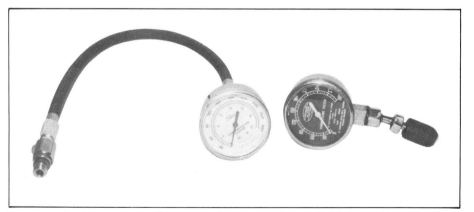

If you are buying a compression tester, then a screw-in one (left) though more costly, is a better deal. It is less hassle to use and you can do an extra test which is difficult to perform with the push-in gauge.

If compressed air isn't available, inexpensive Mity Vac leak-down tester is a good alternative. Although it "pulls" a vacuum on the cylinders rather than pressurizing them, results are just as valid.

If you have a yen to own your own leak-down tester then here is a sample of what is available (usually through a good speed shop). Manley unit has an extra gauge to read supply pressure. This makes it quicker to set up for testing and a little more expensive than the Moroso unit. Figure one of these leak-down testers costs about 3 times the price of a good compression gauge. To use a leak-down tester you will need a compressed air supply of 80 psi minimum.

the cylinder, a valve could be leaking. If you have solid lifters (found only on high-performance engines) check the valve lash to make sure it is correct. With hydraulic lifters, try backing off the nut in the rocker arm half a turn to see if the situation improves. If neither of these tests does anything to raise the cylinder pressure, chances are you have leaking or burned valves.

The very minimum you have to do now is to remove the heads. Should this prove to be all you have to do, skip most of the book and just read the parts dealing with the heads. If you have to take the heads off, you will be able to verify the condition of the bores positively by measuring them. This can be done by the ring-and-feeler method detailed in Chapter 6. Head disassembly and inspection for problems are also dealt with in the same chapter.

THE LEAK-DOWN TEST

Having alternately praised and condemned compression tests in the last few paragraphs, let me tell you about the *leak-down test*. This tests the sealing qualities of the cylinder with compressed air. Incidentally, this system has many advantages over a compression test.

A leak-down tester is not generally found in your supermarket's automotive section. Though there are exceptions, a leak-down tester is incorporated into the more sophisticated equipment seen around professional tune-up shops. The advantage of a leak-down tester is that outside air and variable internal specifications of the engine don't affect its readings. The only thing that it measures is how much air is leaking past the rings, valves, etc. This is important information. A compression tester measures such things in a very roundabout way. It also measures a lot of other things you don't really need to know. On this basis, the leak-down tester is by far the most accurate method of establishing whether or not the engine's cylinders need attention. A typical leak-down tester is incorporated into the Sun electronic engine analyzer. On such a machine — and I am quoting the Sun machine only because this may vary with other equipment depending on how it is calibrated — an engine which is leaking 20% of the test pressure definitely needs attention. A good cylinder will have between 5% and 10% leakage.

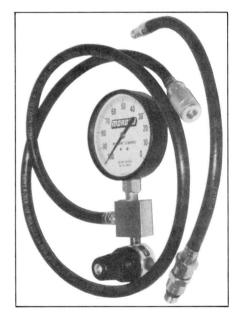

MPG & PERFORMANCE

It could be you have checked out all the foregoing, and the cylinders are sealed okay, oil consumption is reasonable, plugs show no signs of ailing, the MPG figures are not too bad but the engine's performance is below par. This may seem very improbable, but it is quite common on high-mileage, small-block Chevys that have seen regular servicing, like oil changes every 3000 miles and filter changes at the same time.

Regular servicing greatly extends engine life, but the cam and lifters still tend to wear about three times faster than the rest of the pieces. Not many small-block Chevy cams and lifters last 130,000 miles, but the rest of the engine will if cared for properly.

DETERMINING CAM WEAR

The result of such an imbalance of wear between components is that you may end up with a camshaft having a low lift on one or more lobes. To make accurate checks on this you really need a dial gauge but on many occasions the wear is so bad on the cam and lifters you can easily detect it with a machinist's scale or even a short ruler.

When wear can be measured with a ruler, performance will be notably affected. To detect any cam and lifter wear, you will need to start the engine, or crank it over a while to make sure the hydraulic lifters are completely filled with oil. With solid lifters, this is not necessary. Next, remove the rocker cover and spark plugs. Use a dial gauge or dial caliper to measure the valve lift if possible (see nearby photo. Place the tip of the gauge on or by the spring retainer. Then turn the engine over by placing a wrench on one of the front pulley bolts, so the valve travels from closed to full lift. Note the difference in the two measurements, between closed and full.

What Should the Lift Be? — Here comes the snag. Since small-block Chevys have been produced, there have been many camshafts with different timing and lifts. Add to these the almost countless aftermarket performance and economy cams which have been used since 1955, and you can see that quoting a lift figure is nearly impossible. However, all is not lost. The lowest lift Chevy cam you are likely to find is 0.334-inch (just under 11/32 inch) lift. It was used in very early models and you are not likely to

find many cams of this type in use today. If the lift is less than this, the camshaft is worn.

This second piece of information is probably more important. Experience has shown a Chevy cam never wears out *all* its lifters or lobes. Here is what happens. First of all, the lifters and cam lobes do not wear at the same rate. When a lifter/cam profile combination starts to wear, fine metal particles get into the oil. Most engines use a bypass filter, so some of these particles are fed under pressure to the engine. Fine metal particles in the oil accelerate the wear on the particular lifter and cam profile that started the situation. Before you know it, the engine is minus the valve lift on one valve. The particles will cause the other lifters and lobes to suffer accelerated wear, but one or two lobes and lifters usually stay in better shape than the rest. The result is you can measure all the valve lifts and compare each one to the best one.

If there is a variance of 0.030 inch (thirty thousandths) or more between the lift of each valve, plan on buying a new cam and lifters. Performance may not have suffered much, but the variation indicates the cam is on the threshold of annihilating additional lobes and lifters, so replacement is essential to restore performance.

KNOCKING SYMPTOMS

The most obvious time to investigate the well-being of your small-block Chevy is when it starts making noises it shouldn't. Better still is to investigate before any small "knocks" become severe "clanks." A small-block Chevy with hydraulic tappets should run quietly with no more than a murmur from the valve train if all is perfect. If you hear any tapping noises, it is almost too late for the components concerned. With the aid of a long screwdriver, (or if you want to be fancy, an automotive stethoscope) you can detect possible trouble sources before they get too far worn. The

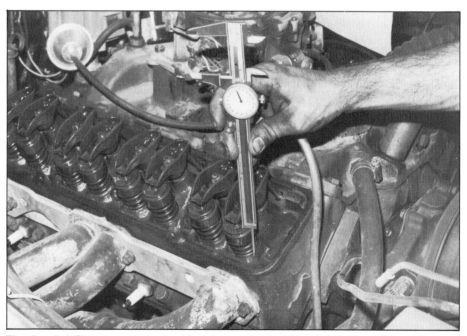

The dreaded Chevy cam-wear problem being checked for with a dial caliper. The technique is to measure each valve's lift and make a comparison. Here it is being done with a dial caliper. In bad cases you can measure the wear with an ordinary ruler.

stethoscope shown in a nearby photo is typically a $10–$15 item. It is far better than the screwdriver for listening to your engine's possible ailments.

Starting at the top of the engine, the first temptation is to listen in on the valve cover. In actual fact what you can hear at this point is of little use for the simple reason that the large air space between it and the rest of the engine means that you'll have difficulty deciphering exactly what you are listening to. A better place to listen in is at the valve-cover screws—any one of them will do. If you listen to all four of them on any one side, you will probably find little difference in the noise because cast iron is relatively good at conducting sound vibrations. What you should hear when you listen on the valve-cover screw is basically clacking noises—all of them about the same. This is because you are listening to the valve train and if the hydraulic tappets are doing their job right, all the noises should be even. On engines with solid lifters, there is considerably greater noise. If you have a maladjusted lifter or one on a cam lobe which is wearing out, you will notice a little louder action when that particular lifter operates.

If you listen to the distributor you can often tell a lot. By putting the probe on the distributor base, you should hear a very pronounced whirring with a hollow clacking noise superimposed. The clacking frequency will be considerably higher than that found when listening at the valve-cover screws. The reason is you are hearing the effect of all 16 cam lobes being transmitted to the distributor via the distributor drive gear. Also you will be hearing the points operating, but this is a lot less noise than you would expect. Again, if there is any pronounced clacking or at least the lack of a clack when there should be, you have an indication that all is not well in the valve train.

If you listen to the fuel pump or the area surrounding it, you will hear a knocking noise. This is caused by normal pump operation, so ignore it.

A quick check can be made on the water pump, although it's not something that you need overly concern yourself with here because a water pump change can be made without pulling the engine. However, if the water pump is listened to, it should make a smooth whirring sound with occasional small clicks, and I mean *small*. If the clicking is very pronounced and easily audible, you could have a bearing going out in your water pump.

Now for the block. If you put the probe somewhere down on the block, preferably around the base of the pan or just below the head, you may be able to hear several noises ranging from a dull thud to a relatively heavy knock. The heavy knocking could well be a rod bearing going out; the dull thud could be the effects of piston slap in a very worn bore. Overriding this you may hear a rumbling sound. This generally indicates the main bearings are badly worn. If it is rod bearings or main bearings which are suspect when you listen, a good check is to remove the oil-pressure switch just behind the distributor, connect an oil-pressure gauge to the hole, start the engine and note the gauge readings. At idle your oil pressure should be 15–20 psi. At 3,000 RPM it should be 35–40 psi. Anything less than these figures indicates that bearings or oil pump are worn out.

If just one or two cylinders are causing a problem, they can be identified by disconnecting each spark-plug cable in turn. When the plug from a knocking cylinder is disconnected, the intensity of the noise will be drastically reduced.

If you take steps to remedy the

Rod journal and piston wear can be detected and the cylinder at fault located with an automotive stethoscope. To determine the extent of valve-train wear, unless really bad, needs an experienced ear. The problem is knowing what noises are normal to valve-train operation.

situation early, it could well save you a lot of money. Chevy cranks do not generally wear that much unless oil pressure is allowed to drop severely. I've seen small-block cranks that have 190,000 miles on them that didn't need to be reground. If metal-to-metal contact does occur through low oil pressure caused by large clearances, it will damage the journals, thus necessitating a regrind. If you detect the problem early enough, you may only need to install new bearings. This can save you a fair amount of money.

SUMMARY

To conclude this section I have made up a chart, Figure 1-1, to lead you through a logical sequence of events to pinpoint whether a complete or partial overhaul is needed. The chart does not detail tune-up procedures. The reason for this is discussed in Chapter 10 which outlines why you need professional tune-up assistance.

ACKNOWLEDGEMENTS

A book, especially a technical one, is always the result of the efforts of many people. My special thanks must go to Denny Wycoff, who spent countless hours helping with numerous facets of producing this book, from technical information to helping set up the photos.

Valuable contributions were also made by Bill Nelson, Bill Wheatley, Kevin Rotty, Don Wood, Sam Ellison and John Redgate.

I am also indebted to Jerry Goodale, Art Fisher, Bill Naumann and Steve Clifton for making their workshop facilities available and for spending the time to set up machines for photographs.

Bill Howell of Chevrolet Product Promotions came up with the answers to several difficult problems. Thanks Bill.

Thanks also to Calvin De Bruin of Sealed Power Corporation and to Terry Davis and John Campanelli of TRW. I am also indebted to Bob Lopez and Mike Derella of Federal Mogul for their generous assistance.

I am especially grateful to Len, Charlie and Jim, who always managed to find the tools I lost while taking photos.

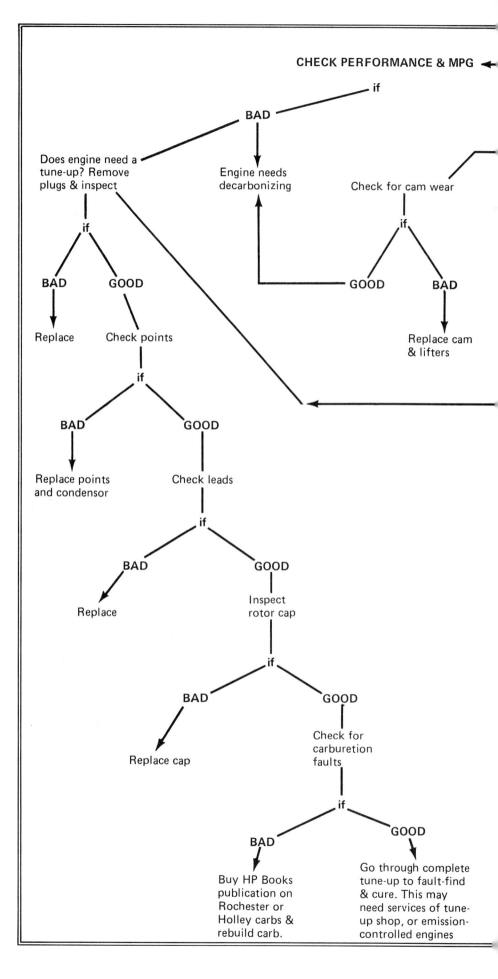

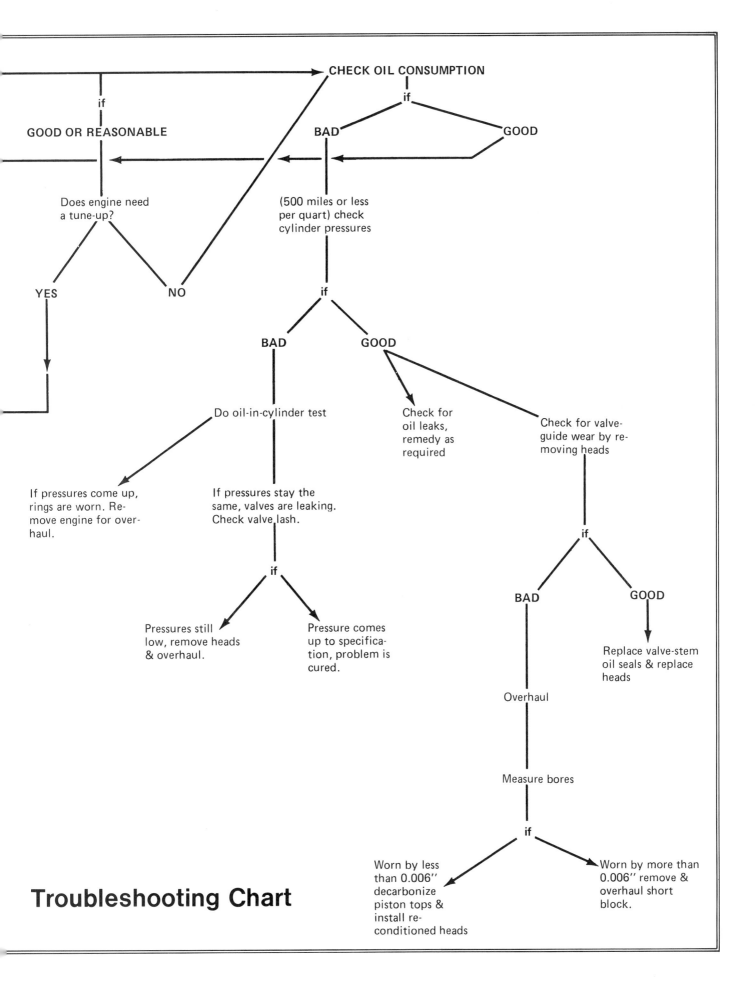

CHECK OIL CONSUMPTION

if

GOOD OR REASONABLE   BAD   GOOD

Does engine need
a tune-up?

(500 miles or less
per quart) check
cylinder pressures

YES   NO   if

BAD   GOOD

Do oil-in-cylinder test

Check for
oil leaks,
remedy as
required

Check for valve-
guide wear by re-
moving heads

If pressures come up,
rings are worn. Re-
move engine for over-
haul.

If pressures stay the
same, valves are leaking.
Check valve lash.

if

if

BAD   GOOD

Pressures still
low, remove heads
& overhaul.

Pressure comes
up to specifica-
tion, problem is
cured.

Replace valve-stem
oil seals & replace
heads

Overhaul

Measure bores

if

Worn by less
than 0.006"
decarbonize
piston tops &
install re-
conditioned heads

Worn by more than
0.006" remove &
overhaul short
block.

Troubleshooting Chart

2
SMALL-BLOCK FACTS & FIGURES

The 283 CID engine was the result of a bore increase over the 265 CID engine. This 1957 model uses heat shields around the plug caps. Modern silicone rubber withstands higher temperatures so the shields are not needed.

I am putting this chapter in because it could save you a lot of money. You could pull your engine apart and find all the parts except one are OK for further use and that one part may have to be replaced. The small-block Chevy has been produced for many a year in numerous cubic-inch-displacement (CID) sizes. Parts from one size engine can sometimes be used on another size—and sometimes they can't. You might have a 302 CID with a cracked block. Your pistons, rods, crank, and everything else may be pretty good. There is a 283 CID block down at the wrecking yard. Can you use it? Will it stand overboring to the 302 CID size, or not? Questions like this need answers. You can often use this terrific parts interchangeability to your advantage. On the other hand, there are drastic pitfalls to avoid.

BLOCKS

265 CID Engine—Back in 1955 the "mouse motor" really was small. The first-year's production of 265 CID blocks from 1955 to the beginning of '56 had no oil filter nor any provision for one. Avoid using one of these blocks. An engine without an oil filter needs oil changes far more often if it is to have a long service life. Another point to watch on early blocks, that is blocks right up to the introduction of the 283 CID in 1957: on all early 265 CID blocks, oil was fed to the lifter galleries through two holes in the rear camshaft bearing. Oil fed the lifter galleries when a slot in the rear camshaft bearing journal lined up with these holes.

283 and Later Blocks—With the introduction of the 283 a modification was made around the rear cam-bearing bore in the block. An annular groove provides a constant oil supply to the lifter galleries so the slot in the cam was no longer required. If you end up using an early block, machine the slot in the camshaft *or* have the groove machined in behind the bearing. Fail to do this and your valve lifters will get no oil and neither will the rocker arms.

Overboring Early Blocks—So far as overboring is concerned, all early 265 blocks will stand boring one-eighth inch (0.125 inch or one hundred and twenty five thousandths) oversize. One type of 265 block produced around 1957 had slightly thicker cylinder walls. It is identified by a capital letter "C" at the end of the serial number on top of the front of the block. In 1957 the 283 CID engine was introduced. Essentially it is an overbored 265, so early 283 blocks will not stand overboring too much and plus 0.060 inch (sixty thousandths) is the absolute maximum.

In 1958 a new 283 block with thicker cylinder walls was introduced. It can be identified by the engine-mounting bosses cast into the side of the block. These blocks could safely be bored to 4.000 inches when new. Occasionally, rust may have corroded the water-jacket side of the cylinder walls so that the 1/8-inch oversize to make a 4-inch bore can uncover porous areas in the cylinder wall. A 1/8-inch (0.125 inch) oversize on a 283 gives 301.6 CID. From '59 to '62 all blocks were basically the same and all will stand boring to the 4.000-inch size. 283 blocks cast from 1963 to 1967 when production of this CID stopped, had thinner cylinder walls and should only be bored 0.060 inch.

Oil Seal Change—In 1959 the rear-main-bearing seal was changed from a graphite-impregnated rope-type seal to a neoprene lip seal. The lip seal is a far better method of keeping the oil from coming out the rear main bearing. If you have the slightest excuse for changing your block, get this type of rear seal. It is very difficult to put a neoprene seal in a block that originally has a rope-seal.

The 327 Block—The popular 327 engine was produced from 1962 through 1967. A lot of pattern changes were made at the factory to produce this block for this engine. In essence, all the principal dimensions were the same. The biggest change was the underside of the block where the bores meet the crankcase area. This was relieved to clear the 327 CID crank's longer stroke. The 327 CID was achieved by increasing the standard bore size to 4.000 inches

On blocks prior to the introduction of the 327, the casting at the base of the cylinders is flat as indicated by the position of the lower edge of the white card. With the 327 and later blocks, the depression indicated by the screwdriver was cast into the block to clear the larger counterweights on the longer stroke cranks.

With the white card removed, the full extent of the radius at the bottom of the cylinders can be seen. Blocks without this radius cannot use cranks with strokes longer than 3 inches.

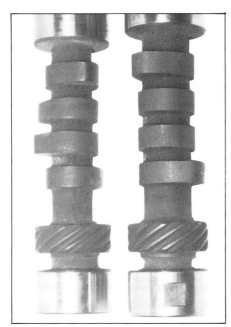

Early cam on right has a slot to supply oil to lifters, valves etc. The back cam bearing has two oil holes. As the cam rotates, the slot connects these holes to supply squirts of oil to the lifter galleries. Late cam on left is used in blocks with an annular groove underneath the rear cam bearing to supply constant oil pressure to the lifter galleries.

using a crank with a 3.25-inch stroke as opposed to the 283's 3.00-inch stroke. If you have a 327 or bigger engine in need of a new block, you cannot use the earlier 283 CID block because the crank counterweights will not clear the inside of the block. In '62, some 283 blocks were produced with the relieved crankcase area like the 327 blocks. This meant a 327 crank would drop into one of these blocks without any clearance problem.

302 & 350 CID Engines—These are essentially engines which came from the factory as longer and shorter-stroke versions of the 327 CID unit. The 302 was built primarily because of the 302 CID limit for the Trans-Am racing series. It was produced in 1967 with a small-journal crank and in '68 and '69 with a large-journal crank. The 302 engine uses the 3-inch stroke of the 283 and the 350 CID engine uses a 3.48-inch stroke. Both engines, of course, use the 4-inch bore.

With all 4-inch-bore blocks, that is 302, 327 and 350, it is best only to bore 0.040-inch oversize. Many 0.060-inch oversize pistons are available for these blocks. If bored to this size, there will be about a 2

percent chance of scrapping the block due to thin or porous cylinder walls.

307 CID Engine—This engine was introduced in 1968. A 283 bore with a 327 stroke gave 307 cubic inches. Boring one of these blocks to 4-inches gives 327 cubic inches. A 4-inch bore on a 307 usually leads to a

Make a note of these holes if you have to change blocks for any reason. They mount the clutch-pivot ball. All blocks will have the rear hole and blocks from around 1965 on will also have the front hole as shown here. After 1965, some vehicles such as Chevy II and Chevelles used the front hole. If your vehicle needs the front hole, be sure to buy a block with one there. Blocks without the hole are also without the cast-on boss to accommodate a hole, so you cannot drill and tap a block which did not originally have this clutch-pivot-mounting hole.

failure rate of about 1 in 10 due to porosity of some cylinders. These odds are not as good as they sound so be sure you have a good reason before choosing this route. As in the case of the 350 engine, the 307 block is notched at the bottom of the bores to give connecting-rod clearance. These are sufficiently large to allow the use of a 350 crank in a 307 block. You can only use a 350 crank in the 307 block if the block is bored to 4 inches and 350 pistons are used. The 307 took the place of the 283 and production of it ceased in 1973.

262 CID Engine — Introduced in 1974 and discontinued in mid-1976, this was the smallest small-block produced to date. The 3.671-inch bore is smaller than the early 265 or 283 engines; the stroke is longer at 3.1 inches. This engine block can be bored up to +0.030 inch over, but no more than that.

267 CID Engine — In 1979 a 267 cubic-inch small-block was introduced. It has a 3-1/2-in. bore and the 3.48-in. stroke of a 350. This engine was to be a fuel-efficient, small-block V-8. Unfortunately, it was not received too well and, consequently, was dropped for 1982.
The 267 has several differences in areas related to it's reduced displacement. For one, the

If you're hunting for a block by casting number, this is where to look. In case you don't recognize the spot, it's above the oil filter on the bell housing flange. Because dirt collects here, you'll probably have to scrape off the dirt to read the number.

combustion chambers are considerably smaller than other small-blocks produced in that era; they look similar to the 57 cc heads used on early 265/283s. Although it has the same size journals, the crank is counterweighted for lighter 3-1/2-in.-diameter pistons. This gives the 267 crank a rather spindly appearance when compared to a 350 crank.

305 CID Engine — In '76 another odd bore size was introduced at just under 3.75-inches in diameter. Its long stroke crank is from the 350 engine introduced back in '68. Again, this 305 block can stand boring to +0.060 inch only.

400 CID Engine — Introduced in 1970, this block differs from the others in the use of a bigger bore and larger main-bearing journal bores. If you have a 400 CID engine, and the block is scrap for one reason or another, then you are going to need another 400 CID block to replace it. None of the others will really do. It also uses shorter rods as discussed in the connecting rod section on page 16. If you have to replace a 400 block it's a good idea to remember that they were available with either two- or four-bolt main bearing caps. The four-bolt main bearing block was used until mid-1973 for all applications. Two-bolt blocks were used from then on for all applications as the factory considered these adequate, even for trucks.

Should you require a four-bolt block for any reason you will find they can be difficult to obtain. If you have a 400 four-bolt block and the main caps are in good condition, but the block is beyond repair for some reason, those caps can be transferred to a 1974 or later 400 two-bolt block. The caps will require machining after they have been installed. They will need to be align-bored and honed and the extra bolt holes must be drilled in the block and tapped. You will have to decide whether or not this is a financially feasible alternative by comparing the price of a new block versus the price of installing the four-bolt mains. Generally, four-bolt mains aren't necessary for most rebuild applications.

Rod & Main Journals From 1968 — From early 1968 on, another change was made in the block design. This change was required because of the change in crankshaft design. Until then, Chevy V-8 cranks had 2.000-inch diameter rod journals with 2.300-inch diameter main-bearing journals. Bearing bores in the block were sized to accommodate these. In '68 the crank sizes went up to 2.100 inches for the rod-bearing journals and 2.450 inches for the main-bearing journals. This meant blocks had to be machined accordingly. Therefore, all blocks produced in 1968 and later have larger main bearings than previous Chevy small-blocks.

BLOCK IDENTIFICATION

The best way to identify a block casting when hunting for a specific one is by the *block casting number*. This is normally located in two areas; on the flywheel flange at the back of the block on the right side when viewed from the front of the engine, or in the area directly underneath the cam sprocket. Of course that's not an easy one to read when an engine is together, so the one on the back of the block is the one to check. However, there are some easier ways of roughly identifying what you are looking for without having to store a whole batch of numbers in your mind. If the engine is out of the vehicle, you can establish whether or not the engine is pre-68 or '68 and later engine by looking at the crankshaft flange where the flywheel or torque converter plate bolts on. If it is a small counterweighted type flange, it's a '68 or later engine. If it's a plain round diameter, it's a pre-68 engine. Of course this won't actually tell you the displacement, but it will establish whether it has small or big bearings.

As far as 400 CID blocks are concerned, you can tell a four-bolt block from a two-bolter by the number of freeze plugs on the side of the engine. Three freeze plugs along the side indicate the block is a 400 with four-bolt main caps. Two freeze plugs indicate a two-bolt unit. To pinpoint blocks any further than this, you'll need to check the block casting numbers. The chart on this page should help you do this without tearing down the engine to measure bore and crank sizes.

There are two more factors you should consider. In fact, they are essential when replacing a block.

First of all, some blocks have clutch-linkage mounting bosses cast in just over the filter housing and by the rear freeze plug. If your block has a clutch-linkage mounting at these points, you must get a block with similar bolt holes to accommodate such. The other factor concerns blocks for the Chevy II. In this installation there was insufficient room between the steering gear and the oil filter, and blocks for this model had the filter moved up by 2-1/2 inches. To avoid any problems, you should replace such a block with a similar one.

CRANKSHAFTS

Given what I've discussed so far, it's obvious that the small-block Chevy can be interchanged quite a bit. Much the same can be said for crankshafts. All 265 cranks—the 3-inch stroke cranks—were forged steel. All 283 cranks to late 1965 were also forged. From late 1965 to 1967, when 283 production ceased, cranks could be cast-iron or forged steel. Forged cranks are generally for truck engines. If you have to replace the crank of a pre-62 engine which has no crank counterweight relief at the bottom of the bores, use a forged crank. Cast cranks can be installed but the block may require grinding on the front main bearing web by the bottom of the bores to clear the front counterweight on the crank.

All cranks up to late 1967 had small journals as mentioned earlier. With the introduction of the large journal, the use of cast cranks became more common. In fact, through '68 and '69, most passenger car cranks were cast, regardless of which engine they were for. Truck units could be equipped with either forged or cast cranks, the forged cranks being the most common. 1968 327 CID engines used the large-journal forged crank in most truck applications and in the Corvette.

BLOCK CASTING IDENTIFICATION

CASTING NO.	CID	YEARS USED	USED IN
360851	262	'74-76	Monza
* 3703524	265	'55	Passenger cars
3720991	265	'56-57	Trucks & passenger cars
14010280 14016376 471511	267	'79-82	Passenger cars
3731548	283	'57	
3556519 3737739 3849852	283	'58-61	Trucks & passenger cars
3789935 3849852 3864812	283	'62-64	Trucks & passenger cars
3849852 3849935 3896944 393288	283	'65-67	Trucks & passenger cars
See Note 1 See Note 2 389257	302 302	'67 '68-69	302 Camaro 302 Camaro
14010201 14016381 14010202 14010203	305	'80-84	Passenger cars & light trucks " "
460776 460777 460778 361979	305	'78-79	Passenger cars & light trucks
3914653 3914636 3932373 3970020	307	'68-73	Trucks & passenger cars
3959512	327	'62-63	
3782870 3789817 3794460 3852174 3858180	327	'62-64	Trucks & passenger cars
3892657 3782870 3903352 3789817 3858174 3892657	327	'64-67	Trucks & passenger cars
3791362	327	'65-67	Chevy II
3970041 3814660 3970010 3914678 3932386 3955618	327	'68-69	Corvette Camaro and other high-performance applications
3855961 3932388 3958618 3970014 6259425	350	'68-76	Passenger cars (2-bolt mains)
3956618 + 3970010 3932386	350	'68-79	Truck and high-performance applications (4-bolt mains)
14016379 366245	350 350	'78-79 '78-79	Passenger cars & light trucks (dip stick in pan)
140029 14010207	350 350	'80-84	Passenger cars
3951511	400	'70-73	Heavy-duty trucks & passenger cars (4-bolt mains)
3951509 3030817	400	'74-76	(2-bolt mains)

* First six-month's production used mechanical cams, not hydraulic.
\+ Sometimes machined for 2-bolt mains.

Note 1: Small-journal 302-CID engine uses 327 block.
Note 2: Large-journal 302-CID engine uses 350 block.

ENGINE & CRANK SPECIFICATIONS (inches)

CID	YEAR	BORE	STROKE	Rod-Journal Dia.	Main-Journal Dia.
262	'74-76	3.671	3.100	2.100	2.450
265	'55-57	3.750	3.000	2.000	2.300
267	'79-82	3.500	3.480	2.100	2.450
283	'57-67	3.875	3.000	2.000	2.300
302	'67	4.000	3.000	2.000	2.300
302	'68-69	4.000	3.000	2.100	2.450
305	'76-	3.767	3.480	2.100	2.450
307	'68-73	3.875	3.250	2.100	2.450
327	'62-67	4.000	3.250	2.000	2.300
327	'68	4.000	3.250	2.100	2.450
350	'67-	4.000	3.480	2.100	2.450
400	'70-	4.125	3.750	2.100	2.650

The crank with the round flywheel flange is a pre '68 item while its neighbor with the counterweighted flange is a '68 and later big-journal unit.

In 1970 forged crankshafts were used in the high-performance engines for Corvettes, Camaros and a few other Chevys.

The 302 crank with its competition background was forged. It was offered in small-and large-journal forms depending on whether it was made in '67 or '68, or '69. Though forged cranks were first used on Camaros and the Corvettes, as time went by only Corvettes had them. In 1978, Corvettes came in line with the rest of the Chevrolet passenger vehicles and were fitted with a cast-iron crank. The '76 and later 305 CID engine with its 3.736-inch bore uses the 3.48-inch stroke of the 350. The 305, along with the 267, also shares the 350's stroke. Like the 267, the 305 crank has lighter counterweights than the 350 because of lighter pistons. If balanced to suit, a 305 crank can be used in a 350. This requires adding weight to the counterweights, usually by welding. On the other hand, the 267 crank cannot be used in a 350, even when correctly balanced; it can't handle the higher power output of a 350.

The 400 CID engine uses main-bearing journals of a size peculiar to the 400 CID engine only, so simple crank interchangeability is not possible with this engine.

If You Have To Replace A Crank—
If you find that your engine requires only new rings rather than a rebore

and new pistons, then any crank replacement must be with one of the same type. If you get one with different size bearings, it won't fit. If you get one with a different stroke length, the pistons will either come out of the top of the bore or not come far enough up the bore. With the standard block height and rod length used on all engines (except the 400), any change in stroke length must be compensated for in the piston construction by the position of the wrist pin relative to the piston crown. Matching the wrong pistons to crank stroke will mean poor performance or an engine which won't go together—period.

PISTON PIN-TO-CROWN HEIGHT	
CID	PIN HEIGHT (inches)
262	1.750
265	1.800
267	1.560
283	1.800
302	1.800
305	1.560
307	1.675
327	1.675
350	1.560
400	1.715*

*Used with 5.56-in. rod instead of 5.70-in.-long rod.

Piston-pin height is measured from center of wrist-pin bore to crown of piston.

You may find you have a damaged forged crank in your engine. Some people are wary of changing forged cranks for cast cranks, believing the cast ones to be inferior. Unless you have a very high-performance small-block Chevy, this really isn't the case. For applications up to 6500 rpm, the cast crank is as good, possibly even superior to the forged crank. They seem to suffer less breakage and last at least as long in terms of wear. So if you find a cast crank in good condition, have no hesitation in using it in your engine so long as it has main- and rod-journal sizes which will work with your block and rods. The stroke length must also be the same as the one you are replacing as well.

If you find you need another crank as well as a rebore, you can use any stroke length you want as long as the crank physically fits in the block. The pistons used must then be those with the correct piston pin (wrist pin) to crown height. This is known as the *compression height*. Be sure you get pistons to match the stroke of the crankshaft. Rods may also need to be changed as some differences exist, as explained in the following paragraph.

CONNECTING RODS
Except for the 400 CID unit, which uses a shorter rod than all the others, all of the rod center-to-center

Crank casting or forging numbers are usually about this position. If you are looking for a crank you don't necessarily need one with the same casting/forging number. When even a small change in design was made, the factory used a new number.

Difference in pin-to-crown heights (compression heights) and overall heights for different stroke lengths is readily seen here. Left piston is for a 350, one at right is for a 283.

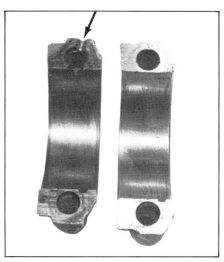

The cap on the left has a spit-hole groove through the bolt hole (arrow). Rod caps from 1968 on do not have spit holes because it was found unnecessary.

distances are the same at 5.7 inches. Interchangeability, however, is not 100 per cent because of the 1968 journal-size change. When you are looking for rods, be sure you are getting the correct ones for your crank's journal size.

Rods to about 1964 had "spit holes" in the rod cap to send a jet of oil up onto each bore. These took the form of a V-groove cut in the rod cap. In practice the bores receive adequate lubrication without the spit holes, so later rods don't have these V-grooves. If you have early rods with spit holes, they can be replaced with the later type should the need arise.

The 400 CID engine uses a rod with only 5.56-inch center-to-center length. Use only 400 CID rods in the 400 CID engine. Any other rods will cause the pistons to come out of the top of the block.

PISTONS

On to the pistons. The effect of increasing the stroke was always accommodated by moving the pis-ton pin farther up the piston, not by increasing the block height as is done by some manufacturers. The pistons must be for the particular engine you have, or rather the crank stroke you have. If the compression height of the piston is too tall for the crank you have, the pistons will come out of the top of the block which means the head won't bolt on. If it's too low, the engine will have a very low-compression ratio and performance will be extremely poor.

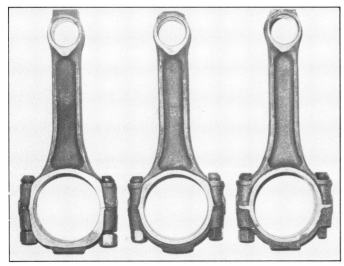

The two rods on the right are pre '68 small-journal rods. On the right is the original 265-283 rod. When the 327 was introduced, it used rods strengthened in the area of the rod bolt heads. This is easily recognizeable as a bump in the side thrust flange by the bolt head cutouts. At first this rod was used only in 327s, but within two years it became standard equipment for all small-block Chevys. Rod at left is the big-journal rod instantly identified by the four "bumps" in the side thrust flange.

Induction-hardened seats seem to be more prone to cracking than do unhardened seats. Cracks most often form in the area between the intake and exhaust port. Black line on the exhaust seat indicates a typical crack position on this type of 350 or 400 head. Cracks like this can often be successfully repaired—at a price!

17

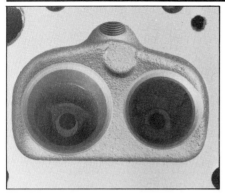

57cc head. This early type head is used mostly on **265** and some **283s**. Easily identified by the recessed plug.

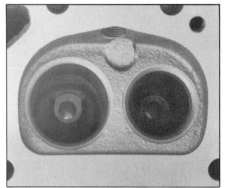

64cc heads. Typical heads used on early high-performance engines from about 1962 to semi-high-performance engines of the early '70s. All have the round shape on the plug side of the chamber. The most common ones have the area adjacent to the spark plug angled off (arrow). This chamber shape is also used on the 262 head.

COMPRESSION RATIO

HEAD VOLUME	PISTON CID	F/T 262	F/T 265	F/T 267	F/T 283	F/T 302	F/T 305	F/T 307	F/T 327	F/T 350	1 DISH 350	2 DISH 400
57cc	*		9.0	9.0	9.4	9.8	10.0	10.1	10.5	11.2	9.2	9.7
64cc	*		8.25	8.2	8.6	9.0	9.2	9.3	9.7	10.3	8.6	9.1
69cc	*		7.8	7.8	8.2	8.5	8.8	8.9	9.2	9.9	8.2	8.7
76cc	*		7.2	7.2	7.6	8.0	8.1	8.2	8.5	9.0	7.7	8.2

*The 262 engine uses a head with 60.5cc chamber volume. This gives a CR of 8.5 on the 262 CID engine. Casting number 354434 identifies this head.
F/T indicates Flat Top pistons.
[1] Typical dish volume for a 350 dished piston is 17cc.
[2] Dish volume for a 400 piston is 24cc.
Note: These compression ratios were figured with a composition-type head gasket. If a steel-shim gasket is used, add 0.1 to each ratio, i.e., 8.2 becomes 8.2 + 0.1 = 8.3 with a steel-shim gasket.

To determine approximate compression ratio with flat top or in the case of 350 and 400 CID engines, dish pistons, you will need to compare the cylinder head chamber shape with these shown here. There are basically five combustion shapes. On the basis of volume, these can be split into four groups. Chamber volumes quoted are the middle-of-the-road figures for any particular group. Production tolerances may create volumes as much as 2-1/2cc above or below the quoted figures.

FIGURE 2-2

69cc head. Typical low-compression head, generally for use on smaller CID engines. Its squared-off shape is radically different to the 57 and 64cc heads. Plug hole is almost flush with the chamber wall.

76cc head. This chamber type is found in low compression, emission-control heads for 305, 307, 350 and 400 CID engines. Identification points to distinguish it from the 69cc heads are the raised valve seats and the pronounced raised area around the spark-plug hole.

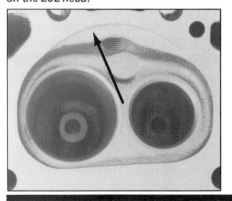

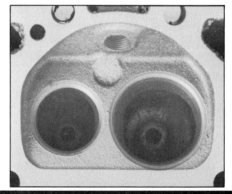

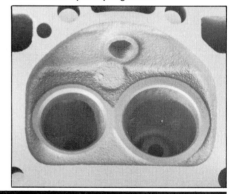

CYLINDER HEADS

This is a likely area where you may find it necessary to buy a replacement from the dealer or wrecking yard. Some cylinder heads crack. Early heads around '68 - '69 using the 2.02-inch valve are prone to crack in the chamber. This usually occurs 45° from the spark plug on the inlet valve seat through to the water jacket.

400 heads can crack between the steam holes if they are overheated. If the head gasket blows due to head warping because of high running temperature, the head will crack almost for sure. This problem occurs less frequently on engines using composition-type head gaskets rather than original equipment steel-shim head gaskets. If you see a set of 400 heads, check that they aren't cracked in the areas indicated in the photo, page 17.

Heads designed for non-leaded fuel have induction-hardened seats. This is the case with 350 and 400

chart compiled with assistance from A.E.R.A.

CYLINDER HEAD IDENTIFICATION

CASTING NO.	YEARS USED	USED ON		CASTING NO.	YEARS USED	USED ON		CASTING NO.	YEARS USED	USED ON
333882	70-76	400		3792563	65-67	327		3931633	68-73	307
354434	75-76	262		3795896	63-72	283-307-327		3931635	68-76	350
	76-79	305		3798996	63-67	327		3931637	68-69	327 & 327 Corvette
358741	76-79	305		3814480	60-67	283-327		3931638	68	327 truck
3030817	74	400 two bolt		3814482	62-67	327-350		3931639	68	302
3636839	55	265		3817680	59	283 4 bbl & F.I.		3932373	68-73	307
367450	75-76	262		3817681	62-67	327-350		3932386	68-76	327-350-350 (4 bolt) & 327 Corvette
3703524	55	265		3817682	61-62	283 2 bbl		3932388	68-76	350 (2 bolt)
3713358	55-56	265 truck		3836839	55	265		3932441	67-72	327-350
3713569	55-56	265 truck		3836842	57-67	265-283-327		3932454	68-69	307
3725306	56-57	265		3837064	56-62	265-283		3932882	76	400
3720991	56-57	265		3837065	55-56	265 truck		3946812	69	350 truck
3731262	56	265 2x4-bbl carb Corvette		3837739	57	283 and 283 truck		3946813	69-70	350
3731548	57-62	283		3848720	57-58	283		3947041	69-70	350
3731554	57	283 car & truck		3849852	57-67	283		3951509	74	400 (2 bolt)
	58-62	283		3849935	65-67	283		3951511	70-73	400 (4 bolt)
3731539	57-61	283 truck		3852174	62-64	327		3951598	70-71	400 2 bbl carb
3731544	55-61	265-283		3854520	62-67	283-327		3956618	68-76	350 (4 bolt)
3731556	57	283 truck		3855961	68-76	350 (2 bolt)		3958618	68-76	350 (2 bolt)
3737739	57-62	283 and 283 Corvette F.I.		3858174	65-67	327		3964286		350
3737775	62-67	283-327		3864812	57-67	283 and 283 truck		3970010	68-76	350 (4 bolt)
3740997	57	283		3867802	57-60	283 F.I. Corvette		3970020	68-73	307
3743096	62-67	327 GMC truck		3876132	62-67	327 & 327 Corvette		3970126	67-70	327-350
3747363	57-62	265		3876775	60-67	283-327		3973487	68-71	350 hi-perf applications
3748720	57-58	283 1x4 or 2x4 bbl carb or F.I. Corvette		3884520	60-67	283-327			71	350 trucks & passenger cars
3748770	55-61	265-283		3981462	62-67	302-327-350		3973493	72-76	400
	58-62	283		3891492	64-67	327		3986339	68-76	307-350
	57	283		3892657	65-67	327		3991492	69-70	350
3748772	58-62	283		3896944	65-67	283		3998916	72	400
3755537	57-62	283		3911032	68-69	327-307		3998991	68-76	350-307
3755539	58-62	283 truck		3912264	58-62	283 car & truck		3998993	68-76	350 low-perf cars & trucks
3755549	57-62	283 car and truck		3912265	63-64	283		3998997	72	400
3755550	57-62	283		3912311	67	350			78-79	305
3755585	62-67	327 GMC and truck		3912313	65-67	327			78-79	350
3756519	57-62	283 and 283 Corvette F.I.		3914636	68-73	307			80-84	350
3760116	59	283 1x4 bbl carb or F.I. Corvette		3914660	68-69	327 & 327 Corvette		468642	78-79	350
3767460	62-64	283 or 327		3914678	68-69	327 & 327 Corvette			80-84	350
3767462	62-67	327		3917264	67	302		517513	79	267
3737465	60-61	283		3917290	68-69	307-327		6259425	68-76	350 (2 bolt)
3767754	60-61	283		3917291	68-69	350-327		6260856		350
3767792	60-67	283 car and truck			67-70	302-327		14014415	80-82	267
3770126	67-70	327-350		3917292	68	327		14014416	80-84	305
3774682	60-64	283-327 cars and trucks		3917293	68-69	307		14022301	80-84	305
3774684	62-64	283-327 Chev. trucks & GMC		3921175	66	327 (350 HP)		14022601	80-82	267
3774692	58-64	283		3927185	68-76	307-327-350				
3782461	62-70	307-327-350		3927186	68-72	302-327-350				
3782870	62-67	327 & 327 Corvette		3927187	69-70	302-350				
3782879	62-67	327 & 327 Corvette		3927188	69	307-327-350 light truck applications				
3789817	62-67	327 & 327 Corvette		3928454	68	307				
3789935	57-62	283		3928455	68	302-327 (325 HP & 350 HP)				
3790721	64-67	283		3928494	68	327 hi-perf 4 bbl & 350				
				3928495	68	327 std. & 327 (250 HP)				

FIGURE 2-3

heads from about '74 on. Some are recognizable by a lump in each exhaust port. This cuts down exhaust flow so some exhaust is retained in the chamber to reduce emissions. Exhaust seats on these heads have a tendency to crack. The casting number to look for on these heads is 333882. It is possible to replace this type of head with a similar head not having induction-hardened exhaust seats. However, if you do this, you'll have to run an unleaded gasoline suitable for both emission-controlled engines and non-emission type ones.

Compression Ratios — If you are specifically after more horsepower, assume that the heads get better up to 1969. Those in the late Sixties are better than those in earlier years. However, after 1969, most heads are low-compression, emission-type ones. If you have a choice between big-valve, low-compression heads and small-valve high-compression heads, choose the high-compression ones unless it is for heavy truck or R.V. use. As long as you keep the compression ratio below detonation levels, the higher compression ratio will be better for normal road use. Consider anything between 8.5- and 9.0-to-1 as a *maximum* compression ratio if an exhaust heated intake is used. Higher compression ratios than this are not compatible with today's octane-poor gasoline. You may disagree, but you'll be very unhappy with a higher compression ratio unless special precautions are taken.

If you have to buy heads, there are a few things to watch for, especially if you are looking in a wrecking yard.

First of all, there are a number of chamber capacities. To find out the capacity of any particular head casting chamber, refer to the photos, page 18. If you are replacing one type of head with another, it's a good idea to know what the compression ratio will be. In Fig. 2-2, I calculated a typical compression ratio with a normal flattop piston, the most commonly used piston in a rebuild. Heed what I said previously about the limits on compression ratio. To avoid going too high on the compression, don't use the smallest chamber heads on the larger displacement engines such as the 350 and 400 CID types. If you use heads from any other engine on a 400 it will be necessary to drill the two extra 1/8-inch water holes in the gasket surface area between each combustion chamber. A 400 head gasket can be used as a template for this job.

Make sure whatever head casting you choose has a combustion chamber volume similar to the heads you are replacing so that compression ratio does not exceed 8.5- or 9.0-to-1. The only time you can run over this 9.0-to-1 limit is when you are using one of the stock high-performance Chevrolet cams in your engine. These have enough overlap to effectively "kill" the extra compression and thus avoid detonation. Even with these longer period cams, I suggest 10-to-1 as the absolute top limit on compression ratio for a stock rebuild.

Valve Sizes— The next point to consider is that quite a few high-performance small-block Chevy engines use the 2.02-inch intake valves. Sometimes these heads are not easily available. However, in a lot of cases, heads equipped with 1.94-inch valves are basically the same casting. You have two possibilities for a replacement head should you have one or both heads unsalvageable.

First of all, if your 2.02-inch valves are in good condition, a 1.94-inch casting can be machined to take the larger valves. However, a point to be considered is: the difference between the 1.94-inch valve and the 2.02-inch valve in terms of performance is almost negligible, except for high-performance use. If the 1.94-inch valves look good, don't hesitate to use them.

Accessory Mounts— The next thing to watch out for are the accessory mounts on the head. Some high-performance heads have accessories (such as the air-conditioner brackets or alternator brackets), mounted in front of the engine, rather than alongside. Accessory mounts on these engines bolt to the front of the heads. The head castings are reinforced in this area so the bolt holes are supported strongly. If you are replacing heads which have these accessory mounts, you will need to replace them with similar heads. You cannot drill and tap non-accessory-mount heads to convert them. If you are looking for a particular set of head castings, a point

If you have to replace heads on a Camaro or Nova, you must make sure you have the type with the accessory-mounting holes on the front. The heads shown here are virtually identical except for those all-important holes (arrows).

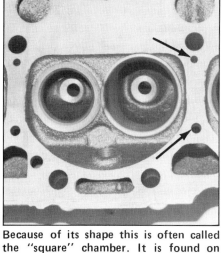

Because of its shape this is often called the "square" chamber. It is found on most low-compression emission engines. Pre-emission era low-compression heads are similar but the plug protrudes from a flat instead of raised surface. Example here is a 400 head. These often crack at the steam holes between each cylinder (arrows).

to remember is that although the casting number may be identical to the one you are looking for, it may not necessarily have the same size valves. Here I refer you to the chart, Fig. 2-3 on pg. 19. You may find that although you locate the right casting numbers, you may find the heads have smaller or larger valves when you remove them from the engine. You will have to decide whether or not you are going to run with those valves or not. You may lose performance, depending on which way you go. Generally speaking, the larger valve heads will give better performance than smaller valves at any given compression ratio.

Chamber Capacities— The next point I am going to cover is an extension of the first point, namely *chamber capacities*. If you are rebuilding a small-block Chevy under 300 cubic inches, it's a good idea to use the smallest chamber size which gives the desired compression ratio. Try to avoid using domed pistons to raise the compression ratio because your heads have too large a chamber volume. A much better alternative when replacing heads is to use the

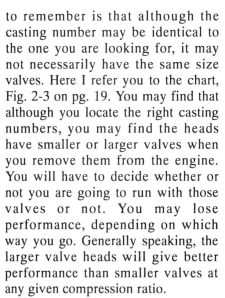

Most higher performance high-compression engines used this chamber shape. Early high-compression engines used a similar shape with smaller volume chambers to produce compression ratios between 8 to 1 and 9 to 1 with their smaller displacements.

smallest chamber volume you can with flattop pistons. At any given compression ratio, your engine will run better with flattop pistons than it will with domed ones. Flattops are much less expensive as well.

Some early small-block Chevys came with domed pistons as standard. If this is the case and the heads are good, don't bother to replace the heads as it will be less expensive to use replacement domed pistons.

If you are head hunting, this number identifies the casting. Once you have narrowed the search to the right casting number, check that the valve sizes are correct for your engine. Remember one head casting type may be used on several different specifications of engine, each possibly using different sized valves.

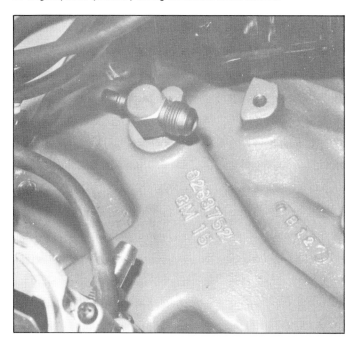

Manifold casting number is normally on one of the runners to the back cylinders. Though this number will help you identify a replacement, do not assume the same casting number means an identical manifold, because it does not! One particular casting type may have been machined several ways to suit different applications. After you have matched the casting number, check that all the vacuum take-offs, heat-sensor holes etc., are what your engine needs.

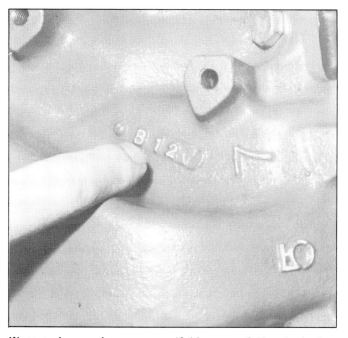

Want to know when your manifold was cast? Here is the key. First letter indicates month (A = January, B = February). Next number or pair of numbers denotes day of the month. Last number tells year it was produced. If you have one ending in a 5 or a 6, you will have to make an intelligent guess as to whether it was made in the fifties, sixties or seventies. Example shown here was cast in February (B) on the 1st day of the month in a year ending in 2. As it happens, it was 1972, the giveaway being the holes for smog equipment.

3
TOOLS & MACHINISTS

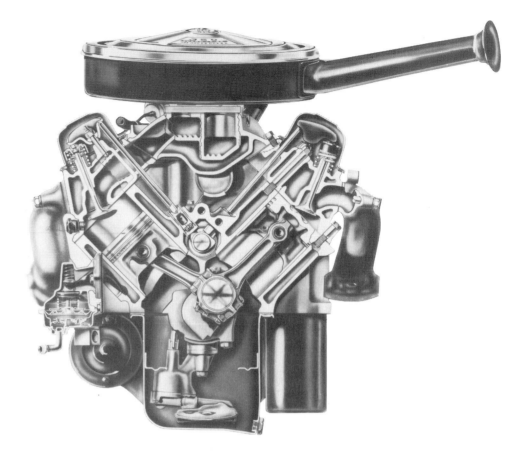

After 12 years, the small-block Chevy had grown from 265 to 350 CID through bore and stroke increases. 1967 engine shown here has the canister oil filter as the spin-on cartridge filters were not introduced until 1968.

Before you can put any engine together you are going to need some tools. Fortunately, the small-block Chevy is less demanding in this area than many other engines, so you will only need a few tools. Basically you need the tools shown in the accompanying photograph. These include a torque wrench covering the 30-85 pounds-feet range. You will also need 1/2-, 9/16-, 5/8-, 11/16- and 3/4-inch wrenches, open-end and box, or you can use a combination set with an open-end on one end and box on the other. Add to this a 9/16-inch deep socket and a ratchet. In fact the small-block Chevy engine is mostly taken apart with a 9/16-inch tool. For the pan bolts you will need a long speed handle and 7/16- and 1/2-inch sockets. Additionally you will need an 18-inch long bar to use as a lever, plus a hammer, a gasket scraper, 1/8 and 5/16-inch-diameter punches and a Phillips-head screwdriver and possibly a couple of other screwdrivers. To remove the spark plugs you will need a plug wrench. Spark plugs come in two sizes, both

with the same thread. One type of plug requires a 5/8-inch-deep socket, the other a 13/16-inch deep socket. You will also need a set of plastic or rubber sleeves or short lengths of plastic tubing to fit over the rod-bolt threads. These threads are either 11/32- or 3/8-inch diameter, depending on the specific engine. Those are the basic conventional hand tools required for disassembly. You will need additional tools to remove the engine from the car. These will vary from model to model and I won't even attempt to list them but a typically equipped tool box will cover most of your needs.

Special Tools — There are some specialized tools you'll need as the work progresses. A *valve spring compressor* is needed to tear down the heads. To check crankshaft sizes you need a *micrometer*. To remove the crankshaft torsional vibration damper, you must have a special puller. For installing piston rings at the time of assembly you need a *ring expander* and you have to use a *ring*

compressor to put the pistons into the bores. You can rent some of these tools. If you rent a micrometer, be sure to get the standards that go with it, because there is no guarantee the micrometer has not been mistreated before. A micrometer reading 0.002 inch (2 thousandths) out is about as useful as a piece of string a foot too short.

Depending on circumstances, you may have to rent an engine hoist for a day. Don't try to lift an engine on the beam of the garage roof! There is no substitute for safety.

Machine Shop Services — Apart from tools, you are going to need the services of a machine shop. Be sure you are going to a good one. Don't look around for the cheapest place, although I won't say a cheap place can't be good. If you have never used a machine shop before for engine work, ask around to find where you can get a good job done at a reasonable price.

Now here is a point which may save you getting some equipment.

Many auto machine shops will measure your crank and block for wear free of charge. Some shops will also tear down your heads if it is part of a valve and guide job. This could save you the price of a spring compressor.

Those things should be considered when you are deciding which machine shop to use.

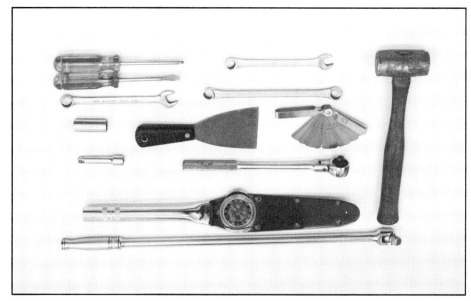

These are the basic tools you'll need to disassemble a small-block Chevy.

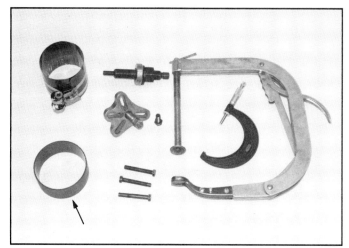

You'll also need some special tools, especially for assembly. The **B&B Taper sleeve (arrow) piston assembly installer is my preference over a conventional ring compressor. It's far faster, easier and less likely to break a ring. Along with whatever ring compressor/piston installer you choose, you'll also need a valve spring compressor, crankshaft damper puller and three micrometers covering the range 0-3 inches.**

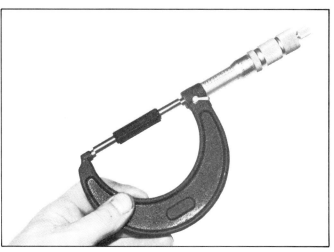

Before using a micrometer you are not familiar with, check its accuracy with a standard.

4
ENGINE REMOVAL PROCEDURE

1969 327 CID engine mounts the alternator on brackets bolted to the head. The effect of emission regulations can also be seen in the form of exhaust-manifold heating of the inlet charge. Thermostatic valve in the air cleaner balances the flow of cold air and hot air to maintain an even temperature over a wide range of operating conditions.

In this chapter, I will discuss the proper method to remove the engine. I do not mention emission equipment in any detail. This is because such equipment varies so much from year to year. However, the basic principles of emission equipment are generally similar across a broad section of models, including all those made by General Motors.

EMISSION-CONTROL EQUIPMENT

Emission equipment is often overlooked and sometimes removed. I like to breathe clean air so I am going to make my recommendations. There are probably emission controls on your engine. Make a note of how they come off so you can re-install them correctly when you put the engine back in. *Do not indiscriminately remove these devices.* Although many emission-equipped cars tend to have lower performance than their non-emission-equipped counterparts of earlier years, they will, in some cases, perform worse without the emission equipment for the simple reason that carburetors and distributors are carefully calibrated to work with the controls. If the equipment is removed, then the carburetor and distributor will probably be wrong, resulting in less performance and worse fuel consumption than you would otherwise get. Furthermore, in many areas of the United States, you won't be able to license your car without it.

Quite frankly, emissions equipment is beyond the scope of this book, but it's going to be with us from now on. If you have an emissions-equipped car, it's better that you learn something about it now than never, because it is here to stay.

Because most emission equipment is on the outside of an engine, you will not find many references to it in the rebuilding procedure.

REMOVING THE ENGINE

Taking the engine out of your car is probably the biggest and most cumbersome part of engine rebuilding. If you tackle it sensibly and in the right sequence, the job can be simplified greatly. A little planning will help. Since 1955 the small-block Chevy has resided in many different vehicles, so I am going to explain the general procedures for removing an engine, and these will be similar for other models within the Chevrolet family.

Before you actually start work on your car, clean the engine. This will make it a lot easier and pleasant to pull the engine, and it will also avoid heaps of crud all over your garage or workshop floor. A typical car wash with an engine degreasing bay is a good bet, although they are scarce nowadays because of problems with the grease seeping into the groundwater.

Having cleaned the engine, the next thing to do is to park the car where you intend to work, and make sure you park it on something sufficiently firm to take the weight of a jack and axle stands for those operations requiring the car to be jacked up so you can work underneath. From here on, I will detail everything in numbered steps, so let's go.

1. Park the car in a manner so it won't need to be moved until the new engine is installed. If the engine is non-HEI equipped, take off the coil lead from the distributor to the coil, and the lead running from the coil center (that's the high-voltage lead) to the distributor. If HEI equipped, remove the supply plug from the side of the distributor. Remove the leads from the battery so it is isolated. Use a puller designed for this if you have to. Don't wreck the battery post by trying to hammer or pry the cable connection loose. Now cover the battery with a rag or otherwise protect it so you won't accidentally create a short between the (+) terminal and (-) ground.

2. Drain water and oil into a receptacle and dispose of properly.

3. Scribe around the hood hinges with a sharp object. This will give you a reference point for alignment when the hood is re-installed. Do it now or you will wish you had later. Undo the front hood bolts on the hood-securing mechanism. The reason for undoing the front ones is this makes it easier for a second person to support the hood while the rear ones are undone.

4. Get a helper to hold the center of the hood while the rest of the hood bolts are undone.

5. Lift off the hood and stand it up somewhere well out of the way, making sure it won't fall over or be damaged. Wire the front hood latch to a stud or nail so the hood can't be knocked over accidentally. It costs money to repair a hood, even if you are the one who dents it by stumbling over it. The wind often does a bit of damage to an unsecured hood, too. If there are small children, I suggest securing the hood in a lockable shed or anywhere they can't get at it when you are not looking. The same goes for anything else you don't want to have disappear.

6. Remove the fan belt by loosening the alternator and lifting the belt out of the pulley grooves.

7. This next step is designed to save you a lot of knuckle busting later on, but the sequence requires changing slightly depending on whether or not you have a plain fan or a viscous-clutch-type fan on your

Use a large container to catch the oil as it tends to go in all directions when the plug is removed.

Scratch some marks on both hinge and hood to help find its position when the time comes to put it back on. Then remove the front bolts first when you start to remove the hood.

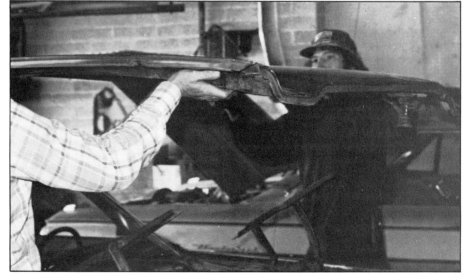

When all the bolts are out, lift the hood off. Store it away from your work area to reduce chances of accidental damage.

Loosen generator/alternator bolts, move alternator towards the engine and remove the fan belt.

Undo the fan shroud from the radiator and tip it back like this so you can get at the bolts. Some radiators are too close to allow doing this with a ratchet and socket but a box wrench will usually work.

Remove the fan and the shroud. Where space is limited keep the fan inside the shroud and lift the two out together.

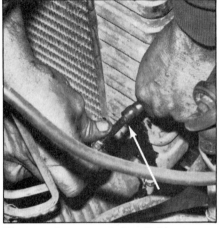

To save the transmission fluid on automatics after removing the lines to the radiator, connect the lines with a CLEAN hose as is being done here.

When all the bolts have been taken out, the radiator can be removed.

motor. To remove the plain fan, undo the bolts securing the fan shroud and move the shroud back so you can get between it and the radiator to undo the four bolts securing the fan. With some clutch-type fans, you may find you can get between the fan shroud and the radiator to get at the bolts securing the fan before the fan shroud is removed, so check to see if you can do it that way. Anyway, whichever method you use, you should end up with the fan shroud and fan removed. Lift the two out together. Remove the top hose if it is in the way.

8. If you have an automatic transmission, undo the automatic-transmission-cooler connections to the radiator, and using a suitable piece of hose, connect the transmission lines to stop dirt getting in. You can, if you wash it thoroughly, use the overflow tube from the radiator in a lot of instances. Of course if it's an old worn-out hose, don't use it because it may introduce dirt into the system.

9. Remove the top and bottom hoses from the radiator and engine or just the bottom one if you have already had to remove the top one in a previous step.

10. The next step is to remove the radiator clamp. This locates the top of the radiator to the body and is held in place by three or four bolts. On earlier models, up to 1964 on passenger cars and as late as 1966 on some trucks, you may find the radiator held in with four bolts, two down either side. Should this be the case, release the radiator by undoing these.

11. Having released the radiator, lift it out, taking care not to damage it by bumping it into anything as you lift it out. On some cars you may think you have enough room to work with the radiator in. Don't try it, as even a gentle bump from the engine could damage the radiator.

12. You should now have a clear field to work on to remove all the accessories at the front. If there is air conditioning, take off the pump and lay it to one side. If it looks like it will fall back in the way, use welding rod, bailing wire, twine or an old coat hanger or whatever you have available and tie it to one side. Do not disconnect the lines to it, otherwise you are going to have a job having the whole air-conditioning system recharged and you may have to buy new parts because air and moisture got into the system.

13. Remove the alternator/generator. It is not always necessary to remove the wires connected to it. Undo the securing bolts, lift it to one side and tie out of the way. When equipped with a smog pump it is easier if both alternator and smog pump are left on the engine and the wiring marked and removed from the alternator.

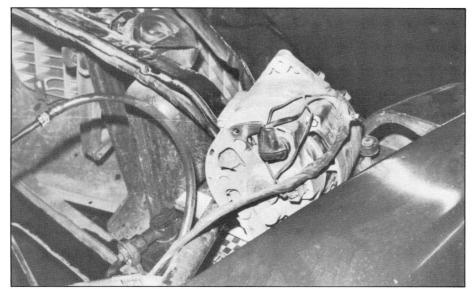
Lay the wired up alternator to one side but if the engine is smog pump equipped both smog pump and alternator should come out with the engine.

the engine, then replace the bolt in front of the block with a longer one. This will press against the pump pushrod and stop it from falling out. Tighten finger-tight only.

18. Remove the motor-mount bolts. Those on the fuel-pump side are always taken out from the back of the

mount. There may be a nut welded to the motor mount itself so it's just a question of putting a wrench on the bolt, undoing it, and sliding it out. Those on the other side may be installed from the back or the front, depending on other installation features. Also some are easier to get at from the top and others from underneath. Look at the situation and think through it to see the best way for your car.

19. Remove the distributor cap to prevent it from getting broken and also

14. Remove the power-steering pump. Again, this need only be unbolted from its position and held to one side. Leave the fluid lines attached. Just be careful to position the pump with the filler cap up so the oil doesn't leak out.

15. Pull off the fuel-pump supply and return line and plug them with some suitable object such as an old spark plug. Some tanks will siphon if the supply line is left unplugged.

16. Remove the fuel-pump line on the outlet side of the fuel pump—the one to the carburetor. Be sure to use two wrenches so you do not strain the line in undoing the smaller compression nut. The nut on the fuel line should ideally be turned with a *flare-nut* or *tubing* wrench because the nut is sometimes made of soft metal. A tubing wrench contacts the nut on five flats, instead of the two flats you'd be turning against with an ordinary end wrench. It's always cheaper to buy a tubing wrench than to buy the line with new nuts after you've damaged it with an end wrench. Having removed this line, you can then remove the fuel pump from the engine block. Place the pushrod and the fuel pump to one side.

17. As a matter of interest, if you have taken off the fuel pump mounting plate, and you want to keep the pushrod in place while you remove

WARNING! Don't break any fuel-line connections near an open flame because of the potential fire hazard.

Now you can get at the accessories on the front of the engine. Here the power-steering pump is being removed.

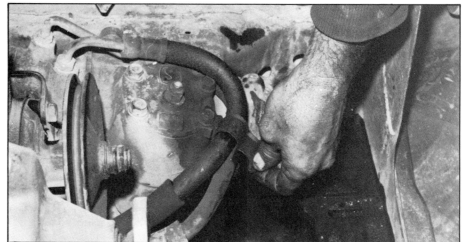
Do not disconnect the oil lines from the power-steering pump. Just release them from any securing clips.

27

Lay the pump to one side, keeping the filler opening up.

When you remove the inlet side of the fuel pump, be sure to plug the fuel line as some systems will siphon and spilled gasoline creates a fire hazard.

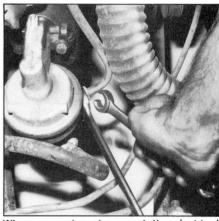

When removing the metal line (tubing) from the fuel pump, use two wrenches, one on the large nut and the other on the sleeve nut. Here I am about to use a tubing wrench on the sleeve nut.

remove the throttle linkage from the carburetor. If you have a manual-transmission vehicle or an HEI distributor, it is best to remove the complete distributor at this stage.

20. Remove the exhaust-manifold-securing bolts at the head. The importance of this step will depend upon the type of exhaust manifolds you have. If you have regular Chevrolet cast-iron ones, you have the options: You can either remove them from the heads now—if it looks like a simple enough job—or remove the exhaust pipes from the manifold at the connection a little lower down. With some engines which use the exhaust to actuate the choke mechanism, it will be easier to remove the exhaust manifolds *after* the engine is out of the chassis.

Tubular headers must be removed at this stage because the engine will not come out of the chassis with them still in place.

21. Jack up the car on the *frame* and pull the mufflers clear of the exhaust manifold. If your car has headers, remove the mufflers from the immediate area of the transmission, as this is the next part to work on.

22. Remove the dust cover from the converter if yours is an automatic, or clutch housing if you have a manual-transmission model.

23. Mark the flex plate and torque converter with a dab of paint in one spot so they can be returned to the exact relative position on assembly. This is important, so don't skip it or you'll be very unhappy when you put everything back together again and your engine vibrates badly because you destroyed the balance. An engine coupled to an

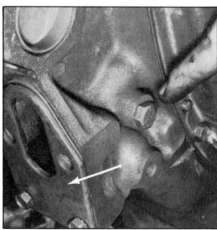

Replacing this bolt with a longer one holds the fuel-pump pushrod in place while the engine is removed. It also prevents the fuel pump from working if you forget about it, so don't leave it in! A bolt over 1-inch long will lock it. One under 1 inch will not. Only tighten just enough to hold the pushrod if that's your intention. Leaving the end plate (arrow) in place also prevents the pushrod from dropping out.

automatic transmission will come out with only the flex plate attached to the crankshaft. The converter stays attached to the automatic transmission. Separate the flex plate from the torque converter by undoing the three bolts. To turn the engine over on automatic-transmission cars, temporarily reconnect the battery positive (+) lead after checking that nothing is likely to short out. Use the starter motor to turn the engine so you can get at each successive bolt holding the flex plate and converter together.

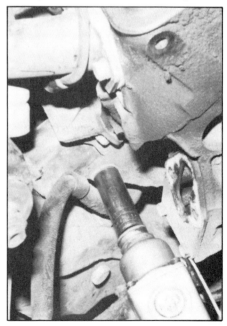

Once you can get at them, removing the motor mounts is easy. Here an air impact wrench is being used but any ordinary hand wrench will do.

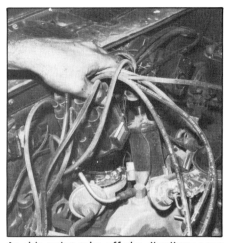

At this point take off the distributor cap to prevent its getting broken. If it has seen better days, junk it. If you have an HEI then pull the whole unit from the engine by undoing the clamp bolt under the main body of the distributor.

Leave cast-iron manifolds on the cylinder heads. They can be more easily taken off after the engine is removed. If you have tubular headers, unbolt them from the heads before trying to remove the engine.

Jack the car up and *support it on stands on the frame, not on the suspension.* Next, release the headers from the rest of the exhaust system. Or, unbolt the exhaust pipes where they join the stock cast-iron exhaust manifolds.

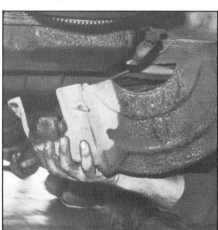

Remove the dust cover from the converter housing.

After you have marked the converter and flex plate so they can be reassembled in the same relation to one another, undo the bolts holding them together.

Take off the starter motor. In many cases this is easiest from under the car. Don't let it fall in your face when it comes free. It's heavy! Wear goggles or safety glasses to keep dirt out of your eyes when working under the car.

If you are working alone, you won't be able to reach the starter button from under the car. In this case, turn the engine over by engaging a screwdriver in the flywheel/flex plate ring gear and lever it around, using the bell housing as a pivot. Once these bolts are undone, the drive from the engine to transmission is disconnected. Disconnect the positive lead to the battery.

With a manual transmission, undo the bellhousing bolts, and in case I forget to tell you later on, mark the clutch to flywheel with a dab of paint on both at one spot so the clutch pressure plate goes back on the flywheel in the same place. You can do this after the engine is out, as the clutch and flywheel are still attached.

24. Whichever model you have, undo all the bellhousing bolts at the top and all except one at the bottom.

25. At this stage, climb out from underneath and remove the ground lead from the battery. Take the battery out of the car because you can clean it easier and get at the battery box or tray to do any cleaning or repairs which may be required.

26. Remove the starter leads. If these are very dirty, clean them because you will need to know in which order they go back. It's fairly

Using a suitable engine hoist which can be rented for the job, lift out the engine.

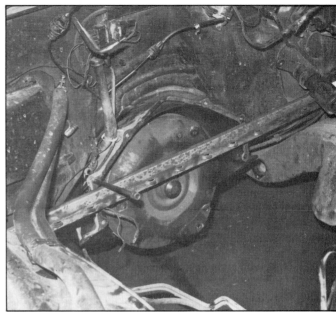

Once the engine is out, you can support the transmission with a piece of wood, metal, tube or whatever you have. This prevents loss of transmission fluid and prevents damage to transmission mountings and couplings.

obvious because the leads are all different sizes, but if you have any doubt, use masking tape to make short flags on each lead. Write on the tape so you'll know where they came from. Next remove the starter motor. Now, without fail, support the transmission with a jack, blocks of wood or what have you.

27. Undo two diagonally opposite intake-manifold bolts and using two similar but longer bolts, secure your engine-lifting chain at these points. One should be near the front of the engine and the other at the back. Attach the lifting chain from a suitable engine hoist or lift and put a little strain on the chain by starting to lift the engine very slightly. **Do not use the beam in your garage unless you know it will take 750 pounds IN COMPLETE SAFETY.**

Undo the last remaining bellhousing bolt, then lift the engine out. With manual-transmission models you will have to wiggle the engine and bring it forward so the clutch disconnects from the transmission input-shaft splines. With automatic-transmission cars, only a small amount of forward movement will be required to free it from the torque converter.

28. Remove the engine to the place where you are going to strip it down. Before you release it from the hoist, check to be sure you drained the oil. If not, do it now before letting the engine down to the floor. Congratulate yourself on getting this far. You did drain the oil, didn't you?

5
DISASSEMBLY

The clue to when this engine was made is the oil-filler tube in the inlet manifold. Engines from 1969 on had the oil filler in the rocker covers. This is a 302 CID Z28 Camaro unit built in 1968. It is equipped with a smog pump and the alternator is mounted from the head casting.

The ability to take things apart is a talent most people seem to possess. I'm not going to go into detail on how to take a small-block Chevy *apart*. Instead, I'll focus on what to look for while you are *disassembling*. This can tell you what may need to be done in the rebuild.

First, I'll assume you have the engine out of the car and all accessory equipment is off. This is merely a question of undoing the right nuts and bolts and taking them off. Talking of nuts and bolts, get some boxes so each group of bolts such as manifold bolts, pan bolts, etc., goes into its own marked box to avoid confusion at assembly.

Crankshaft Vibration Damper —
Make your first task the removal of the crankshaft vibration damper. For this you must have a puller designed for the job.

At this point the front pulley may still be attached to the crankshaft vibration damper. If so, you have to remove the pulley before you can fit the puller to the damper. This is done by removing the three securing bolts,

and on some high-performance engines you will also find a fourth bolt at the pulley center. It goes through a large flat washer into the crankshaft nose. Removing this can be a problem unless you lock the crank to prevent it from rotating. To do this, insert a large screwdriver into the flywheel or flexplate gear teeth, then lever against the block. Holding the crank locked, remove the bolt.

It's now time to use the puller and this is where your first complication can arise if you're not careful. The three lines in the crankshaft vibration damper can be tapped either 3/8-inch coarse (UNC) or 3/8-inch fine (UNF). There seems to be no rhyme or reason why they should be one or the other. When you attach the puller be sure you use the right thread. Check the threads on the bolts you have just removed. Also on very early small-block Chevys you may find the vibration damper has only two holes to attach the puller. Some 1955-57 dampers also had the pulley groove built into the damper. If you

have this type and it needs to be replaced, replace it with a newer style damper plus a new sheet-metal-type pulley to drive the accessories. Be sure to get a pulley with the correct fore-and-aft groove position as any misalignment will cause belt and possibly crank thrust bearing problems. So far as the puller is concerned, its use is simple enough. A precaution you have to take when using it is to ensure that the screws or bolts going into the damper itself engage at least 3/8 inch. If they don't engage with enough threads, the force you have to use to extract the damper may be more than those threads will withstand and they will pull out. This will leave you with a damper well and truly fixed to the front of the crankshaft, and that will present you with severe removal problems. Also check that the puller you are using will not damage any crankshaft threads. If the draw bolt of the puller does not have a cone in the end to match the one in the crankshaft nose, then reinstall the crank bolt so the draw bolt will bear against the crank bolt.

Transmission Components—With manual-transmission vehicles, progressively remove the bolts holding the pressure plate to the flywheel *a turn at a time* then remove the clutch cover and disc. The flywheel, or if you have an automatic-transmission vehicle, the flexplate, can now be removed. To do this lock the flywheel or flexplate by inserting a large screwdriver into the gear teeth and use the block as a stop to prevent rotation. Now undo the six high-strength bolts securing the flywheel or flexplate to the crankshaft.

Distributor—If you haven't already done so, remove the distributor after undoing the clamp bolt and removing the clamp.

Though I told you earlier, you may have overlooked disconnecting the wire that goes from the distributor to the coil. If you haven't undone this, you will not be able to remove the distributor, so disconnect it now and pull the distributor out, then make your very next job the removal of the coil bracket. On some engines, typically those with two-barrel carburetors, you will find the coil-bracket-securing bolts also hold down the throttle-cable bracket so when you remove the coil bracket, you will also be removing the throttle-cable bracket.

You did drain the oil before you took the engine out of the car, didn't you? If you didn't, you have a heavy cleaning problem unless you can hoist the engine while you drain the oil now!!

Covers—The next step is to remove the covers from the engine—rocker covers, oil pan and the timing-chain cover. Now you see inside the engine and get a good idea as to how dirty it is. A really dirty engine indicates oil changes have not been made frequently enough. Needless to say, this also indicates the engine will probably be in a lot worse condition than would otherwise be the case. If the engine is very clean or even reasonably clean, there is a fair chance that you are going to have a pretty easy time and a not very expensive job when it comes to rebuilding. If the engine is really dirty, then you could have some major things wrong, but don't despair. In many instances Chevy engines which have had the most abused life still seem to have many of their parts live through it and survive for many more years. Anyway, back to the teardown.

Intake Manifold—Remove the bolts holding the manifold in place and remove the entire manifold assembly. On those engines with exhaust-heat-operated chokes, disconnect the heat tube from the exhaust manifold before removing the intake manifold. In many cases, the intake manifold will need hot tank cleaning because of the deposits on the underside on the exhaust-heat passage. To reduce heating of the oil, the exhaust passage is equipped with a heat shield. If this is the type that almost fully shrouds the heat passage, as on most passenger-car manifolds, the shield must be removed to clean the deposits. This is easily done by using a punch as shown in Figure 5-1 and removing the rivets. The shield on some truck manifolds is not as large, and normal cleaning can be done without removing it from the manifold.

Rocker Arms and Pushrods—Next, remove all the rockers by undoing the adjusting nuts. Keep each nut, rocker and ball together by slipping the set of three pieces onto a piece of wire and twisting the ends. As you remove each, inspect it to see if it is scored. If there are heavy score lines on the ball or on the ball seat of the rocker, discard both now because they aren't going to be good enough for further use. The same also applies if that part of the rocker arm which bears on the end of the valve shows more than about 5 thousandths wear (0.005 inch). This you will have to estimate by

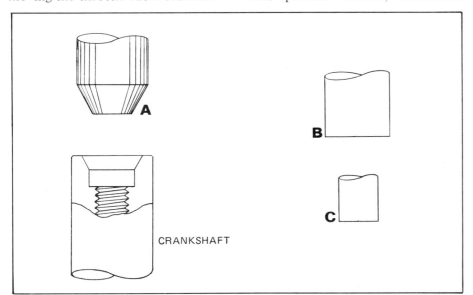

Thoughtless use of a damper puller can damage threads in the crankshaft nose. If the puller you are using has a screw end like B or C, install the center crankshaft bolt so the puller can operate against the bolt head. If the cone on the end of the puller screw is like A, and fits the crank cone, you don't need the crankshaft bolt installed.

You need a puller to remove the harmonic balancer. On high-performance versions you'll have to remove the securing bolt in the crank nose first. Puller-attachment threads in the damper are 3/8" but some are fine thread and some are coarse. Use the correct bolts to fit the threads.

Believe it or not, some engines are even dirtier than this. If yours is, expect the worst when you examine it for wear. Oil in this one was too thick to flow out of the pan when the plug was removed. No wonder the engine had to be rebuilt.

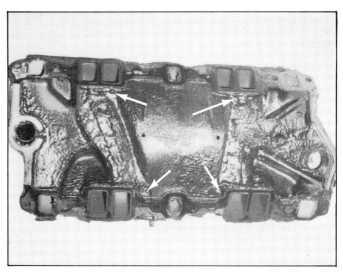

The underside of an intake manifold collects sludge. The only way to get at the worst of it is to remove the shield by taking out the four rivets in the positions arrowed. When rebuilding, the shield must be reinstalled as it covers the exhaust-heat passage. Oil splashing directly on this passage would cause an even higher rate of sludge formation.

eye and maybe make a comparison with a 0.005-inch feeler gauge.

Now pull out each pushrod and keep it in order with its respective rocker. The simplest way to make sure this order is maintained is to drill 16 11/32-inch holes in a piece of wood. Number the holes and note whether they are intake or exhaust. When you put the pushrod into the respective hole, place the rocker ball seat and adjusting nut over the pushrod.

Cylinder Heads—Cylinder heads can now be removed. Just undo each set of 17 bolts holding the cylinder head down. When it actually comes to lifting the head from the block, you may find the gaskets tend to stick the block and head together. The separation technique is to place a long wrench handle in an inlet port and lift at the far end to give maximum leverage. Thus usually breaks the head free without any trouble. Mark the heads and gaskets

RIGHT and LEFT to assist in identifying problems.

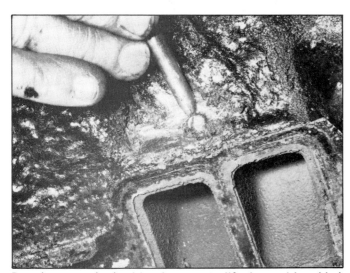

By using a punch, the drive-rivets can be lifted out with a chisel-shaped tool and the shield separated from the manifold. When it's time to reinstall, the drive-rivets can usually be reused as the spiral thread cuts a new groove.

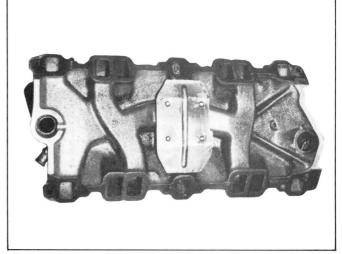

Most truck manifolds have a small exhaust-heat-passage shield and the manifold can be cleaned without removing the shield over the exhaust-heat passage.

Damaged exhaust-valve seat is bored out . . .

. . . and seat insert (arrow) is driven into place. Seat is then ground to correct angle and width. Photos by Ron Sessions.

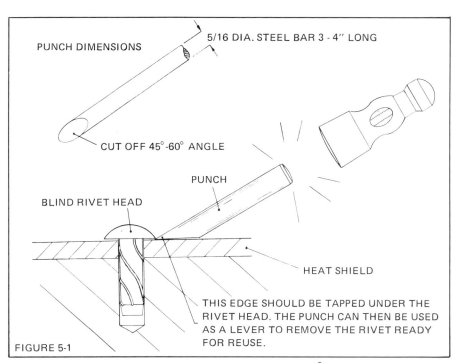

PUNCH DIMENSIONS

5/16 DIA. STEEL BAR 3 - 4″ LONG

CUT OFF 45°-60° ANGLE

PUNCH

BLIND RIVET HEAD

HEAT SHIELD

THIS EDGE SHOULD BE TAPPED UNDER THE RIVET HEAD. THE PUNCH CAN THEN BE USED AS A LEVER TO REMOVE THE RIVET READY FOR REUSE.

FIGURE 5-1

A piece of 5/16-inch to 3/8-inch steel rod cut at about 60° makes an ideal tool for lifting out self-tapping rivets which hold the intake manifold exhaust head shield in place. The technique is to drive the sharp edge of the tool under the rivet head, then lever the rivet head up to remove it. *Do not* cut off the rivet head.

VALVE-SEAT WEAR

With the EPA mandated elimination of tetra-ethyl lead—commonly called *lead*—from gasoline, increased exhaust-valve-seat erosion occurs. Engines originally designed for use with unleaded fuel have *induction-hardened* or *inserted* valve seats. However, all engines, whether they have hard seats or not, face the problem of using only unleaded fuel. This can mean that even if the valve seats, particularly the exhausts, have survived so far, simply refurbishing them to restore their original shape does not guarantee adequate durability.

The elimination of tetra-ethyl lead, though, is not the only source of exhaust-valve-seat wear. Worn valve guides, a situation itself aggravated by worn rocker-arm tips, can accelerate seat wear for both intake and exhaust valves. If seat wear is due to worn guides the solution is to simply fix the guides, recut the seats, and go about business as usual. However, an increasing proportion of seat wear is going to be due to lack of lead lubrication on the exhaust seats of both head and valve. The subsequent reconditioning procedures with early heads with soft exhaust-valve seats require that hard seats be installed. This requires boring out the original seat and installing an insert with about a 0.0045-in. interference fit. The seat is driven into place. It is then ground to the correct width and angle.

To remove the rockers, undo the securing/adjusting nut in the center. These are self-locking so expect them to be hard to turn—any which are not hard to turn should be thrown away.

Valve Removal—At this stage, if you have a valve-spring compressor, you can strip down the head. If you haven't got one, your motor machinist can do it for you, but he may charge for the work. My advice is: get a valve-spring compressor because if you ever have to do this job one more time, you will break even on the cost.

Guide & Seal Wear—Now the thought may cross your mind that your heads don't need any work. If this is the case, it will be very rare. Most Chevys wear out the valve guides. Once the guides start to wear, the seats also start to wear. This leads to bad sealing and the result is performance loss and high oil consumption due to oil going down the guides, plus greatly increased chances of detonation. Another area to inspect is the underside of the umbrellas that go over the springs. Very often the spring will wear the underside of the umbrellas. Eventually the outer part of the umbrella will drop free and oil consumption through the guides will increase.

Valve Wear—As I have just said, the valve guides will more than likely be worn; the valves themselves may still be usable. Have the valve stems measured. If they show no more than 0.002-inch wear, you can reuse them.

An inexperienced mechanic managed to remove this head, or at least most of it, without removing the eight short head bolts on the outside of the engine! The deed was accomplished mostly by using wedges, brute force and total ignorance!

I consider 0.002-inch wear the top limit if you are working on a tight budget: 0.001-inch wear if you can afford to buy new valves.

Another thing you should look for on the valves—and this depends mainly on whether you have a hydraulic or a solid-lifter cam—is the condition of the *valve seat surface.* With hydraulic cams, the valve seat has a relatively easy life and normally lasts 100,000 miles without showing undue damage. On the other hand, engines with solid lifters tend to "beat" the valve seat surfaces much more because of the tappet

clearance and the fact that the valves hit the seats harder. Very often this creates a groove in the valve seat face. To a degree, the valve can be re-machined (ground) to get rid of this groove. If it has gone too far, you should consider replacing the valve. If it cannot be ground to clean up and leave sufficient margin as shown in Figure 5-2, buy a new valve.

DISASSEMBLING THE BLOCK

Now let's get back to the block disassembly. The next move is to number-stamp all the connecting rods so their respective halves may be kept together. Do not overlook this simple step. Many an engine has had a short bearing life due to mixed-up rod caps. 1/8-inch steel numbering stamps will work fine for stamping the upper part of the rod and the rod cap as will a center punch and the requisite number of indentations.

Now follow this sequence, one bore at a time, and be sure you follow this because you will save yourself the cost of a reground crank if you do. Turn the crankshaft until the cylinder you are working with has the piston at BDC. First, remove the rod-journal cap you intend to start on. Next, place a rubber or plastic sleeve over the rod-bolt threads to protect the journal from scoring as you take the piston out. If the journal is obviously mutilated from lack of oil, this precaution is a waste

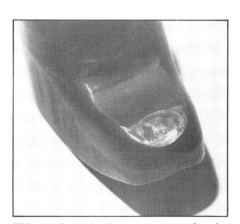

This rocker tip has worn too far for further use. With hydraulic lifters it can cause noise one moment and the next it will hold the valve slightly off the seat because an unworn part of the rocker tip is contacting the valve.

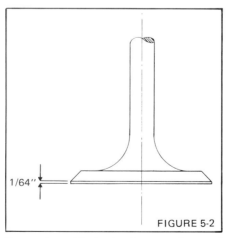

1/64″

FIGURE 5-2

Grooved or pitted valve faces can be saved by regrinding. If regrinding reduces the margin shown here to less than 0.015-inch (1/64-inch) then the valve should be replaced.

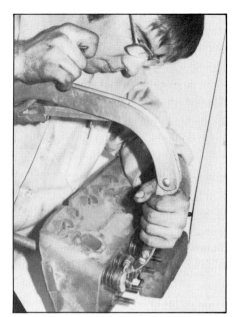

Almost all Chevy heads need rebuilding when overhaul time comes around. The guides wear out. Stripping the head requires a valve-spring compressor.

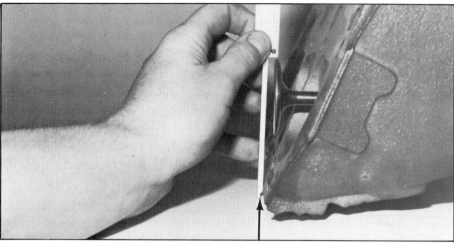

Position the end of the valve stem level with the valve spring end of the guide. Move the valve head up in the direction of the arrow and measure the distance to the surface the head is resting on. Move the valve head down and remeasure the distance. Subtract the larger measurement from the smaller then divide by 3. The figure you have left is the *total* valve guide clearance. If more than 0.005 inch clearance exists, consider a guide job.

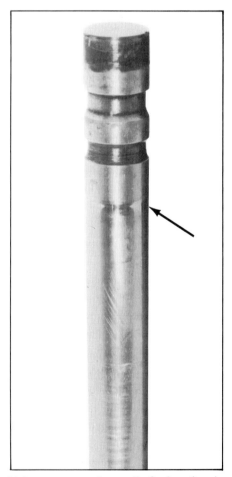

Valve-stem wear is usually far less than in the guides themselves. Even so, under severe conditions, a step may form and that means scrapping the valve.

of time. However, Chevy cranks do not wear very quickly. They may have suffered the toughest sort of life, yet still not need a regrind. You won't actually know in most cases until you put a mike on it. You won't be happy if you find it didn't need a regrind, but has to be ground because of the damage you inflicted with the rod bolts.

Removing Pistons—If there is large "lip" or *ridge* in the upper end of

the bore you will find it difficult to remove the piston through the top of the bore. More than likely, you will have to find a suitably stout bar and drive the piston out with a hammer. Should this be the case, you can forget about saving the piston for rering and reuse, because the piston will be smashed and the bore will be far past a rering job to recover its performance. If the ridge is small, then the piston will usually

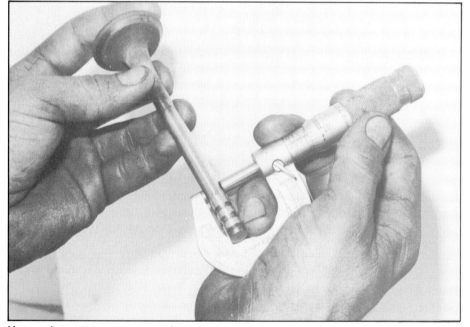

Use a micrometer to measure the valve stem on a worn and unworn section to see how much wear has taken place. With a bronze liner in the guide, you can get away with 0.002-inch stem wear, but 0.001-inch is much more acceptable. Inadequate guide jobs with 0.002-inch wear on the valve stem will not last. Valves can be an expensive item. Always spend whatever it takes for the best guide job as it can possibly save you the price of a set of valves.

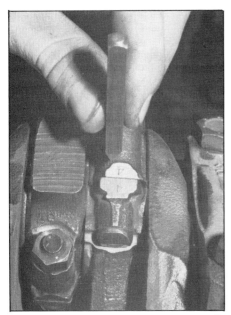

Before you attempt to remove any rods, caps or anything mark everything so that you know with what and where it has to go back. If you don't do this, you may have to buy new parts because you won't know which pieces match.

come out without any undue trouble. To ease the situation it is often a good idea to remove the carbon deposit build-up from around the top of the bore. A three-cornered scraper makes light work of this job.

Having told you about simple piston removal, consider the situation where piston removal is difficult, yet the bore and piston are still OK for further use. Under such conditions, you obviously don't want to damage the piston to make it unusable. If you suspect bore wear hasn't gone too far and yet you are unable to remove the piston easily because of a very pronounced wear ridge, then check the wear by comparing the ridge with a feeler gauge. When you find one that's close—say 0.003-inch—then double that dimension to estimate the wear (0.006-inch in this case). Better yet, use the more accurate ring-and-feeler-gauge method to measure the bore wear. This method of measuring the bore is explained in detail in the following chapter. If it is worn around 0.006-inch, and the piston won't come out easily, stop right there. Load up

your engine and go to your local machine shop and have them ridge-ream the tops of the bore to remove the ridges. When this is done you will be able to remove the pistons and continue with disassembly.

The ridge on the top of the block is not the only thing that could stop you from removing the piston easily. When you have removed the cap and slipped the rubber sleeves over the rod bolts, all appears to be straightforward. You start to tap the piston up the bore and then, more than likely, you find the piston comes to a halt. The temptation is to strike the piston harder until it does go up the bore as you originally intended. Resist this temptation because you may wreck your block. More than likely you will find your rod has dropped as it came off the rod journal so the head of a rod bolt is caught on the edge of the bottom of the bore. This isn't easy to see and many first-time small-block Chevy builders scrap their blocks by not realizing the rod is hung up. They go on driving the piston out and take a chunk out of the block, cracking the bore as they do it. All you need to do is raise the rod slightly until it travels up the bore and then removing the piston is no problem. This may require tapping the piston head so the connecting rod goes back down the bore a little way.

Once the piston is out, *put the cap on the rod and replace the nuts so everything is kept together.* Discard the bearings. Even though the crank may not be worn, bad oil and infrequent changes will damage the bearings nevertheless. They will almost always be worn. Besides, the cost is negligible and there is no good reason to reuse the old ones. This is no place to save money.

Checking Piston Wear Patterns— As you remove each piston from the engine, gently wipe the piston skirt and inspect the *wear pattern* on it. This is important to do right away. Do not wire-brush the piston to decarbonize it because you need to inspect the skirt wear pattern to establish whether the rod is bent or distorted. If the wear pattern is centrally placed on the piston skirt as

shown in the photo, you can assume that rod is true enough to be reused. Inspect each piston carefully this way. Important: This applies whether you plan to reuse those pistons or not.

Crank & Cam Timing Gears— When you have removed all of the pistons and made the checks just outlined, turn your attention to the crank and cam timing sprockets. First undo the bolts securing the cam timing sprocket to the cam. Take out the bolts, remove the cam sprocket and its chain, then inspect the sprocket. Chevrolet normally installs a nylon-faced cam sprocket to minimize engine noise. These are adequate in cool climates but wear and reduced reliability are greatly accelerated in hot climates. The nylon is also prone to cracking. If it does crack, the sprocket won't last much longer. It is a good safety precaution to replace a nylon-faced sprocket even if it appears new. However, your engine might have been torn down and

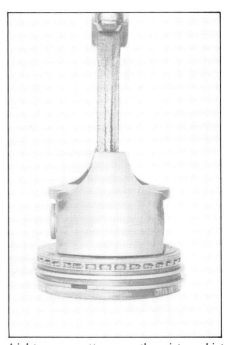

Light wear pattern on the piston skirt tells a story. Centered as shown here, it's a good indication the rod is not bent or twisted. If it is to one side or the other, make a note to pay special attention to that rod when checking rod/piston/pin alignment.

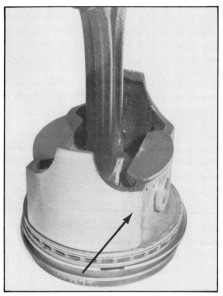

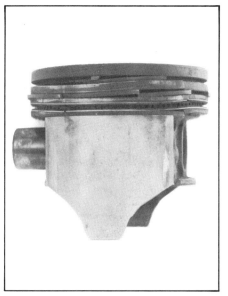

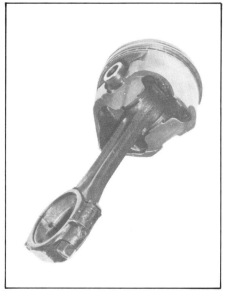

Here is another tell-tale sign. This piston has heavy scuff marks from a partial seizure caused by overheating. As a result the piston skirt may be on the point of collapse. The rings will surely have lost their temper if they are of cast iron. Other possibilities due to the overheating are weakened valve springs and cracked heads. Check out *all* of these possibilities before using any of these components in the rebuild.

Dentonation and overheating led to the end of the road for this piston. Anytime you see this, check your heads for cracks and rod journals for ovality.

A rare occurrence. Due to a mis-sized wrist-pin bore, the pin in this rod crept out and eventually made contact with the bore. When this rod came out it had cut a 1/8-inch-deep groove up and down the bore. The block was saved by sleeving that cylinder.

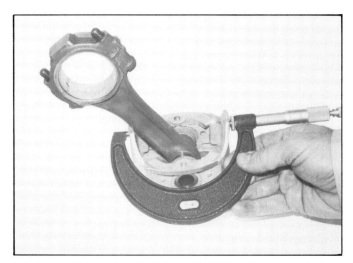

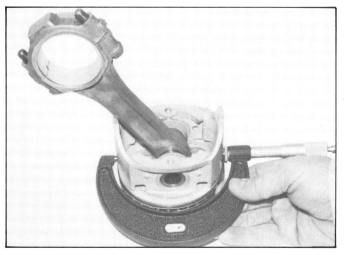

Carefully measure the size of the piston at the open end of the skirt as shown at left. It should be between 0.0005-inch to 0.002-inch larger than the size measured 90° to the pin axis at pin height as shown at right. If this is not the case, the piston skirt may be ready to collapse.

Used gear on right illustrates typical fate of nylon-faced gears. Bad lubrication contributed to excessive wear and the gear teeth are breaking up. With a little chain wear this can proceed to the point where the chain can jump a tooth, with possible disasterous results to the valves and pistons.

It may be difficult to see, but the screwdriver is pushing out a lifter.

rebuilt at some stage earlier. Remember, Chevy engines never die—they just fade until they get rebuilt. In such a case, the previous engine rebuilder may have installed a steel sprocket. These last much longer. Just check the sprocket teeth to see that the wear has not progressed too far on them. If it has not, then assume it is okay for further use. So far as the timing chain itself is concerned, junk it! If you have bad lubrication in the engine or it has seen lots of miles, it is definitely worn.

Crank Removal—The next step is to remove the main-bearing caps after numbering them 1 through 5, starting at the front of the engine. Then take out the crank and discard the bearings.

Cam Removal—Once the crank is out, push all the lifters out of their respective bores. Then—and only then—can you pull out the camshaft. This is made easier by temporarily putting the cam sprocket back on the cam. Unless the engine is obviously in bad shape, try not to damage cam bearings as you remove the cam. You'll cause the least damage to cam bearings if you turn the engine so you are lifting the cam straight up to get it out.

BLOCK CLEANING

Here you reach the point for another decision. That is, the method you will use to clean the engine block and cylinder heads. If the engine is not too dirty inside, and I mean not too dirty, then you can wash it with engine-cleaning solvent and water. Some car washes will let you take your engine to one of their bays and do the cleaning there. However, if the engine is very dirty inside, then hot-tanking is the best solution for cleaning it.

Saving Cam Bearings—Now here's the problem: Many hot-tank solutions will erode aluminum-compound bearings. In most cases this is the type of cam bearings you have in your block. Hot-tanking with certain high-powered cleaners will ruin these bearings, even if they were okay for further use, which they usually are. This means these bearings must be removed and replaced. Even if the bearings are not worn they should not be left in while the block goes into the hot tank. With the exception of very early blocks that used a slotted cam, there are grooves behind the cam bearings that collect deposits of sludge and grime. This is just one of the reasons why blocks should be hot-tanked.

If the block needs to be hot-tanked, remove the cam bearings. Then, remove the three drive-fit plugs that are above the cam-bearing bore at the front of the block.

It is not practical or even desirable to work on an engine or its parts which are this dirty. Either farm out the cleaning or be prepared for considerable time in messy degreasing.

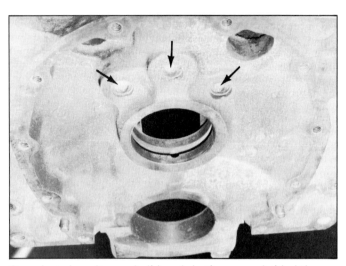

One place deposits can build up is in the groove behind the rear cam bearing. To be certain this is properly cleaned out, the cam bearings must be removed. Plugs (arrows) must also be removed to clean out the oil galleries.

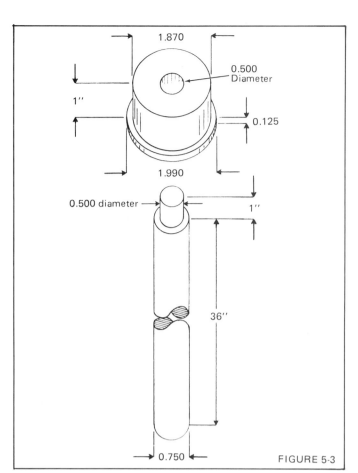

FIGURE 5-3

If you intend to remove and install your own cam bearings you will need a tool like this.

This is important because deposits collect behind them. Also remove the three plugs at the opposite end of the oil galleries at the back of the block. This will allow you to run a brush through each passage. The rear cam-bearing plug and waterjacket freeze plugs can be difficult to remove, so refer to the photos to see how to go about it.

Have the block cleaned. Most engine shops will charge about $50 for hot tanking, plus approximately $40 for installing presized new cam bearings. I recommend that you have the shop install the cam bearings rather than try it yourself. The procedure is too difficult and there is no margin for error.

Some reconditioning shops have high-pressure-spray engine cleaners. This is a tank containing a rotating platform for the engine components. Solvent at very high pressure is directed at all angles onto the block. Not only does this have the benefit of the solvent to clean the block but also the solvent strikes the block so hard that it removes deposits with a very pronounced scouring action. The solvent used in some spray cleaning tanks does not destroy bearing material. Unless you have a block which has really clogged-up oil passages, it may not be necessary to remove the cam bearings. Here, your best plan is to seek advice from whomever you take the block to for cleaning. They will have a far better idea of just what their spray tank can cope with and what it can't. It may also be wise to check whether or not the chemicals they use will damage your cam bearings, be-

cause not all these tanks use non-corrosive cleaning chemicals.

With a spray tank, you may be able to leave your cam bearings in but you certainly can't leave the main oil gallery plugs in. These will have to come out no matter what sort of cleaning tank is used.

Having your block cleaned in one of these spray tanks may save you money. My advice is to do a little phoning around to find out which shop has one and whether or not you can leave the cam bearings in. It could be that you will save the cost of installing new ones.

As far as results are concerned, these spray tanks make the blocks come out like new. My own experience with them is that they do a really good job and are well worth

The first block cleaning step is scraping off all old gaskets.

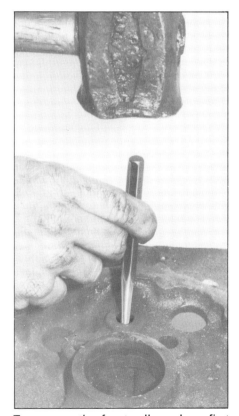

To remove the front gallery plugs, first drive in a tapered punch.

Hold a large lag screw or bolt in a pair of Vise-Grip pliers and screw into the plug.

With the tire lever against the Vise-Grip pliers, lever out the plug.

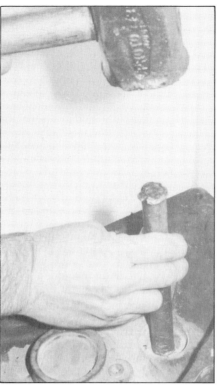

To remove the freeze plugs, first drive them into the block.

When the plug is down in the water jacket tap it off to one side as shown here.

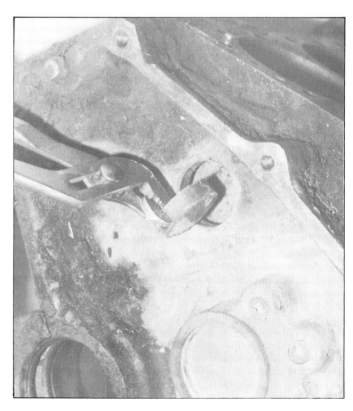

Grip the edge of the plug and lever against the side of the block.

Lean on the pliers and out comes the plug!

Most engine rebuilders have a cleaning tank. This "boil-out" tank cleans the block and anything else placed in it right down to the bare metal.

After hot-tanking, the block is washed off with water at high pressure. Then the water is blown off with high-pressure air. In humid climates a rust inhibitor should then be applied to the block surfaces to retard rust formation.

the effort finding an establishment with such a cleaner to do your block.

Here's another point worth noting. Some places will put the heads in with the block and get those roughly cleaned off at no extra cost, since they have to run the tank to do your block anyway. Again this is a point to be checked. Cleaning the heads at this stage is no real advantage except in situations where they need no further work on them because the guides are in good order. Usually it's not really worthwhile cleaning the heads until all the work is done on them. But, if you can get them clean for nothing it will mean that the heads will be that much less messy to handle.

Cleaning The Block Yourself—Don't attempt to clean the block yourself unless you are prepared to spend many hours doing it thoroughly.

With new engines, even minute particles of grit can cause wear problems because of the small clearances between bearings and journals. If you are wondering how the clunker you are stripping down tolerated so much dirt in the oil, just remember, old worn-out engines have big bearing clearances. Big clearances allow more debris to pass through the bearings without necessarily making the situation much worse. This is not true with new bearings. The parts and work place must be kept scrupulously clean when you are rebuilding your engine if the job is to last as long as you would like.

CLEANING THE CYLINDER HEADS

At this stage, it's not really necessary to clean the cylinder heads unless you had them hot-tanked at the time the block was done. The most important time to clean the heads is after all the machining has been done on them, because they are going to get grinding dust and machining dirt on them anyway whether you clean them now or later. The only reason for cleaning the heads now is to make any cracks that may be in the head a little easier to see. Most cracks will be self-evident, but you will be dollars ahead if you avoid spending good money on a bad head.

Personally, I would at least give the heads a good dousing in engine-cleaning solvent and a quick hosing to get the worst of the deposits off.

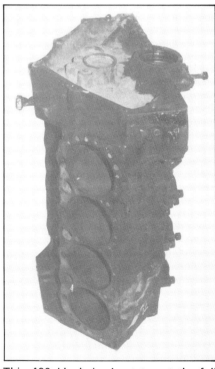

This 400 block is about to get the full cleaning treatment in a jet-spray tank.

Though you usually pay more to get a block cleaned in a spray-jet tank, it does a very thorough job and is generally worth the extra cost.

Before a block is removed from the turntable in the high-pressure-spray tank it is washed down with water to remove the cleaning chemicals.

This is the 400 block after it has been cleaned in a spray tank.

6

RECONDITIONING THE PARTS

The biggest displacement production small-block Chevy—the 400 CID engine, was introduced in 1970. This low-compression engine was designed to meet the horsepower and emission requirements for heavy vehicles. For about two years, these engines had four-bolt main-bearing caps. Later engines used only two bolts to support each main cap.

THE BLOCK

If you are to build a good reconditioned engine at a price not too near the sky, the trick is to know when a used part is OK for further use and when it should be junked.

Just because the block appears to be a strong hunk of cast iron, don't assume that it's indestructible, because it isn't. There are factors other than whether or not the block can be rebored, which may determine its further usage. These must be checked out before you even look to see if the block needs a rebore. Generally speaking, the most common problems a small-block Chevy can suffer in the block department are caused by inexperienced small-block-Chevy builders. The first thing you should look for are cracks in the block main-bearing webs where the main-bearing bolts screw in. Cracks in this area are a sure sign the bolts were overtightened by a previous builder. This problem is more common on two-bolt main bearing blocks although it can happen on

four-bolt blocks if the engine was previously put together by a King Kong rebuilder.

If any cracks are found, scrap the block. It's OK to cry a little.

The next thing to watch out for is the handywork of a heavy-handed rod/piston remover. Remember from the stripdown how it was possible to catch the rod bolt on the bottom edge of the block as you were pushing the piston out? When the piston comes to a stop because a bolt is caught on the edge of the bottom of the bore, it's amazing how many people are convinced the piston has become tight in the bore. They then continue to hammer on the piston until it finally comes out, usually with a chunk of bore as well. This can cause a crack in the bottom of the bore which may go farther up the bore than just the area where the piece has been smashed out. Check this. If in doubt, have your block pressure tested when you take it to be rebored.

The third common complaint is— has the engine ever been run with a

blown head gasket? If it has, and they usually blow between cylinders, then it could well be that the hot gases have scoured away the cast iron and left the block in need of a heavy decking job (machining the damaged head-gasket surface). On 400 engines where the block thickness between each cylinder is small due to the large bores, running with a blown head gasket will cut a substantial groove into the block.

On the smaller bore engines, it isn't quite so much of a problem. However, the moral is, if you have a head gasket blow on a small-block Chevy, don't drive it. Some engine rebuilding shops have facilities to weld up blocks which have worn in this region. The block face is then remachined and a rebore is done on the cylinders to clean up any weld which may have slopped into the bore and to straighten any upper-bore distortion.

Those are the three most likely things you will find on a small-block Chevy. However, you should check all threads, dowel holes and

In case you really didn't believe that it's possible to remove a hunk of bore while stripping the engine, here is the irrefutable evidence.

anything else that looks like it has something which fits to it and may be a source of problems. Check that there are no cracks, no stripped threads, etc. Then and only then can you turn your attention to other aspects of the block.

Usually the biggest increase in fuel consumption and loss of power is caused by worn cylinder bores. Reboring the cylinders and installing oversize pistons is the most obvious way to cure the worn-bore problem. It is also the most expensive. In some instances you can spend less by following other courses of action. It all depends at what point you elected to do this rebuild and how much wear had already occurred.

BORE-WEAR MEASURING

To rebore or not to rebore? This is the question. You can establish this by measuring the amount of wear on both the bores and the working surfaces of the pistons.

Let's check out the bores first to see how much wear your block has. This will be one of the major factors influencing whether or not you need to bore the block. First, clean out the bores, especially the top of the bore where carbon deposits gather in the area above the top ring. Using a wire brush, clean it off down to the metal so you can establish the size the bore was prior to the wear. Now at this point a snap gauge or inside micrometer is a useful item to have, but not essential. If you have either of these two items, measure the amount of wear that has taken place on the bore. With the snap gauge you will need an outside micrometer to measure across the gauge points to see what size you have in both the worn part of the bore and the unworn part of the bore. Measurements should be taken at 90° to the crankshaft axis and then parallel to the crankshaft axis and measurements should also be done at top, middle and bottom

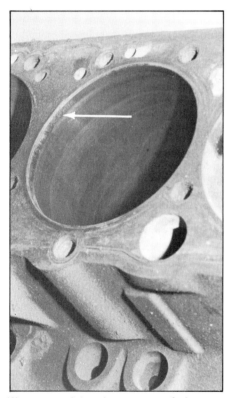

Wear caused by the passage of rings up and down the bore leaves a "step" or "ridge" at the top of the bore (arrow). If small, due to little wear, this step can be removed by ridge-reaming. Bore shown here has gone too far for that and needs reboring plus new pistons.

Measuring the bore with the inside micrometer to see how much wear has taken place.

Inside micrometers are subject to wear on their measuring pads, so the wise machinist/builder checks the inside "mike" with the appropriate outside "mike" to get a more accurate and reliable measurement.

of the bore so you can establish the shape the bore has worn to. Most bore wear occurs from side to side rather than from front to rear of the bore. This is due to side thrust on the piston generated by crank rotation.

You say you don't have a micrometer? If you don't have either an inside micrometer or a set of snap gauges, don't despair. You can get a good idea of the amount of wear that has taken place by the piston-ring-and-feeler-gauge technique shown in the accompanying photos. Here is an example of how it works:

Ring gap measured at the top of the worn portion just below the ridge

= 0.062 inch (62 thousandths)

Ring gap measured at the top of the bore on an unworn section (on ridge)

= 0.030 inch (30 thousandths)

Difference

= 0.032 inch (32 thousandths)

Then $\dfrac{0.032 \times 7}{22}$

= 0.0102 inch (10.2 thousandths) wear

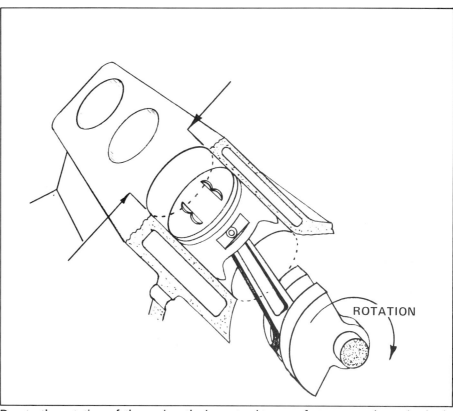

Due to the rotation of the engine, the bores tend to wear faster across the engine in the direction of the arrows than parallel with the crank. The outer cylinders of each bank also tend to wear more than the inner pair, possibly because of a longer warm-up time.

Another technique to establish bore size or to measure wear is to use a dial bore gauge. Correctly used, these are very accurate.

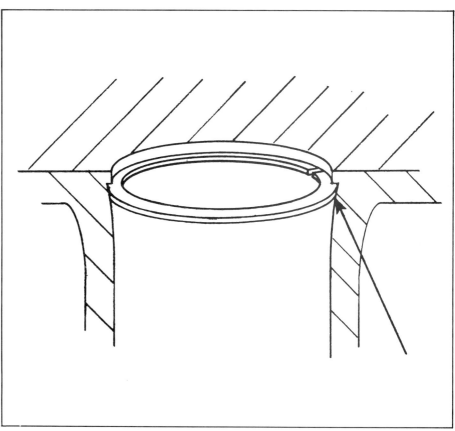

When checking for maximum wear with the ring and feeler method, be sure the ring is positioned up against the bottom of the wear ridge.

47

In the absence of precision measuring equipment, the ring and feeler-gauge method can be used. Though simple, it gives a surprisingly accurate wear measurement. First, put a piston ring at the top of the bore on the unworn section and measure the ring gap. Clean any carbon from this part of the bore to avoid getting a false reading.

Next, using the same ring positioned on the worn part of the bore below the ridge, remeasure the ring gap. Subtract the first measurement from the second. Multiply this by 7 and divide by 22. What you are left with is the average diameter increase due to wear. On this engine I took measurements at the top, middle and bottom of the section traveled by the top ring.

The figure you are left with is *average diametral bore* wear — in this case — 0.0102 inch. Because this is the *average* wear, a rebore will be needed at a lower wear figure than that indicated by the snap gauge or inside-micrometer measurement method. Measuring with the snap gauge or micrometer indicates the maximum wear which has taken place, and this is really what determines whether or not the block needs to be rebored.

Example — A particular engine must be rebored when the wear gets to 0.0055 inch when measured with a micrometer. If measured by the piston-ring-and-feeler-gauge method, then in all probability it would need to be rebored when 0.004-inch wear is detected. This is because there may be 0.006-inch bore-wear across the engine but little bore-wear along the longitudinal axis. This can show up as an average wear of 0.004 inch when the actual maximum bore-wear was 0.006 inch.

PISTON-TO-BORE CLEARANCE

If the bores have worn more than 0.006 inch when measured with a snap gauge or inside micrometer, or 0.004 inch when measured with the ring-and-feeler-gauge method, then the block needs to be rebored. Experience has shown that a small-block Chevy with about 0.006-inch wear at the top of the bore will, when rebuilt with a good set of moly rings, run up to 50,000 normally driven miles. At the end of 50,000 miles, they are generally down 10-15 percent on power and are using oil at about 500 miles to the quart. Chevrolet's own wear limits for *reringing*, as opposed to reboring, are smaller than those I quote here. The factory generally figures an overhauled engine should run at least 100,000 miles. In many cases, if you are working on a tight budget, an engine which will run respectably for 50,000 miles will get the job done. In most cases that's going to represent two or three years driving. Approximately 0.006-inch bore wear represents roughly 50,000 miles of remaining life when new rings are installed. Bores worn less than this will give a longer life but more wear shortens the life drastically and it very quickly gets to the point where the rings will never seal well right from the start.

With excessive wear in the bore, you quickly realize that a rebuild without a rebore is not very economi-cal. If you try to rebuild an engine worn beyond this limit, the engine will be short-lived. Before finally deciding whether to rebore or not, check the total piston-to-bore clearance as described a little later on. If it measures less than the quoted figures, your engine may not need a rebore. It now depends upon the condition of your pistons and I will come back to these in a moment. Right now you need to check whether the rest of your block is serviceable and what may or may not need to be replaced.

CAM BEARINGS

Earlier I mentioned different methods of cleaning and the fact that some methods may not only clean out the dirt from your engine, but also clean the camshaft bearings of their bearing material. The point I want to make is, you may not need new cam bearings if the engine has been well cared for. If this is so, you can save yourself both the price of hot-tanking and the cost of new bearings by cleaning the block yourself. If you clean the block yourself, be sure to remove all the deposits from the groove behind each of the five cam bearings or the front four of pre-57 blocks. A piece of wire jiggled through the cam oiling hole, plus liberal doses of kerosene or a good quality degreaser, may do the job. The

Cam bearings may not be too worn. If this is the case and the engine is not too dirty internally, it will be worthwhile cleaning it yourself as this will save the cost of cam-bearing replacement due to hot-tank erosion of the bearing surfaces.

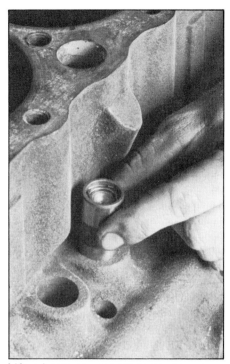

Lifter bores are not prone to wear, even after high mileages. Easiest way to check them is to check whether a *new* lifter (tappet) is a reasonably snug fit.

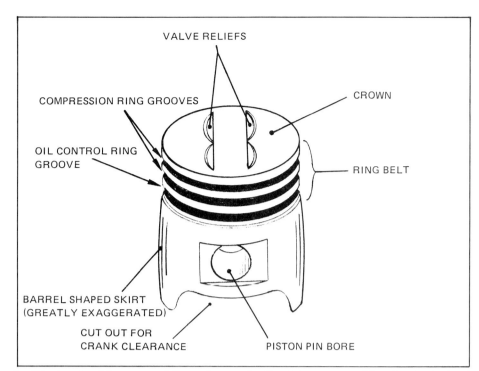

In this drawing I have named the various parts of a piston so you will understand what I am talking about.

problem is that you have no real way of knowing, short of removing the bearings, whether or not the grooves are clean. Stubborn deposits require the removal of the cam bearing. However, if it gets to that stage, you are probably better off paying for block cleaning and having new cam bearings installed. On the small-block Chevy, the bearing housings are bored with sufficient accuracy so that driven-in presized bearings will do the job. This does away with the need for an expensive align-boring operation and allows using simple drivers to make the installation.

LIFTER (TAPPET) BORES

These almost never wear, but a simple check can be made by oiling a new lifter and inserting it into each of the bores to see that it is a slop-free slide fit. In the unlikely event that the lifter bore has worn you will have to scrap the block.

PISTONS

Even after considerable mileage your pistons may still be reusable. Wear occurs in four places:
1. On the piston skirt due to its rubbing up and down the bore.

2. In the ring grooves due to the continual rubbing of the rings as they flex in and out and take the inertia and gas loads during normal operation.
3. Piston-pin bores due to the angular motion of the rod.
4. Piston skirt collapse due to overheating.

TOTAL PISTON CLEARANCE

If engine silence is not a prime consideration, quite a large increase in piston-to-bore clearance due to wear can be tolerated. One point I am going to stress is reringing old pistons and using them in old bores usually means a shorter life due to the initial extra clearance caused by wear.

Usually, most wear takes place on the bore—not on the skirt of the piston. Your first job is to check the skirt wear or the piston skirt-to-bore clearance. The easiest way to do this is to remove the rings from the piston and place the piston in the bore. Then, using a feeler gauge 90° to the piston-pin axis, check to see how large a feeler gauge can be inserted between the bore and the piston.

Check this at various positions up and down the bore to establish just what the largest piston-to-bore clearance can be. If the largest clearance exceeds 0.008 inch you need a rebore; Between 0.006 and 0.008 inch you are in that twilight zone where you really have to make up your own mind. Under 0.006 inch, you can rering and expect a reasonable life of up to 50,000 miles before you need to recondition the engine again.

As the small-block comes from the factory, it can have as little as 0.0008 ± 0.0003-inch clearance between the piston and bore, to as much as 0.0027 ± 0.0003-inch. The small clearance is for cast-aluminum pistons used in regular passenger car and truck engines. The large clearance is generally for forged aluminum pistons in high-performance versions of this engine. With the high-performance engines, you may find, although you have a bore wear under 0.006-inch, the total clearance is over 0.008-inch due to the bigger initial clearance between the bore and skirt of the original piston. Don't be tempted to run with

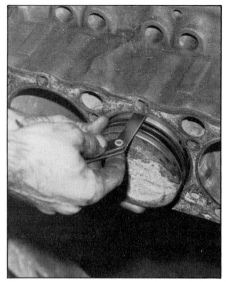 

Piston-to-bore clearance is the deciding factor as to whether or not a rebore is required. With the rings removed from the piston, this clearance can be checked with a feeler gauge. Place the feeler gauge alongside the piston as shown in left photo. Then push the gauge and piston down the bore so the skirt is on the worn part below the ridge. Remember you are checking *skirt* clearance, not the clearance around the ring belt, which is very much more.

over 0.008-inch total clearance because it won't work for long.

GROOVE CLEARANCE

Once you have established that the piston-to-bore clearance is satisfactory, you need to check how much the ring grooves have worn. You may find it difficult to visualize how ring grooves wear since a very slow rotation in the groove is the only relative motion between ring and piston. This is the case for a new engine but as time goes by new factors become involved.

At the time of ignition and combustion, the top ring sees a very much increased outward load due to the gas pressure getting behind it. The second ring sees very much less than the top ring because the top ring has sealed most of it off from the second ring. This high outward force from the top ring during ignition and combustion causes the first half-inch or so of the bore from the top of the stroke down to wear much quicker than the rest of the bore. When the bore wears in this tapered fashion, the ring as it maintains contact with the bore, flexes in and out of its groove. This is the major cause of wear in the ring groove. Grooves which have

worn more than a few thousandths will mean that the rings will have a harder time sealing. This leads to more blow-by, loss of power, increased oil consumption, high oil contamination and generally greater engine wear. With a small-block Chevy you should regard about 0.004 inch on the compression rings as the absolute limit of ring-groove clearance. On the oil-control ring, 0.0055 inch can be tolerated, although you will rarely find the oil groove worn anywhere near that limit. As the nearby photo shows, checking the ring groove is simple enough. You place a new ring in the groove and check the remaining gap with a feeler gauge. Do this at sever-

al points around the circumference of the ring groove. Doing this with a segmental oil-control ring is more difficult. Here the easiest thing to do is to assemble the old ring into the groove. You will find if the wear is 0.0055-inch maximum with that, then it will be less with a new ring.

PISTON PIN BORES

With a press-fit piston pin it is difficult to remove the pins from the piston to check how much the surfaces have worn. Fortunately for us, these surfaces wear very little. The easiest way to check them is to see if there is any detectable slack in the pin bore when you twist the crown of the piston one way and

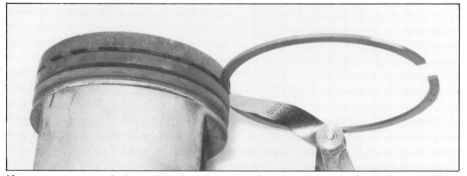

If you are contemplating using the pistons again with the new rings, then you must check the ring-groove clearance as shown here. This should not be more than 0.004 inch (4 thousandths). Any more than this and you are wasting your time because rings won't seal very long in a worn groove, so junk the piston.

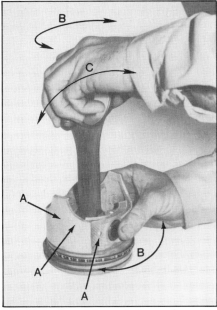

Checking the piston pin-bores for wear and cracks. Any cracks usually occur in the areas indicated by the arrows A. To check the pin bearing in the piston, first try twisting the rod and piston back and forth in opposite directions indicated by arrows B. Next, try holding the piston against the bench top and try rocking the rod sideways in the direction of arrow C. If any movement is felt due to wear in the pin bore, or any cracks are evident, junk the piston.

the rod the other way. The clearance should be so small that you should not be able to detect any apparent movement except in the direction the piston should swing. See photo at left.

PISTON SKIRT COLLAPSE

If an engine has overheated, especially one with forged pistons, the piston skirt may be at the point of collapse. When the engine overheats, the skirt expands until all the clearance has been taken up in the bore and the sides of the piston are forced against the bore. If a piston has been through this phase, it should be discarded because it will not last much longer. The usual telltale sign is score marks towards the edge of the thrust area of the piston and fine cracks in the wrist-pin-boss area. The edges of the thrust area do not normally touch the bore. If it has wear marks on it, there's a fair chance the piston has been overheated, so discard it.

A Rebore is Best—To restore the performance of a cylinder, a rebore is best because it restores it to like-new condition. If you use new pistons with the moly rings you can expect a life of 100,000 miles. Understandably, a rebore with

new pistons is the most expensive way to do the job.

CLEANING YOUR PISTONS

If you have decided that the pistons are fit for reuse, your next move is to clean them thoroughly. There is little point in putting back pistons with carbon on their crowns and deposits in the grooves. There is one method that you must *not* use for cleaning pistons, and that is with a wire brush in an electric drill. The material from which pistons are made is too soft to withstand wire-brushing from an electric drill-mounted brush. It will take the edges off the ring grooves and destroy their sealing ability. What you can do, so long as you don't overdo it, is wire-bristle the piston crowns with a hand brush, but this should only be used as a final cleaning technique. First you should gently scrape the piston crowns with a blunt screwdriver to get the worst of the carbon off. Then, clean out the grooves, using a piece broken from an old ring or a proper ring-groove cleaner. Take great care not to score the sides of the ring groove that the rings seat on. If you do scratch these surfaces, it will lead to *blowby*, which is just the thing you are trying to avoid.

RE-RINGING PISTONS

I assume at this stage that the cylinder wear is such that a re-ring job will do the trick. If the pistons are in good condition and the ring grooves and piston-pin bores aren't worn, then the cost of re-ringing the piston, ridge-reaming and honing the block, will be about a third the cost of a rebore, new pistons and rings. This situation assumes the pistons are OK, except for rings. If ring grooves have worn, this can also be remedied. A machinist can machine the ring grooves, widening them to allow groove inserts to be installed. Groove inserts are generally 0.060-inch wide and this takes up the extra clearance after the groove has been remachined.

If you have to do this to get your pistons back into proper working order, then the cost of a "GI 60" (0.060-inch groove insert), plus

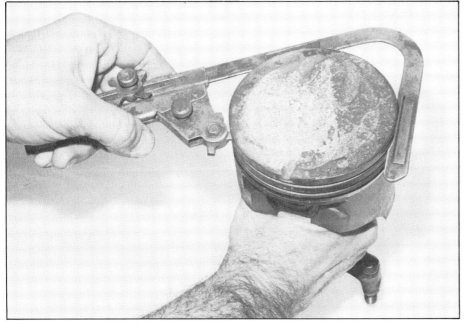

As an alternative to an old ring, you can use a ring-groove cleaner as shown here. If it looks like the pistons can be reused, DO NOT remove them from the rods, just leave in place and clean them thoroughly.

re-ringing the piston, plus having the block ridge-reamed and honed, will come to approximately 50 percent of the cost of a rebore and pistons. If the job is done properly it should be good for 50,000 miles.

PISTON KNURLING

Lastly, consider the situation where piston clearance is just a little too large for the piston to be used as it is. To cover this eventuality, there is a process known as *knurling*. With this process a knurling tool is rolled into the piston skirt which raises the metal. This has the effect of taking up some of the excessive clearance. Piston knurling is really a makeshift method of getting pistons to fit. It usually doesn't last very long and your piston-to-bore clearance may open up to where it was before in as little as 10,000 miles. If the bore has too much taper, then that 10,000 miles may be reduced to a mere 3,000 miles. It hardly makes it worth tearing down the engine. If you needed to do ridge-reaming and honing, plus rings and a knurl-ing job to get going again, this will have cost you approximately 50 percent of a rebore and pistons. And, you may have only done a "temporary" repair. On the other hand, if your pistons also needed groove inserts as well as knurling, then this will cost you about 75 percent of a rebore and new pistons. This is an uneconomical proposition in view of its probable short life. Both from the point of view of reliability and economics, if you cannot get away with a straight re-ring job, ridge-reaming and honing, then it is best to rebore the cylinders and install new oversize pistons to fit. Basically, the cheapest cast-iron rings for a Chevy will cost about 25 percent of the price for a new set of pistons and rings.

RIDGE-REAMING & HONING

Do not fall into the trap of thinking you can re-ring a set of pistons without getting the ridge-reaming and honing operations done at your local machine shop. First, if you do not de-glaze the bore by honing, new cast-iron rings will take many thousands of miles to seal and during that time oil consumption will be high and power will be down. Second, if the ridge is not removed from the top of the block, the new ring, which has no wear on its top corner comes slightly farther up the bore, hitting the ridge. It usually takes only a short mileage before the top ring is broken.

Unlike cast-iron rings, moly rings do not take very long to "bed in" on a glazed surface but they are just as susceptible to being smashed by hitting the wear ridge. This means you could, if you were using moly rings, get away with just ridge-reaming. I don't recommend this! It is only a real advantage if you are replacing a piston while the engine is still in the car. Because honing is not absolutely essential, you avoid getting grit in the rest of the engine. Therefore, the only operation you have to do is ridge-reaming. In your case, the engine is out of the car and the performance of the ring will be much better if the cylinder is fine-honed .

At this stage you should have enough information to establish whether or not your engine is going to be rebored with new pistons, or re-ringed. If you entrust this work to a competent machinist, you should have no problem.

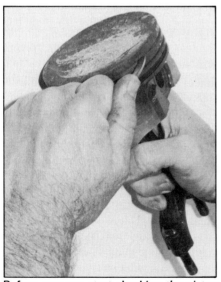

Before you can start checking the piston for ring-groove wear, the grooves must be cleaned. This can be done with an old piston ring plus a little care and some hard work.

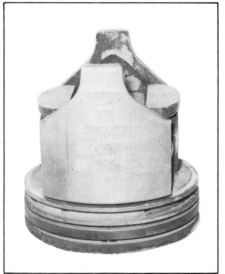

This is what a knurled piston skirt looks like. Raised metal at the edge of each indentation helps take up excessive clearance on very worn bores. Don't plan to use this process as a long-term cure for big bore clearances.

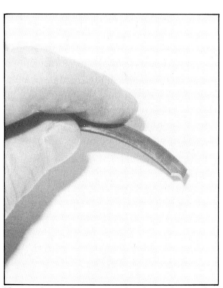

If you intend to use a broken piston ring to clean the ring grooves, grind it to this shape to make the job easier.

Here is a ridge-reaming tool. Removing the ridge stops ring breakage caused by the new ring hitting the wear step formed by the old ring.

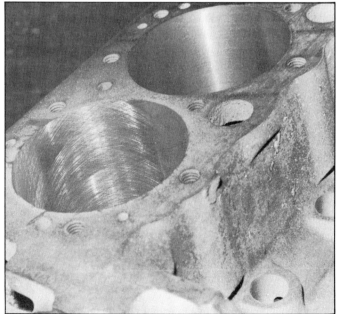

For rings to seal properly, whether new or old, the bores must have the correct finish. A honed finish as shown by the nearer bore is the type required. A plain bored or glazed-from-previous-use finish will lead to problems.

Many of the better-equipped motor machine shops will have a hone such as this Sunnen power stroke hone. These produce good consistent results on bores for accurate size and finish quality.

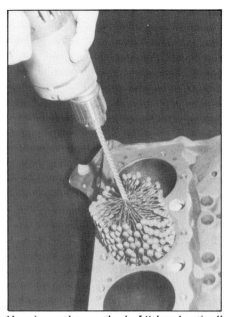

Here is another method of "glaze busting" a used bore. This brush hone produces a suitable finish for new rings to run on. It takes about 30 seconds to hone one bore with this tool.

If the engine has suffered a blown head gasket, especially on the block side of the gasket, it will be necessary to reface the block decks (head-gasket surfaces).

Ideally, the decks should be machined parallel to the main-bearing housings. Here the operator uses a special gauge to check the accuracy of his work after the block decks have been machined.

CHAMFERING THE BORES

The one simple check you should make when you get your block back from boring is to see whether or not the bore tops have been chamfered. Some machine shops do this, others expect the builder to do it. Whatever the case, the job needs to be done. To remove the sharp edges, make a small chamfer with a sharp file. This gives a lead in when installing the new piston/ring assembly. Without this chamfer you will find installing the pistons more difficult and a greater possibility for broken rings.

The next set of do's and don'ts to consider will come at assembly time.

CONNECTING RODS

A rod can suffer several ailments that will lead to bad engine performance and short engine life. The one most people think of first is a cracked con rod. After prolonged use, a connecting rod may develop a crack from a manufacturing defect. The rod itself may last 100,000 miles and then break because the flaw developed into a crack. In other words, connecting-rod fatigue can lead to a sudden termination of the rod's usefulness. If this happens, you wreck an engine. If rods have seen a lot of use, a crack test such as Magnaflux testing is a good idea to see if there are any flaws to cause the annihilation of the rod and the rest of the engine.

Connecting Rod Distortion— Less obvious is the effect of a distorted rod. For a smooth-running, efficient engine, the rods must be accurate. A rod can have two errors in its accuracy. One is *twist* and the other is *bend*. These errors cause vastly increased bore friction. Piston rings and bores will wear faster. Horsepower will be down and fuel consumption will be up because of the increased friction. Because the piston is not square in the bore, the effectiveness of the rings will be reduced and therefore oil contamination due to blow-by will be increased—and so will oil consumption. Both of these will eventually cost you money.

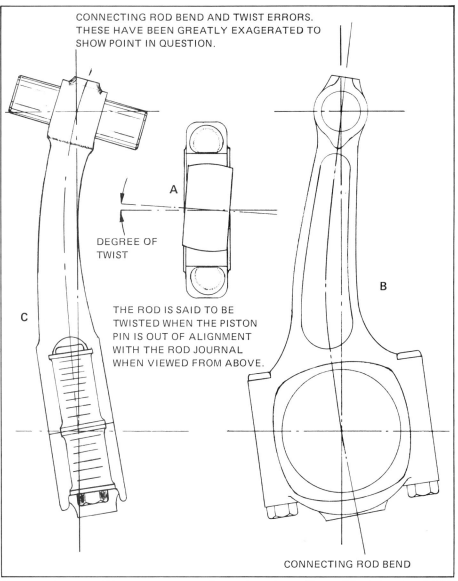

CONNECTING ROD BEND AND TWIST ERRORS. THESE HAVE BEEN GREATLY EXAGERATED TO SHOW POINT IN QUESTION.

A

DEGREE OF TWIST

THE ROD IS SAID TO BE TWISTED WHEN THE PISTON PIN IS OUT OF ALIGNMENT WITH THE ROD JOURNAL WHEN VIEWED FROM ABOVE.

B

C

CONNECTING ROD BEND

Here are three possible errors a connecting rod can have. The rod in A is twisted. This error in a close fitting piston causes increased friction. A rod bent as in B has little effect on engine performance unless it is bent to the point of being obvious. A rod bent as in C prevents the rings from sealing properly. Although I have shown each of these errors separately, a rod will usually have a combination of all three.

In the drawings I show an exaggerated bend and twist in a rod. You may have a rod with a combination of both.

Checking Connecting Rods—Your motor machinist has a fixture which will check con rods. This shows which are out of alignment, and the machinist can bend the rod until the fixture shows the rod is straight. Some checking fixtures require disassembling the rod and piston. Others can check alignment with the piston on or off the rod.

Separating Connecting Rods and Pistons—Unless you intend to replace the pistons **DO NOT remove the pistons from their rods!** Removing the pistons imposes severe stresses on the piston and in most cases it can become permanently distorted. If you are replacing pistons, then the rod must be removed from the piston by using an arbor press to push out the piston pin. Don't—as I have seen done—attempt to remove the piston with a punch and hammer, as you may end up with a bent rod and a wrecked piston.

Rod Alignment Check—As I pointed out during the disassembly, there is a fairly sure way of knowing whether your connecting rods are true or not. By examining the wear pattern on the piston skirt, you can get a good idea of how accurate the rod alignment is. If the wear pattern is even down both sides of the piston skirt and in the middle of the skirts on each side 90 deg. to the piston-pin axis, you can assume the rod is accurate enough to put back in the engine without further checking. This test is not 100% accurate, but for most practical purposes it is a very good indication. If the pattern is to one side or crooked, have the rod straightened or your rebuild efforts will be wasted.

Rod Journal Bore—There are two more ailments a connecting rod can have. First, the rod journal bore may be distorted. It can be oval-shaped in the up-and-down direction due to the reciprocating and gas pressure loads it has to bear. If this is the case, new bearing inserts in the rod will pinch the journal at the split line and there will be excessive clearance in the up-and-down direction. Low oil pressure and rapid bearing wear will result from this. Before you know it, you will be buying parts again. Fortunately, this situation can be remedied if the distortion isn't excessive. Usually, rod journal bore distortion is small unless the rod has been subject to excessive heat—just what happens when the oil film breaks down. However, these cases are rare.

Spun Bearings—A common problem with small-block Chevys is rod bearings spinning within the rod bore. Experts suggest this may be due to running on low-octane fuel which detonates easily. Detonation can also be caused or aggravated by excessive oil getting past the rings or guides into the combustion chambers. Oil mist contaminates the air/fuel mixture and causes premature detonation under heavy loads. This, plus dirty oil from lack of servicing, subjects the bearings to loads beyond their capability. A rod bearing may then spin in its bore, often scrapping

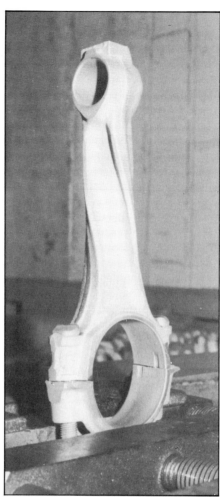

Chevy rods are made of tough material. This one was deliberately bent 90° like this, then straightened. I didn't try using it nor would I recommend such, but it shows that normal rod errors can be corrected by bending the rod. Such alignment work does not weaken the rod.

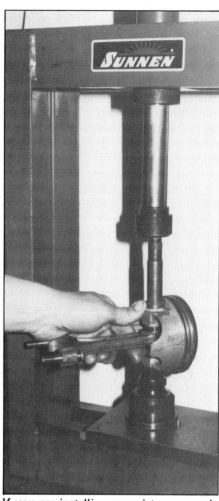

If you are installing new pistons or working on the rods, then the piston pin must be pressed out of the rod on an arbor press. Don't try using a hammer and punch!

the rod—and sometimes the crank and block—in the process.

Rod Journal Bore Correction—If the rod journal bore is only slightly oval shaped, the cap and rod can be ground at the split line. New bolts can be added, the cap and rod assembled, and the nuts torqued to spec. The journal bore can then be resized on a rod machine. Under some circumstances, rods can be

saved when they are as much as 0.010-inch oval on the rod journal, but most engine rebuilders draw the line at half this figure. This machining operation can be done with or without the pistons on the rods. Some engine parts houses sell rods on an exchange basis. You will get reconditioned rods regardless of the condition of your own rods.

The last area of doubt for a used rod is in the little end (pin bore). With

The first operation towards repairing an oval rod-journal bore. Rod-cap faces are being squared on the flat side of a grinding wheel. This closes down the bore.

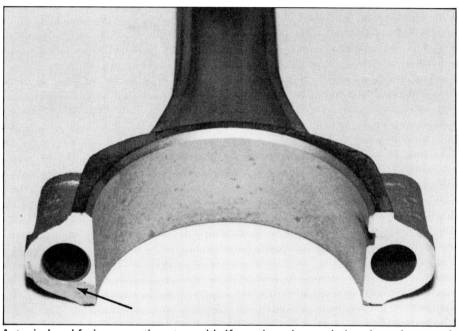

A typical rod-facing operation stopped halfway through completion shows how much out of true these locating faces were. Darker area (arrow) shows the portion not yet cleaned up.

all except a few high-performance Chevy engines, the wrist pin is a press fit in the rod. This press fit presents no problem and as long as the wrist pin stays a press fit, it will continue to present no problem.

Rod Bolts—On many engines, it is advisable to replace the rod bolts at re-build time. The Chevy rod bolt should not be replaced for the sake of re-placement. Under normal conditions,

they are not prone to break and if you do replace the bolts the cap will not line up and the bearing bore will have to be machined. The rule is: if the rod bolts are okay, stick with them. If you have one of those rare rods that needs work, if it needs only one machining operation to put it right, then your best bet is to have it done. If it needs more than one thing done to it, you are bet-ter off buying a new rod from your

Chevy dealer or a replacement TRW rod. Fortunately, small-block Chevys suffer little in the way of rod problems in normal day-to-day use so long as they have not suffered oil starvation. Unless there is a spun bearing, there's an excellent chance the rod will be okay for further use. If you know the engine had a hard life, it may be wise to *crack test* the rods as a precautionary measure.

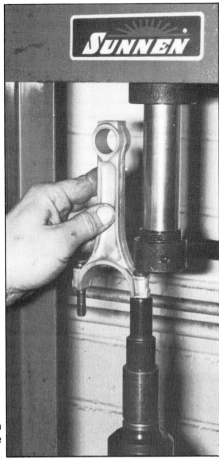

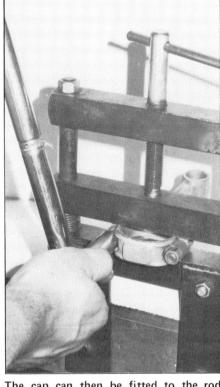

Once both cap and rod faces have been machined square, new rod bolts can be pressed in.

The cap can then be fitted to the rod and new rod nuts tightened up to 30-35 pounds-feet for 11/32'' bolts and 40-45 pounds-feet for 3/8'' bolts prior to machining the rod-journal bore.

Honing the rod-journal bores must be done with care. Doing two at a time, then turning them around and swapping one for the other is a technique machinists use to keep the rod-journal bore square and parallel.

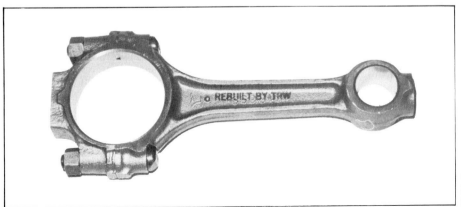

Between honing operations, a close watch on the diameter must be kept so the correct bearing "crush" is achieved. If this diameter is slightly oversize, bearings can spin in the rod, which destroys the bearing, rod and crank journal.

A fully rebuilt rod by a reputable company such as TRW puts you back in the as-new league.

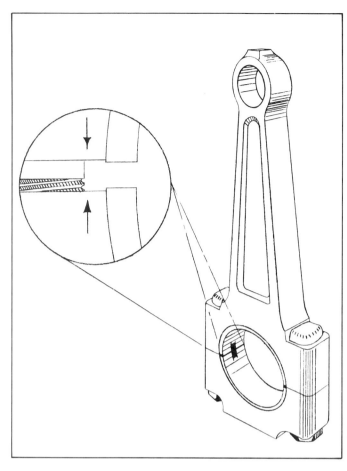

A rod journal bearing housing is always made slightly smaller than the bearing it accommodates. This bearing crush is largely responsible for holding the bearing to prevent it spinning.

Here is the result of a classic mistake—crank journal is damaged so badly that it needs a regrind. This engine has less than 1,000 miles since an overhaul.

This is how the caps came off the crank shown in the previous photo. If you look carefully you will see number 2 cap is on number 1 rod and number 1 cap is on number 2 rod. The cap muddle-up was the cause of the crank failure. Be sure you don't, for any reason, fall into the same trap.

Only install new rod bolts if you have to because the journal bore will need to be trued up when a bolt change is made. Some replacement bolts have plain shanks as shown here. GM replacement parts often have a knurled shank to hold them tight in the rod.

This 100,000-mile crank is OK for reuse without a regrind. With regular and frequent oil changes, many cranks show low wear rates.

CRANKSHAFT

Like the connecting rod, the crankshaft takes a beating. Crank failure often leads to catastrophic results. The biggest enemy of the crankshaft is lack of lubrication or sub-standard lubrication due to too long a period between oil changes. Given the right conditions, the crankshaft will run for many miles with very little wear. Fortunately, Chevrolet designed a highly effective lubrication system. If the engine hasn't been fed a steady diet of dirty oil, crankshaft wear is not usually a problem. In fact, all Chevy cranks—both cast and forged—have extremely good wear properties. A major percentage of Chevy engines can be rebuilt without any need for crank regrinding. All you need to do in these instances is to put in new bearings to give the engine a new lease on life.

Crack Testing—Having removed the crank from the engine, one of the first steps is to have it crack tested or *Magnafluxed*, especially if it is from a high-performance or truck engine. Although it may seem logical that cast-iron cranks are more prone to cracking than forged steel ones, this is not the case. The reason for this is when a cast-iron crank cracks, it usually breaks all the way through instantly and catastrophically; forged cranks usually run quite a while before breaking once cracked. Therefore, you'll likely find cracks in

what you think is a good forged crank.

Crank Regrinding—If there are no cracks, the next step is to check main- and rod-bearing journal wear to see whether your crankshaft needs regrinding. Refer to the chart, Fig.6-1. For this check, a micrometer is essential. When checking journal size on rods or mains, check at several points around the circumference, as the journals often wear out-of-round.

You may measure within tolerance at one point, yet find greater wear at a different position on the journal.

On the question of economics, it always pays to install new bearings if the engine has run more than 50,000 miles. Also, you can sometimes find only a few journals need regrinding and others are in good condition. Do not be tempted to grind only those needing it. If one journal needs grinding, regrind all of the journals and use the crank with new undersize bearings. Don't try to save money here.

Crank Kits—Another possible means of getting a crank back into new working order is by exchanging your crank for a *crank kit*. This is often less expensive than having your crank reground. Some companies specialize in crank regrinding so they can cut the cost because of the tremendous number of cranks they recondition. This means they can offer crank kits at better prices than you may get from your local engine rebuilder. Check your local parts house or even your local Chevy dealer to see if a crank kit is available for your engine. Such kits contain the

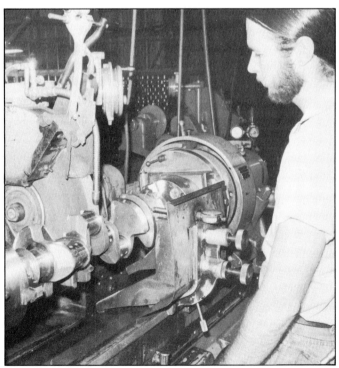

With this type of crank grinder, journals are indexed to get them in the correct angular position and the journal "throw" is dialed in with a vernier slide to give the required stroke length.

	Bearing	Minimum Size of Rod Journal	Bearing	Minimum Size of Main Journal
REGRIND CHART				
Small-Journal Crank	Standard	1.9985 in.	Standard	2.2973 in.
	-0.001 in.	1.9975	0.001 in.	2.2963
	-0.002	1.9965	0.002	2.2953
	-0.010	1.9885	-0.010	2.2973
	-0.020	1.9785	-0.020	2.2773
	-0.030	1.9685	-0.030	2.2673
	-0.040	1.9585	-0.040	2.2573
Big-Journal Crank	Standard	2.0985	Standard	2.4479
	-0.001	2.0975	-0.001	2.4469
	-0.002	2.0965	-0.002	2.4459
	-0.010	2.0885	-0.010	2.4379
	-0.020	2.0785	-0.020	2.4279
	-0.030	2.0685	-0.030	2.4179
400 Crank	Standard	2.0985	Standard	2.6479
	-0.001	2.0975	-0.001	2.6469
	-0.010	2.0885	-0.010	2.6379
	-0.020	2.0785	-0.020	2.6279
	-0.030	2.0685	-0.030	2.6179

Note: 400 crank can have the rear main bearing (no.5) 0.0005-inch less than indicated above.

FIGURE 6-1

bearings for both rod and mains, crank lube and rod bolt sleeves, so bear this in mind when you compare quoted prices.

TIMING GEARS

The small-block Chevy comes from the factory with one of several different types of timing gear setups. Passenger-car engines have either a narrow or wide one of the type shown in the photos. The narrow one is used on 1967 and later engines. Also, the cam timing gear as it comes from the factory will be nylon-faced. These narrow gears wear more than other types and the same is true for the narrow chain. If the nylon gear has a crack in it, then you probably caught the situation just in time. Once the nylon cracks, it quickly separates from the rest of the gear. When that happens you soon end up with no gear teeth on the cam gear.

If your engine has a narrow cam sprocket and chain, then replace the timing chain set (both sprockets and chain) with the wide type. In hot climates and in heavy-duty applications use an all-steel timing gear as these will last considerably longer in high heat situations. At the very least, replace the cam sprocket and chain if you stick with the narrow one.

In most cases truck engines use a roller-type chain which has a good reliability record when it has received proper lubrication. On those which haven't, there will be slack. If there is more than 1/2-inch slack in the chain, replace it. The gears themselves wear a lot slower than the chain, so in most cases a new chain is all that's needed.

CRANKSHAFT VIBRATION DAMPER

You may ask what can possibly go wrong with a crankshaft vibration damper as long as it's not cracked. The most important thing to look for is normal wear on the diameter upon which the oil seal runs. On high-mileage engines, this surface is often grooved due to wear and though it may be sealing when you pull the engine down, the fact that you have disturbed it and possibly replaced a seal means it is likely to leak when you rebuild.

There are two ways you can fix this. First, you can replace the entire damper which is an extreme measure and expensive. Second, if the groove is more than a few thousandths deep, you can recondition the damper by fitting a press-on, thin-walled, sleeve. This makes the sealing diameter larger, but the seal can accommodate this. These sleeves have a hard-chrome finish and a long wear life.

To fit one of these sleeves, use emery cloth or paper on the oil-seal diameter of the damper until it is completely free from corrosion. Then liberally oil both this diameter and the inside diameter of the sleeve and posi-

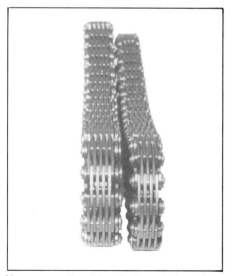

Narrow and wide timing chains. The wider one runs quieter and lasts longer.

Steel gear at left will outlive the nylon-faced aluminum gear, especially on later cars where high running temperatures are created by emission-control equipment.

A narrow and wide crank gear compared. Be sure to use the appropriate one for the chain and cam gear you have.

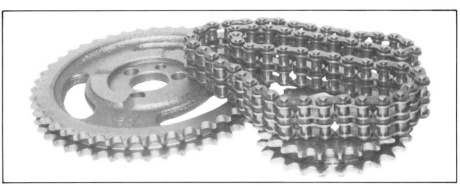

Truck engines use a roller chain with the matching crank and cam sprocket. These are reliable but can be noisier than chains commonly used on passenger cars.

That groove on the oil-seal surface spells trouble in the oil-seal department. Always emery this surface and if the groove is more than a few thousandths deep, replace or recondition the item.

Install one of these reconditioning sleeves to end oil-leak worries caused by a grooved seal surface.

These fit over the working diameter of the harmonic balancer and provide a new working surface for the seal. Here, a sleeve is about to be pressed in place. The bore of the sleeve has been liberally greased to aid the fitting. The slight increase in diameter can be accommodated by the standard front seal.

tion the sleeve on the damper. Then press it on. This can be done in a press or, if you are careful, in a vise.

While you're at it, check the rubber bonding between the outer ring and inner section of the damper. If this rubber, which is vital to the function of the damper, shows signs of distress, replace the damper. If you don't replace a suspect damper on a hard-working engine, be prepared for your engine to at least suffer damper failure, or at worst, damper failure followed by crankshaft failure. Imminent damper failure is usually preceded by movement of the outer ring on the inner. This can be radially, thus putting the timing mark out; and/or fore and aft, sometimes resulting in the ring coming into contact with the timing-chain cover.

CAMSHAFT & LIFTERS

Small-block Chevrolet cams are not noted for a long life, especially in engines which have not had frequent and regular oil changes. When you pull the cam out, about half the time you will find a lobe or two missing or badly worn. The cam must then be replaced. Some engine rebuilders have equipment for re-profiling slightly worn cams to bring them back to like-new condition. In the case of the Chevy cam, it is best to consider an outright replacement, as the cam lobes are usually too far worn for the shaft to be reground satisfactorily.

Also, check parts stores for replacement cam kits. These can be a source for low-cost cams but watch the quality. It gets expensive if you have to haul out your new engine to replace a cheap camshaft!

Alternative Camshaft Profiles — At this point you could consider a camshaft with a profile different from the standard one — one that may give you a power curve more applicable to your needs. There are many camshafts available from the aftermarket designed to put the horsepower in the part of the rev range where you need it most. For instance, a lightweight high performance vehicle can benefit from having the horsepower curve farther up the rev range. In other words, a performance camshaft can be beneficial. A heavier vehicle, especially one used for towing, needs power lower down in the rev range. If you are rebuilding an engine for a recreational vehicle, such as a motor home, then you could use a lot of power down low to get that weight moving. There are special camshafts designed to do just that. An engine machine shop or a speed shop (often they are one and the same) should be able to recommend a good camshaft manufacturer. *Crane, Sig Erson, Iskenderian* and *Competition Cams* are good places to start.

Getting back to the wear problem, when the cam lobes get demolished, the lifters tend to follow suit. There is no cure for worn lifters. You must buy new ones.

OIL PUMP

The lubrication system is one of this engine's strongest assets. The oil pump is a reliable part and there is little reconditioning you can do. Either the pump is okay for more use or it isn't. You can check the end play of the gears with feeler gauges, as shown in the photographs on page 64. You can also inspect the gears and pump body for scoring. If you have any doubt about the serviceability of the pump, replace it, because this is the heart of the engine. If it isn't in perfect condition, your engine will not last.

At this point, it is worth mentioning the Melling and TRW high-volume oil pumps. These are big-block Chevy pumps supplied with a special oil pickup pipe to allow installation without clearance problems in a small-

This often happens to Chevy small-block cams. Arrowed lobe is almost circular on this particular shaft. 5 of the 16 lobes were badly worn.

Cam-lobe failure is usually accompanied by lifter wear as shown here. Remember, the lifter face should appear very slightly *convex,* not concave. WHEN A NEW CAM GOES INTO THE ENGINE, NEW LIFTERS MUST BE USED. WHEN THE OLD CAM IS PUT BACK INTO THE ENGINE, LIFTERS MUST BE PUT BACK EXACTLY IN THEIR ORIGINAL ORDER.

Look for wear on the underside of this cover. Pump gears bear on this face and excessive wear here cannot be tolerated. The pump cover shown has only light surface marks and is okay for further use.

Sometimes debris going through the pump can damage the pump gear teeth. Scores in the teeth make this one a borderline case, but it will be okay if the engine is well looked after and never has to contend with dirty oil.

Another point to watch is the area at either end of the pump (arrows). Big scores here mean scrapping the pump.

The last thing to do is to see if the end float in the gears is excessive. Do this with a feeler gauge between the end plate and the gear teeth. If, when tested with a feeler this is between 0.002-inch and 0.006-inch, then it's okay. If it's more than this and the rest of the pump looks good, have a few thousandths of an inch taken off the pump body face to give the correct clearance.

block Chevy pan. If you use one of these pumps it will be necessary to install the pickup pipe onto the pump. Check that you have clearance with the pan by placing the pan in position without the pan gaskets to see that the pickup screen case clears. If it does not clear, the pan will not seat against the block.

If the engine has already been rebuilt, it may already have one of these installed by the previous rebuilder.

The easy way to recognize the adapted big-block Chevy pump is by a cover secured by five bolts, rather than the four bolts of the small-block pump. Apart from having a greater flow potential, these pumps, due to the greater number of gear teeth on the gears, produce smoother distributor operation. This pump is worth considering if your small block is to see arduous stop/start use in a truck or car, such as in a vehicle used for deliveries.

CYLINDER HEAD

The valve guides on the cylinder heads will almost certainly need to be redone. Because the guides are machined directly in the head, reconditioning or replacing them is not a simple job. If the guides are refurbished, then the valve seats must be resurfaced whether they are worn or not, so they will be in line with the new guides.

Guides can be refurbished in several ways. This is one area where you truly get what you pay for. The least expensive method you choose will last the shortest. Spend more money and you can get guides that may outlast the original factory guides by many miles.

Knurling Guides—The cheapest method of refurbishing is to knurl the guide bore. On a Chevy this may only last 2,000 miles before it is as bad as when you first started. A knurled guide only works if your guide wasn't worn to begin with, and only needs cleaning up. Therefore, I do not recommend this method for reconditioning guides.

Winona Guide Insert—First, consider a coil-type insert in the guide. This involves tapping the guide and putting a bronze coil insert into the guide and

Conventional small-block Chevy oil pump has four bolts securing the top cover. A new one depending on the source, may or may not come with the oil pickup pipe (not shown) and the plastic pump/distributor drive-shaft connector.

The high-volume pump, basically a big-block Chevy pump with a suitable oil pickup for small-block Chevy pans, is identified by five bolts holding the cover. Melling conversion kit comes complete with pickup and plastic pump/distributor drive-shaft connector.

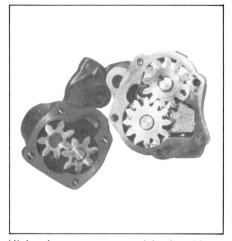

High-volume pump on right has bigger gears with more gear teeth. Increased number of teeth has a beneficial side effect: less distributor vibration leading to less spark scatter.

Here is a trick used on an engine which is a real smoker and has a tendency to oil up plugs. An extension tube is screwed into the plug hole in the head, then the plug screws into the tube. In simple terms, the effect is to cut down the heat conductivity to the head, thus the plug runs hotter and burns off oil deposits more readily. The same sort of effect could be achieved by using a plug one or two heat ranges hotter or curing the large amounts of oil coming past the guides and rings.

Knurling a Chevy cast-iron guide with this type of knurling tool is usually a short-lived remedy for guide restoration.

then reaming to size. This is effective if done properly, however it is not the method I prefer to use for restoring guides.

Cast-Iron Replacement Guide— Another method used by some machine shops is to install a brand new cast-iron guide. To achieve this the guide hole is bored considerably oversize and a replaceable guide is pressed into the enlarged hole. This restores the guides to like-new condition. Install chrome stem valves and you'll have a set of high mileage heads. Be aware that some stainless, non-chrome valves are incompatible with cast-iron guides; they must be used with bronze guides.

Bronze Guides— There are several ways to install bronze guides, but beware. Some types of bronze guides are not that good. Although I haven't tried them all, the ones I mention have yielded good results.

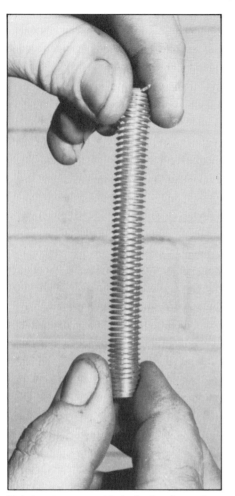

This is a bronze guide helical-coil repair.

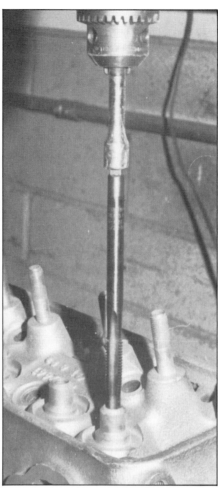

Installing coil guide insert involves tapping out the guide to put in a thread compatible to the insert.

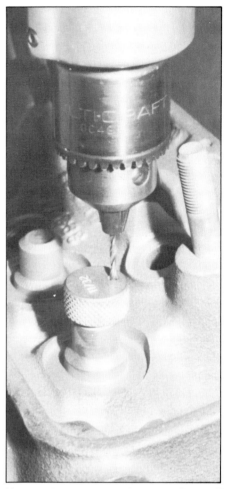

Next, using this little fixture a "notch" is drilled in the side of the guide wall.

The first of these is simply a replacement guide made of a type of bronze that is suitable for about any condition it could possibly encounter. The installation of such a bronze guide follows the procedure as that for a regular cast-iron replacement guide. Essentially, this involves boring out the existing guide, sizing the hole, and pressing in the new guide. The advantage of this type of guide is it allows you a greater choice of valve-stem oil seals. Stock umbrella-type seals mounted under the spring retainers will do fine. However, you may elect to go with *stem* type seals that seal more positively. Such seals, because they limit the amount of oil that gets to the guide and lower part of the valve stem, should be considered only if the

guide used needs little additional lubrication. Bronze guides such as those shown in this book usually fall into this category.

An aspect of bronze guides that you should be aware of is they transfer heat from the exhaust valve better than cast-iron guides. The bulkier the bronze guide and the closer the stem fit, the better this conductivity will be. For example, if 0.001-in. clearance is used — not practical with cast-iron guides — heat conductivity can be double that with a clearance of 0.0025 in. Because the use of bronze guides can significantly aid exhaust-valve cooling, consider using them in an effort to recoup some of the valve-seat life lost due to the absence of tetraethyl lead in gasoline.

Thin-Wall Bronze Insert — Apart from a conventional guide, another effective method of curing wear is to use thin-wall bronze guide inserts. This involves reaming the worn guide anywhere from 0.030 to 0.060 inch larger than the original hole. Into this a split-wall guide insert is installed. A special knurling tool is run though the guide bore to expand it into the cast-iron guide. Finally, the guide is finish-reamed to size. This type of guide repair works very well, producing something that will go 100,000 miles. Although the first two types of guide replacement are satisfactory, bronze replacements are about the best.

Here's how it looks with the notch.

This jig is used to screw the coil insert into the end of the guide.

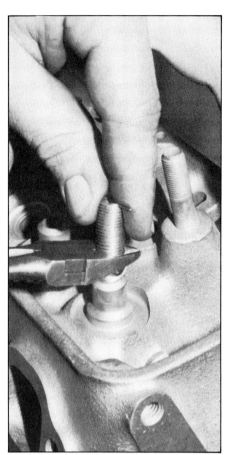

The excess is then trimmed off.

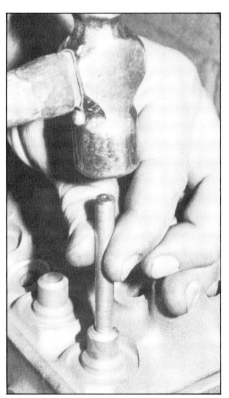

A punch is then used to break the "tang" off the end of the coiled insert.

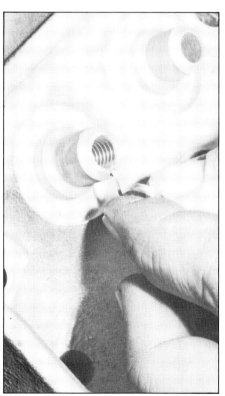

The other end of the insert is turned into the notch to lock it in position.

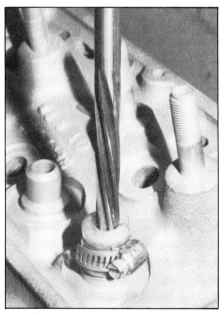

As a final operation, the guide is reamed to size. The sleeve and hose clamp prevent the first one or two threads of the insert from pulling out during the reaming operation.

With the thin-wall replacement guide, the first step is to ream out the guide to accommodate the thin-wall insert.

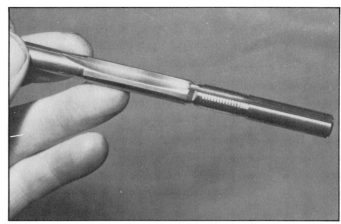

A special reamer is used. The threaded section pulls the sizing section of the reamer through the guide.

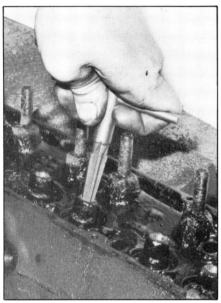

Having reamed the old guide bores to their new oversize, they are then taper-reamed to provide a lead-in for the bronze guide insert.

The bronze guide insert is mounted on a mandrel and sprayed with an anti-seize lubricant prior to fitting.

The next operation is driving the insert into the guide and stopping as it reaches the end of the guide bore.

The excess is trimmed off with this tool.

A knurling tool is used to expand the thin bronze into the cast iron beneath. This ensures that it is keyed permanently in place.

The final operation is to ream to finish size. This head is still very dirty. When all the machining operations are done it will be hot-tanked to get rid of all dirt and machining debris.

Here is a guide I cut through at an angle so you can see a thin-wall bronze guide insert fitted. As you can see from this cutaway, the insert is very thin. The final wall is about 0.015-inch thick.

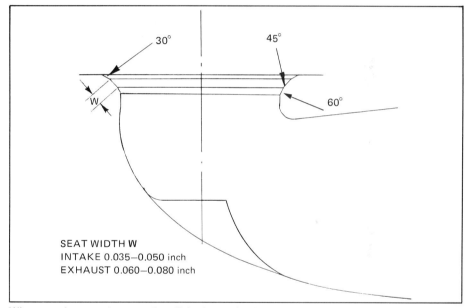

SEAT WIDTH W
INTAKE 0.035–0.050 inch
EXHAUST 0.060–0.080 inch

When a valve seat is recut, it will be larger in diameter and lower in the head. This can restrict airflow into or out of the port unless the seat is top and bottom cut with 30 degree and 60 degree stones or cutters. Due to unleaded gasoline, a head not having hardened seats should be cut at maximum width to help reduce seat recession.

SEAT REFACING

Whenever any work is done on the guides, the valve seats *must* be refaced in the head to ensure concentricity with the guide bores. This means you can expect the price of a seat-refacing job, along with the guide reconditioning. Refacing the seats inevitably makes them wider and in most instances too wide. On engines which have seen very high mileages or those with solid lifters (non-hydraulic), the valve seats may have sunk, due to the incessant hammering. Such seats will need refacing whether or not a guide job was done. Again, this can lead to a very wide seat if the seat is merely refaced at 45°. The correct procedure is to angle-cut the valve seat top with a 30° cutter and the bottom with a 60° cutter. See drawing.

WARPED HEADS

If small-block-Chevy heads have seen long service, it's almost inevitable that they have warped. If I set the limit on warpage at three thou-

sandths, six out of ten heads are warped more than this. If you have a straight edge, you can check warpage with this, plus a feeler gauge. Lay the straight edge diagonally across the head and see if a 0.003-inch feeler gauge will pass under it anywhere. Obviously, the head face must be perfectly clean for such a check. Having checked it from one corner to the other, check it from the two opposite corners, then finally at the top, middle and bottom, just to make sure you've covered the head from end to end.

Such a check doesn't cost much if you don't have your own straight edge. If you have taken the rest of your engine in for reconditioning, the machine shop will inevitably do such a check for you to see whether your heads need refacing.

Just how flat a head needs to be depends on the type head gasket you use in the rebuild. Steel-shim head gaskets, as sold by most General Motors dealers, do not tolerate very much out of flat before they start causing problems. Composition head gaskets, such as those

Valve-seat cutting is commonly done with a high-speed grindstone dressed at the correct angle.

A final check on seat-to-guide-bore concentricity should be made with a special dial gauge as seen here. 0.001-inch run-out should be considered maximum.

When seats have seen a lot of use, they tend to sink. Regrinding the seat makes a very wide seat. So, to avoid too much seat width, they must be angle-cut both in the chamber and port. Arrows here show the cuts on either side of the seat.

produced by McCord, Fel-Pro or Mr. Gasket will take up far more warpage before they give problems. I would say a head as much as 0.005 inch out of true will, under most circumstances, be trouble-free *if a composition head gasket is used*.

ROCKER STUDS

There may be times when rocker studs need replacing. This is normally the case if a rocker has run at an angle and one side of the slot in the rocker has started to cut through the rocker stud. If you have pressed-in rockers the remedy for this is simple, pull out the old stud, tap the hole and install a new screw-in stud. The sequence of photos shows how it's done. If you have to replace screw studs, just unscrew the damaged one and screw in the new one.

A point to watch is that most studs go into the water jacket. When you are installing a screw-in stud, you must use silicone sealer on the threads to prevent water coming in via the thread.

VALVES

Once the guides and valve seats are refurbished, take a careful look at the valves. These can be expensive to replace. If you aren't in a hurry you can mail-order factory-type replacement valves from advertisers that are listed in many do-it-yourself and performance car magazines. Regardless of the price you can get replacement valves for, make sure the original ones are unusable before spending a small fortune on new ones.

First use a 1-inch micrometer to check stem wear very carefully on every valve by measuring and comparing worn and unworn sections. As I said previously, one thousandths (0.001) wear can be tolerated, especially if you have equipped the heads with bronze-type guides. Two-thousandths (0.002) wear makes a valve a borderline case. This should only be considered if you find the cost of new valves more than you can afford.

Oversize Stem Valves — If you need new valves, here is a point to consider. Valves with oversize stems are available. If the guides are worn and you need new valves, you can ream the guides to take the new larger-stem-diameter valves. This is only worth considering if you have

Look for this sort of rocker-stud damage. Uneven wear on the valve tip leads to the rocker leaning so it bears on the stud as shown here. Remedy is a screw-in relacement but it's a machine-shop job.

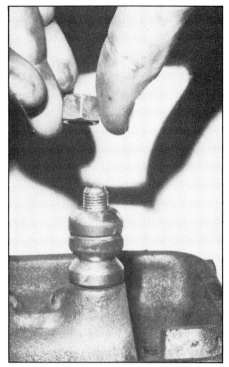

To remove a damaged stud, first make a stack of spacers out of washers or, as I've used here, some old rocker ball seats. Fit a 3/8-24 UNF nut on the thread.

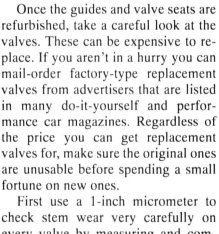

Using a deep socket, tighten the nut down so it pulls the stud out. Don't run the nut so far down that it runs out of threads. When the nut gets close to the end of the threads—judge by the amount of stud sticking out of the top of the nut—increase the number of spacers.

This stud has just been pulled. The amount indicated between the arrows shows how far the stud had to be pulled to remove it.

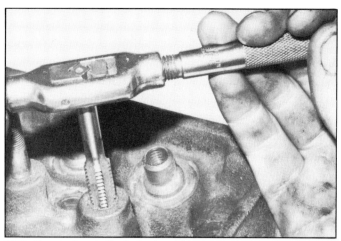

With the stud out, the hole should be tapped 7/16-14 NC. NOW HEED THIS WARNING: The hole must be tapped square with the face of the boss. If the new stud does not go in the same position and is leaning, the rocker will cut into it.

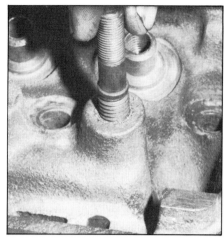

Coat the threads with silicone sealer and screw the replacement stud into the tapped hole.

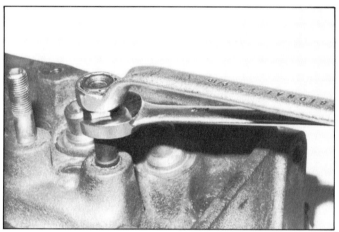

Lock two 3/8-24 UNF lift nuts on the stud by tightening them into each other.

Tighten the stud into the head by turning on the top nut.

One stud-replacement job completed.

A great number of valves can be reused if the valve is refaced on a valve-facing machine.

If the valves are going to be reused, have the stem ends faced square to retain consistent valve-lash settings.

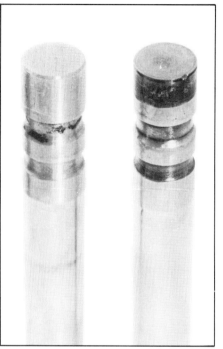

Newly ground valve-stem tip compared to unground tip. Before installing old valve in new guide, file burr from edge of keeper groove (arrows).

to replace most or all of the valves. With this approach there is one further thing to consider, namely that you have not cured the basic Chevy problem of rapid guide wear. You may find you can save money and get better results by asking your motor machinist if he has any good used valves he can sell you for a cheap price. These, along with a bronze guide job, will probably be your best bet. Check the cost of both possibilities *before* you proceed.

Reconditioning the Valves—Turn your attention to the valve heads. Inspect seat faces. If they show signs of damage, your best plan is to have them refaced. Don't fall into the trap of thinking you can lap the valves into the cylinder head with grinding paste. To do 16, if the seats are at all bad, will give you a considerable number of blisters and you will find that it would have

been well worthwhile to spend the extra cash to have them refaced. While you are having the valve seats refaced, also get your motor machinist to square off the stem ends. The reason is, non-square stem ends cause noisy valve operation whether you have solid or hydraulic lifters. In part the same applies to the rockers. These I will talk about later. If you find some valves are just too far gone to reuse, then this does not mean you have to replace the entire set of valves. Just replace the bad ones.

Lapping Valves to Seats—Now comes the all-important fit of the valve onto its respective seat. Depending on the type of equipment your motor machinist used, you may or may not find it necessary to lap (fine-grind) the valves into their seats. Some of the latest modern seat-cutting equipment will produce

a seat which needs little or no work done to it after it has been cut. On the other hand, many machine shops still use older equipment which, although it functions well, produces seats which need final lapping prior to assembly.

Your best plan is to assume all the valves need lapping. If, after gently grinding them for a few seconds with *fine* grinding paste, you find they are showing a grey ground finish around their entire circumference, then they are seating correctly. If this is so you can stop because no further work is needed. Should you find after a few moments grinding that they are not showing a pattern around the entire seat circumference, then you know it may take a few more minutes to produce the correct seat. Either way, you will have not wasted much time by lapping those that did not need it.

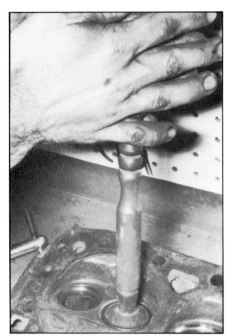

Final job on seats should be to lap/grind the valve lightly to its seat to ensure a perfect seal.

Finished valve seat after lapping should show a consistent grey finish around the entire circumference as seen here.

New spring on right, old spring on left. Use has made the older spring shorter. Spacer leaning against old spring will just about restore new-spring performance. Such a method must not be used with an aftermarket performance high-lift cam as the spring coils may bind or hit at full lift. Usually an aftermarket high-performance cam has the cam grinder's name stamped on it so you can tell it is not a stock cam.

Checking Valve Sealing — As a final check to make sure the valves are sealing correctly, assemble the head temporarily. Hold the valves in place with their springs, retainers and keepers. Install the spark plugs. Block the head so it is level with the combustion chambers up. Then put cleaning solvent into the chambers. If the solvent leaks into any port, you will know all is not well. If, after a minute or so there is no sign of any kerosene in the ports, then the valves are doing their job sufficiently well. Disassemble the head. When you lap the valves, or rather as you are doing the job, keep them in the correct order for each head. A valve ground into one seat may not seal on another. The simplest way of keeping them in order is to punch holes in a piece of cardboard and number the holes, then put each valve into the hole when the lapping job is finished.

VALVE SPRINGS

As you would expect, valve springs are an important part of the valve train. On a high-mileage engine, they may have fatigued, consequently resulting in less force being exerted by

each valve against its seat. To a degree, this isn't bad, but if allowed to continue, the valves will not follow the form of the cam lobes at high rpm. Or, at the end of the closing cycle, they may bounce off their seats. Either way, correct valve action is lost.

On the average, springs which have been on the engine for 50,000 miles or more tend to drop about 10 pounds seat pressure. The way to remedy this is to put a 0.060-inch spacer washer under the used valve spring. This restores seat pressure to about the same load given by new springs.

If the engine has ever been overheated, the exhaust valve springs may have suffered some loss of *temper*, leading to a greater reduction in valve seat pressure. Check this by putting an exhaust valve spring next to an intake valve spring. If the exhaust valve spring is more than 1/16-inch shorter, discard it and buy a new exhaust spring. If it is about the same length, you can use exactly the same procedure as with the intake by fitting the 0.060-inch spacer-washer underneath. These spacers are available through your motor machinist. Some engines, mostly in trucks, use rotator valve

spring retainers on the exhaust valves. Engines with this type of retainer used the same valve spring as on the intake valve up to 1973. From '73 on, the spring used was 1/8-inch shorter and smaller in diameter.

Replacing the Springs — With high-performance Chevrolet cams or aftermarket performance cams, replace the springs with the type recommended for the particular cam you are going to use. Do not use the spacer method to increase spring pressure as in some instances this can lead to *coil binding*. Coil binding occurs when the valve lift uses all the available spring travel, leaving each coil of the spring in contact with its neighbor. The spring is now "solid." Any further valve lift will cause severe damage to the valve train.

Don't be tempted to put heavy-pressure valve springs meant for high-performance engines into an engine meant for ordinary daily use. I think I have made it clear that Chevy V-8 engines often suffer from cam wear. This wear is accelerated by spring pressure which is too high, so heavy-duty springs are not a good

Rotator spring retainer from '73 on used a smaller spring. When new, the spring is 1.9-inch long in its relaxed position. If it is within 1/16-inch of this it can be reused. The 0.060-inch spring spacer can be used with this spring to restore original seat pressure. Rotators are primarily used in large trucks.

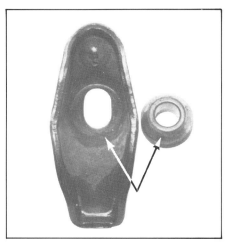

Check the two arrowed areas for scoring. If these parts are scored, consider them scrap.

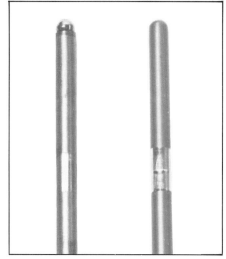

Here is the effect of a possible mistake which I deal with later. This pushrod was damaged by a too-long manifold bolt. If you have a pushrod or two like this, change the pushrods and use 1-1/4'' manifold bolts.

idea unless needed for the camshaft you are using.

If you want to extend the life of a camshaft, put in General Motors' Engine Oil Supplement (E.O.S.) when you fire up the engine after rebuilding—whether you installed a new, reground or original camshaft. It is available at your local Chevy store—and any other GM dealer's parts counter.

ROCKER ARMS

The last components you need to inspect thoroughly prior to assembling the cylinder heads are the studs, rockers and the ball seats on which they operate. First, the end of the rocker which bears on the end of the valve: More than a few thousandths wear or pitting here causes valve train noise, even with hydraulic lifters. It also makes valve clearance adjustments difficult or inaccurate if you are using solid lifters. To keep costs at a minimum, you may be tempted to reface the part of the rocker which bears on the end of the valve stem. These rockers are case hardened. Case hardening gives only a very thin wear surface. Once through the case hard-

ening, the rocker will have a very short life indeed. If the wear is more than a few thousandths, replace the rocker with a new one. Pitted rockers should not be used unless you really can't afford replacements. New rockers can be installed later if you are in a money bind. Inspect the rocker in the area which runs on the rocker ball. Scoring here means the rocker is scrap, together with the ball seat on which it runs.

If you are concerned about your engine not generating power up to its potential, be aware that rocker-arm ratios vary dramatically from their original design. Often original-equipment rocker arms are the worst offenders with the rocker ratio down to 1.43:1 from the intended 1.50:1 ratio. My experience has indicated TRW rockers are best in this respect.

PUSHRODS

Lubrication for the valve train comes through the pushrods from the lifters. Normally, there isn't a lot that can go wrong with a pushrod. On very rare occasions one may become blocked, thus shutting off the

supply of oil to its rocker and valve. Just as rare is a bent pushrod. This will be obvious from the fact that it will show heavy wear marks where it passes through the cylinder head. Another check can be made by rolling it across a flat surface. Any bend shows up as it rolls.

Do not assume because you are using new pushrods that they will be straight. I have had to sift through three sets of new aftermarket pushrods in order to get one straight set of pushrods. My experience on this point is that the genuine GM part here is hard to beat for quality, so if you have to replace a pushrod, get them from your local Chevy dealer.

The last thing you may find wrong with the pushrod is that the ends, usually the upper end which bears on the rocker, start to split. Again, bad lubrication can cause heavy wear at this point. If you find a bent pushrod or one with the ends beginning to break up, then the remedy is replacement. Under normal circumstances, all you really need to do is to wash the pushrods and check that no dirt is left inside them.

7
THE REBUILD

1970 350-CID 370-HP engine. This was the last generation of small-block Chevrolet engines to have any "muscle" worth mentioning. From 1970, increasingly severe emission requirements caused a decline in power output. In 1978 the most powerful small-block Chevrolet developed 210 HP.

THINGS TO DO BEFORE YOU START

Engine assembly is probably the most interesting part of what you are doing. It is also the most crucial. This is the stage where mistakes must be found, because after assembly it is usually too late. The responsibility for finding any possible trouble sources rests entirely with you—the engine builder. If you miss the clues, don't blame the guy who did your machining—the parts man—or anyone else. If something doesn't seem correct, investigate it until you know one way or the other. DON'T RUSH THE JOB! A few extra minutes—even hours—may save days and dollars later on.

When all the component parts have been reconditioned, checked over or replaced as necessary, then you should be in a position to assemble your small-block Chevy. To put the unit together you will also need: An engine-gasket set, a quart of engine oil, a little molybdenum grease, a tube of silicone sealer, a tube of 3M® Weatherstrip Adhesive, a piston-ring compressor, a

brass punch or similar tool, plus the tools you used to strip the engine, especially the rubber or plastic sleeves to go over the rod bolts.

Having all the tools present at this stage is not enough. The other important thing you will need is space to build the engine. What's more, this must be *clean* space. Remember, **DIRT AND ENGINES DO NOT GO TOGETHER**. Get some dirt in the engine at assembly time and your engine will be self-demolishing. When you are not working on your engine, cover it with a large plastic bag to prevent any dirt getting in.

BLOCK PREPARATION

Assuming you are ready to go, let's "take the bull by the horns." Not unexpectedly, you should start with the preparation of the block. I assume you have a clean bare block. In other words, your block was in the worst possible condition and it required hot-tanking, a rebore and so on and so forth. Now more than likely your cam bearings, rear cam plug, freeze plugs etc., will have been installed by a motor machinist.

On the other hand you may have stripped your own block down to the bare minimum, in which case I will detail what you must do to get a bare block into a useable state to accept the moving parts.

DEBURRING OIL GALLERYS

Your first job is to give some attention to the three oil gallery holes in front of the block. The plugs for these holes are prevented from accidentally coming out by deliberately burring over the edge of each hole. This means that if you try to drive in new plugs without first deburring these holes you will score the plug and cause it to leak. The remedy is to deburr these holes first. This can be done with a file if no other tool is available. Ten minutes with a file will do the job. However, a tapered reamer is a far better bet for deburring these holes. It makes the job literally ten seconds a hole. These tapered reamers are available from most industrial supply houses.

Deburring these gallerys will produce some chips or metal bits and some may have strayed into the gallery. Your best plan is to give all

Here are all the components necessary to build up the block ready for installation of the moving parts. Check off the items against the parts list to see that you have them all.

BLOCK ASSEMBLY			
ITEM	NOTES	NUMBER	CHECK
Block (bare)		1	
Front main bearing cap		1	
No. 2 main bearing cap		1	
No. 3 main bearing cap		1	
No. 4 main bearing cap		1	
Rear main bearing cap		1	
Main bearing bolts for pre '68 small-journal cranks	7/16"—14 UNC x 3"	10	
Main bearing bolts for 1968 and later large-journal cranks	7/16"—14 UNC x 3-1/4"	10	
Main bearing bolts for four-bolt mains, long	7/16"—14 UNC x 3-3/8"	10	
Main bearing bolts for four-bolt mains, short	7/16"—14 UNC x 2"	6	
Water-jacket freeze plugs	1-5/8" dia. (cup)	8 *	
Cam-bearing plug	2-3/32" dia. (shallow cup)	1	
Oil-gallery plugs	1/2" dia. (cup)	3	
Oil-gallery screw plugs	1/4" pipe thread x 7/16" long (socket drive)	3	

*400 CID four-bolt main bearing engine requires 10 water-jacket freeze plugs.

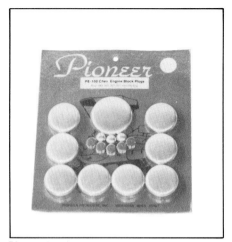

Plug kit shown here will simplify the acquisition of the cam, oil and freeze plugs and usually costs less than purchasing the items separately.

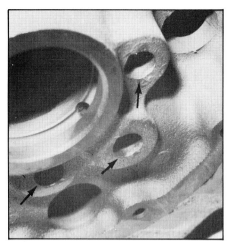

Before you attempt to fit any front gallery plugs, you *will* need to deburr the holes (arrows).

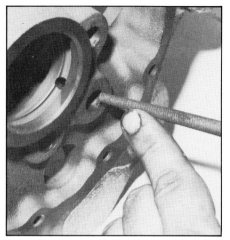

Deburring can easily be done with a file, but don't remove any more metal than is necessary.

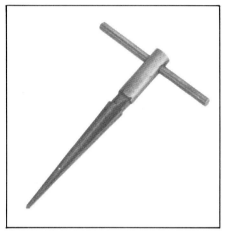

This tapered reamer is available through most industrial equipment suppliers.

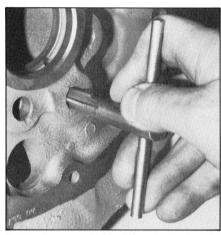

Tapered reamer is ideal for deburring the oil-gallery plug holes. It is quick, easy and produces a neat job.

THE CAM BEARINGS

Now comes the time to install the cam bearings and for this you will require the tool that was used to remove them. Before you attempt to install anything in the block, here is a vital piece of information you must know: cam bearings come in three different outside diameters. Your set of cam bearings will have these three different sizes. Because they vary by only a few thousandths of an inch, it is not easy to identify any apparent difference it is so small. Look at the cam bearings and you will see each has a number. Most cam bearings sold in the U.S.A. are manufactured by Durabond®. These have a number on them such as CH-4-1. Other numbers end in 2 and 3. These numbers signify the bearing size. Going from the front of the engine to the back, you will have to fit the bearings in 1, 2, 3, 3, 2 order. These numbers are the last digits of the numbers on the cam bearings. Cam bearings with numbers ending in 1 are for a cam bearing housing of 2.020-inch diameter. Those ending in 2 go into 2.010-inch diameter in the block. Those ending in 3, go into a cam bearing housing which is 2.000-inch diameter.

The numbers I just quoted are for blocks from 1957 and later using the grooved rear cam bearing housing. If you have a '55 or a '56 block with the two holes in the back cam bearing housing, you will need a

the oil gallerys a good brushing through with rifle or shotgun barrel brushes of the correct size. First of all, brush through the main bearing oilways from the main bearing saddles into the main gallery. Then go round the other oilways as shown in the nearby photos. Lastly, brush through the three main oil gallerys to make sure they are clear of all metal particles.

A couple of gallerys are difficult to get to. As shown in the photos, these are plugged by two threaded plugs with a square socket drive. These plugs are put in at the factory while the blocks are still hot after they come from a hot-tanking operation. The plugs are cold, consequently when the block cools off, it holds the plug very tight, therefore it is almost impossible to remove one of them by merely trying to undo it. The only way I've been able to remove these plugs is to drill them out and retap the hole.

Experience has shown that hot-tanking clears any build-up of sludge behind these plugs. On engines where the utmost cleanliness has been necessary, the removal of these plugs after hot-tanking has produced no sludge, which meant that the plugs need not have been removed in the first place. Once you have brushed through all the gallerys that you can get at, either wash out the gallerys with kerosene, or better still, blow them out with a high-pressure air line.

After deburring, the gallery holes should look like this, i.e., nothing to cause scoring of the plug as it is driven in.

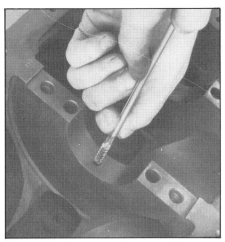

The deburring operation may have got some cast-iron particles in the oilways and if the block has stood for a few days, dust and grit from the air may have collected in some vital places. Just to make sure all dirt is dislodged, brush through the main bearing oil drillings with a barrel brush.

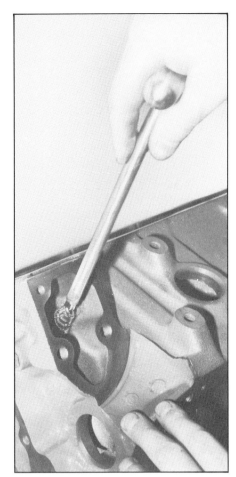

Though not connected to any major oil galleries, brush through the fuel-pump-pushrod hole, as particles collect here.

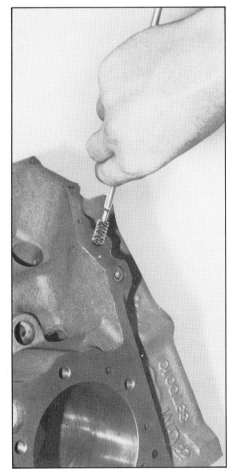

Brush out the oil-pressure-gauge/pressure-sender hole.

This oil passage is difficult to brush out but the hot tank or jet-spray tank cleans it without difficulty.

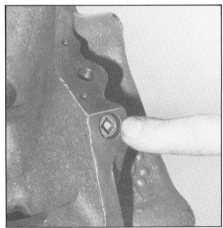

Here are two places that are difficult to get to because the screw plugs are fitted cold, while the block is hot. Fortunately, trapped buildup of sludge behind these plugs ranges from negligible to zero, so you don't really have to remove them.

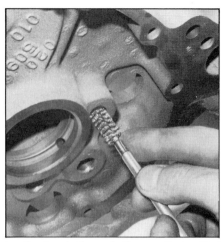

Lastly, brush through those galleries that run from end to end, these being the main and two lifter galleries.

If you have an early engine which requires the wide rear bearing, be sure your cam bearing kit contains such a bearing (left). If it doesn't, you will have to modify a later, narrow-type bearing as described in the drawing.

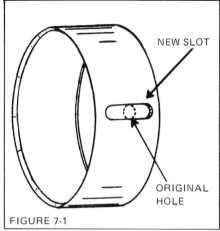

FIGURE 7-1

NEW SLOT

ORIGINAL HOLE

If you have an early block (1955-56 265 CID) and have bearings for the later block, then these bearings can be used if the hole is filed into a 1/2-inch-long slot. When installed, this slot must connect both oil holes in the block.

different bearing set. It will be the same, except the rear cam bearing is wider, being 0.940-inch wide instead of 0.740-inch wide.

If you are pulling an engine apart which was manufactured between '57 and '62, and it has never had the cam bearings replaced, you could find a wide rear cam bearing installed.

This is because the factory must have had a large stock of these wide cam bearings. They can be used in later blocks with no advantage or disadvantage. When they are driven into the block the required depth, the first hole in the cam bearing lines up with the groove in the cam housing and it functions just as if if was the narrower bearing with only one hole. In other words, if you are given the wrong set of bearings, it's of no consequence. You can use the early type rear cam bearing in your later engine with just as much success. If the situation is reversed and you have a late-type cam bearing, which, by the way, is a much more likely possibility, you can use it by filing a slot in the cam bearing. See Figure 7-1.

If you are not using Durabond® bearings, some other manufacturers use different numbering systems to denote which bearing is which size. Refer to the chart and make sure

that you do get all your bearings in the right place. If the bearing type you have is not on the chart you must use a micrometer to determine which size bearing fits where. If you measure the bearings you will find that they are between 3 and 5 thousandths of an inch larger than the sizes I quoted earlier. This is the amount of press fit in the block.

INSTALLING THE CAM BEARINGS

Your first job before putting any bearings into the block is to chamfer the edge of the cam bearing that will receive the impact from the driving tool. Use a 3-cornered scraper. If you don't do this, you may find that the cam is tight in the block—possibly too tight to turn, even with the cam sprocket on. Chamfer the edges of the bearings now and this problem will not arise. It's a lot harder to chamfer or deburr the bearings after they are installed.

Start with the rear cam bearing, double-check that it is the correct number for the rear of the block, position it in the block and drive it into place with a bearing driver of

There are three different sizes of cam bearing outside diameters. Each is identified by its number. Check these numbers with those in the chart and determine which fits where.

the type shown on page 40.

The position of the oil hole won't matter unless you have the early block. If you have the early block using the wide bearing, you must drive the bearing in so the holes line up. Once you have installed the rear bearing, progressively work your way to the front of the block. You may find it easier to install the front two bearings squarely in the block by inserting the driver in the back of the block through the 3 rear bearings. To make sure you

CAM BEARING CHART						
					EARLY	LATE
BEARING NO. from front	1	2	3	4	5	5
Durabond	CH4-1	CH4-2	CH4-3	CH4-3	CH4-4	CH4-2
Federal Mogul	2021DR	2022DR	2023DR	2023DR	2024DR	2022DR
TRW	SH 290	SH 288	SH 287	SH 287	SH 289	SH 288
Michigan Bearing	230CS	231CC	232CS	232CS	233CS	231CS

The above numbers are those stamped on the bearings. *The part number for a complete cam bearing set* for the above brands is as follows:

Durabond: early CH4, late CH8
Federal Mogul: early 1145M, late 1235M
TRW: early SH 287S, late SH 290S
Michigan Bearing: early 73CS, late 950CS

Note: Early is 1955–56
Late is 1957 and later

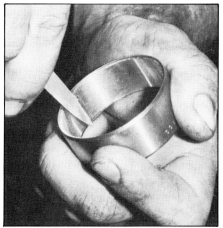

If you are installing your own cam bearing, use a three-cornered scraper or something similar to chamfer the inner edge of the bearing on the side which will take the driver impact.

Using the right size cam bearing driver, install the rear cam bearing first. On early engines using the wide bearing, line up the two holes in the bearing with those in the block.

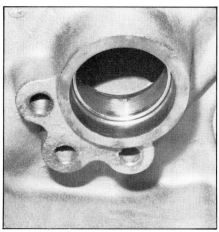

Continue driving in rear bearing until it is just short of step for cam-plug bore.

don't drive the bearings in too little or too far, at each stage refer to the photos to see the position where the bearings should end up when they are in place.

Once all the cam bearings are in place, smear a drop of oil on each of the cam bearing journals on the camshaft and slide the cam into the block to check that it will rotate freely. In 9,999 cases out of 10,000 the cam will rotate with no binding. If the cam should bind, find out why and fix the situation. If all the cam bearings appear in perfect order, yet as you put the cam into its bearings, it appears to be tight, it could be bent. Even if all bearings are perfect, the cam will be stiff to turn. The test is to roll the camshaft across a flat surface to see if there is any visible wobble in it.

If the cam is bent, consider exchanging it for a reconditioned one. A new cam is an ideal solution, but may cost considerably more.

From the inside of the block a correctly positioned narrow rear bearing will look like this. The installed wide bearing comes even with the edge of the casting.

The intermediate bearings look like these.

Starting the front bearing square is the most difficult because there is little for your eye to align the driver shaft with. Use extra care here to achieve correct installation.

The front bearing should be driven in until its outer edge is just level with the inner edge of the chamfer in the block.

With the cam bearings installed, temporarily install the camshaft to see that it turns freely.

The cam plug is much shallower than the water-jacket freeze plugs. A large-diameter punch must be used to install it, otherwise it will distort and leak oil.

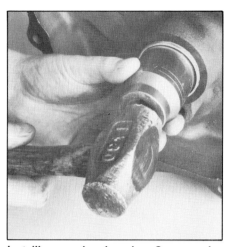
Installing cam-bearing plug: Smear sealer around outside edge, then, using large socket as a punch, drive in plug flush to 1/32 inch below block face.

Having driven the plug in until its outside edge is just below the block face, liberally coat the joint between the plug and the block with silicone sealer.

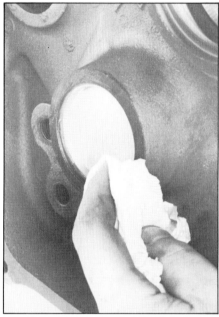
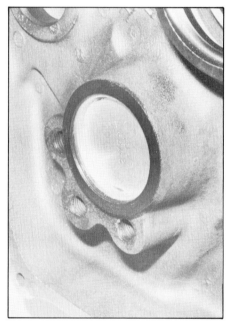
Wipe off the excess sealer with a paper wiper to leave a neat job like this.

BLOCK PLUGS

The first plug that will go in is the rear cam plug. This is a very shallow plug and just a little distortion during installation will cause it to leak. Therefore, care must be taken to install it properly.

First of all, smear the edges of the cam plug with silicone sealer. It only needs a thin smear, not so much that it will get into the bearing in the block. Take a large socket about 1/8-inch smaller than the internal diameter of the cup, and use it as a punch to drive the plug into the hole. Work your way around the edges so as to apply the load at the turned-up edge of the plug, so the plug will not cave in. Drive the plug in until the edge is just below the chamfer on the outer face of the block. Don't drive it in too far or it will butt against the cam when the cam is installed. Spread silicone sealer around the plug-to-block joint. Wipe off the excess, making sure you leave a good bead of sealer around the joint between the plug and block. This ensures there will be no oil leaks at this point.

Now for the 1/4-inch pipe plugs. Smear a generous amount of silicone sealer on the threads. Insert these into the block and tighten them with a torque wrench to about 18 pounds-feet.

Now for the front of the block. Take the 1/2-inch cup plugs and drive these into the three oil gallerys at the front. A word of advice: do not use a punch which is too small or, for that matter, one which is too large. These plugs are quite a bit larger than the hole they are going into. They taper. A punch may fit closely into the cup of these plugs while they are out of the block but as you drive the plug into the block, it will close onto the punch and you will find you cannot remove it from the plug. Use a punch with 5/16-inch diameter as this is neither too small to destroy the plug as it is driven in, nor too large to be gripped by the plug as it closes down to go into the hole. Once the plugs are in, they must be staked into place. A cold chisel will do this job admirably. It may not be as subtle as the original factory burring. Although somewhat uglier in appearance, this gets the job done.

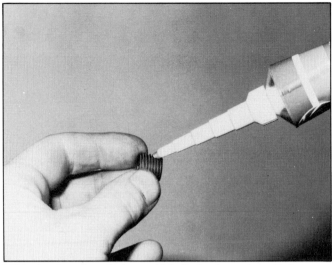

1/4-inch pipe thread plugs which fit in the main galleries *must* have their threads coated with a thread sealer prior to installation.

Put the plugs into the block and tighten them.

If you aren't sure how tight "tight" is, use a torque wrench with an Allen adapter and tighten the plugs to 18—20 pounds-feet.

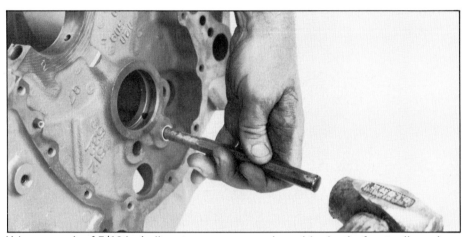

Using a punch of 5/16-inch diameter—no more, no less—drive in the front gallery plugs.

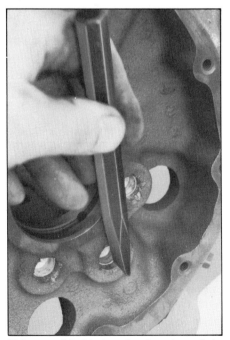

Using a cold chisel, stake the edges of the holes to prevent the plugs coming out.

After staking, the front of your block should look like this.

The next and last set of plugs to go into the block are the freeze plugs in the water jacket. Every bit as much care needs to be taken with these plugs as the cam bearing one, and exactly the same technique can be applied. Smear the outside diameter with sealer and use a large socket to drive the plugs into place. They should be driven in so the top edge of the plug is level with the bottom edge of the chamfer when it is put into the block. Once the plug is in, run a bead of sealer around the plug-to-block joint edge. Wipe off the excess, being sure to leave a visible bead at the joint.

When all the water-jacket freeze plugs are installed, your block will be ready for the installation of the moving parts.

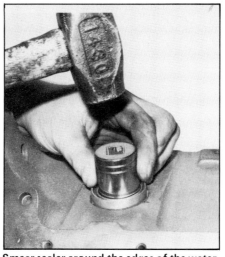

Smear sealer around the edges of the water-jacket freeze plugs and, using a large socket, drive in the plugs by working around the edges at the *bottom* of the cup.

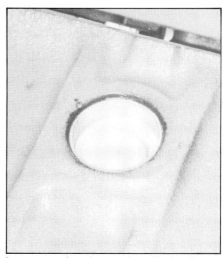

Last operation is to give all the freeze plugs the same sealer treatment the cam plug received. This installed plug has a thin, continuous bead of sealer showing at the joint between block and plug.

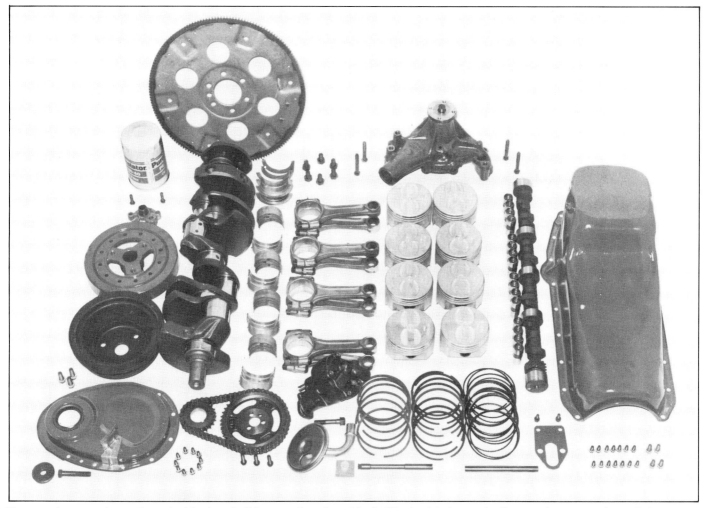

Here are the parts that go into the block to build a complete short block. Check with the nearby list to make sure you have all these parts.

SHORT BLOCK ASSEMBLY			
ITEM	NOTES	NUMBER	CHECK
Block		1	
Pistons and pins	to suit bores	8	
Rings, top	to suit bores	8	
Rings, second	to suit bores	8	
Rings, oil control	to suit bores	8 sets	
Connecting rods		8	
Connecting rod bolts and nuts	to suit rods	16	
Connecting rod bearings	to suit crankshaft	8 pairs	
Crankshaft		1	
Crankshaft main bearings	to suit crankshaft	5 pairs	
Crankshaft vibration damper (harmonic balancer)		1	
Crankshaft keys		2	
Crankshaft pilot bushing (manual transmissions only)	to suit crankshaft	1	
Front pulley	with grooves to suit application	1	
Front pulley bolts	3/8''—24 UNF or 3/8''—16 UNC x 1'' long (check damper for thread type)	3	
Crankshaft vibration damper bolt	7/16''—20 UNF x 2-1/4'' long	1	
Crankshaft vibration damper bolt washer		1	
Camshaft followers (lifters or tappets)		16	
Camshaft		1	
Camshaft sprocket		1	
Camshaft sprocket bolts	5/16''—18 UNC x 1'' long	3	
Camshaft drive chain		1	
Crankshaft gear		1	
Crankshaft rear oil seal		1 pair	
Cylinder head locating dowels	5/16'' dia. x 1/2'' long	4	
Dipstick tube		1	
Dipstick		1	
Flex plate (automatic transmission only)		1	
Flywheel (manual transmission only)		1	

SHORT BLOCK ASSEMBLY			
ITEM	NOTES	NUMBER	CHECK
*Flex plate or flywheel bolts	7/16"—20 UNF length to suit	6	
Oil pump		1	
Oil pump securing bolt	7/16"—14 UNC x 2-3/8" long	1	
Oil pump pickup pipe		1	
Oil pump drive shaft		1	
Oil pump drive shaft adapter		1	
Oil pan	to suit chassis	1	
Oil pan bolts (small)	1/4"—20 UNC x 1/2" long	14	
Oil pan bolt star washers	1/4" dia.	14	
Oil pan bolts (large)	5/16"—18 UNC x 5/8" long	4	
Front cover with oil seal		1	
Front cover bolts	1/4"—20 UNC x 1/2" long	10	
Front cover bolt star washers	1/4" dia.	10	
Front cover ignition timing tag (if applicable)		1	
Oil filter pressure-relief-valve housing	to suit filter	1	
Oil filter pressure-relief-valve housing bolts	5/16"—18 UNC x 1" long or 1/4"—20 UNC x 1-1/2" long (check block and filter for size)	2	
Oil filter case or spin-on cartridge	check pressure-relief-valve housing	1	
Oil filter securing bolt for cartridge type filter (if applicable)	1/2"—13 UNC x 9" for short canister or 12" for long canister	1	
Water pump	extended or short to suit application	1	
Water pump bolts for extended pump	3/8"—16 UNC x 2" long	4	
Water pump bolts for short pump	3/8"—16 UNC x 2-1/2" long	1	
	3/8"—16 UNC x 1-5/8" long	3	
Fuel pump pushrod		1	
Fuel pump spacer plate		1	
Fuel pump spacer plate bolts	1/4"—20 UNC x 5/8" long	2	
Oil pressure switch		1	
Fuel pump		1	
Fuel pump bolts	3/8"—16 UNC x 1-1/4" long	2	

*For safety use only the correct grade bolt from a GM dealer.

BLOCK ASSEMBLY

For many of you, the things I've just described will have already been done at the engine machine shop. Before you go any further, now is the last time to check that there isn't any dirt in the block. If the block has been standing a few days at the machine shop, then the oil that was put on the bores immediately after they were finished may have collected some dust. If so, wipe the bores clean of that oil with a lint-free rag and then re-oil them. Now remove all the main-bearing caps and wipe them clean to ensure the bearing shells will seat correctly in the main caps. Do the same for the bearing bores in the block.

Check Main Bearings—Are the main bearings the correct size for the crankshaft main journals? You will find the size, either standard or undersize, marked on the back. Having established that they are the correct size, install the grooved bearing shell halves into the block. Next, install one-half of the rear main oil seal and be sure it's positioned the right way if it's a neoprene one (see p. 90). Do not oil the back of the bearing shells or the block. Just make sure the bearings are perfectly clean and fit snugly in the block.

Shown here is the relationship of the moving parts within the short block assembly. Though this drawing is of an early engine, it will still serve as a useful guide for later units. Drawing courtesy Chevrolet.

Gasket set contains all necessary gaskets for rebuilding the engine from the intake manifold down. This one contains steel-shim head gaskets. I prefer kits with composition-type head gaskets.

Before doing anything else, see that the main caps are in the right position on the block, by checking the block/cap number you stamped on during teardown.

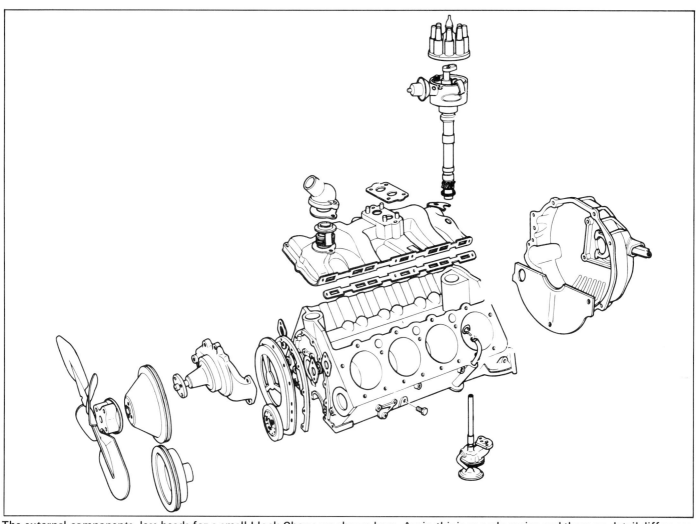

The external components, less heads for a small-block Chevy are shown here. Again this is an early engine and there are detail differences between this and later engines. Drawing courtesy Chevrolet.

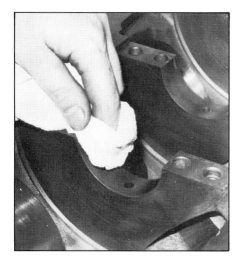

Thoroughly wipe the main-bearing bores, both block and cap. Any dirt trapped here will cause an early bearing failure.

Your box of main bearings will contain four different types of bearing shells. Two wide ones with flanges are the rear main bearings: the grooved one goes in the block, the plain one in the cap. The narrow bearings fit in the other four bearing stations, grooved ones in the block, plain ones in the caps.

Before installing the bearings, check that you have been given the correct size for the crank. This is stamped on the back of the bearing: STD (standard) as shown here; -010 (minus ten thousandths); -020 (minus twenty thousandths) etc.

Wipe the bearings clean and install the *grooved* halves into the block.

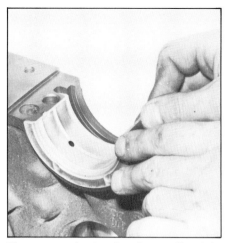
The rear main bearing is usually tight across the inside of the thrust flange. You will probably have to press it in position with both hands. *Do not* use a hammer to install the bearing. Remember it is a delicate, precision component and must be treated as such.

Here's how to install the neoprene-type oil seal. Be sure to put the seal in the right way or your engine will leak oil for sure. Note that the seal "lips" point toward the bearing.

Deburring the crank prior to putting in the keys is important if this operation is to go smoothly. First of all, go across the keyway slots with the file as shown here.

CRANK INSTALLATION

If you are using a new crank or a crank kit, no keys will be installed. If there are none in place, now is the time to put them in.

Your first job is to inspect the keyways in the crankshaft to see if there are any burrs on them. Inevitably there will be, so file these off and then chamfer the edges of the crank keyway grooves with a 45-deg. chamfer. It only need be small; it is really just breaking the edge to give some sort of lead-in to the key which is a drive-fit into the groove.

Your next job is to put a similar chamfer on the key itself. Then, using a punch at least as wide as the keyway,

drive the keys into position. When you have driven them in, they should be perfectly horizontal. Often, you will find after driving in the keys, that it is a tight enough fit to burr one side or the other, sometimes both. This must be remedied by filing off the burrs.

Next turn your attention to the oil-way drillings in the crank main and the rod journals. Check to see if there are any sharp edges where the hole breaks into the bearing surface. If there are, gently remove these sharp edges with a very fine file so that they do not have any chance of scoring the bearing.

With all your filing done, you can

now give the crankshaft its final cleaning before installation. Using a pipe cleaner, a rifle-barrel brush or a suitable bristle brush, clean all the oil holes in the crank. Then fill a squirt bottle with cleaning solvent and squirt this through all the oil holes to remove any particles which may have been left by the brush. Repeat this operation several times until you are absolutely positive that the oil holes are perfectly clean.

Finally, finish cleaning the crank by wiping off excess solvent, grit, etc., with paper towels. Most "shop rags" will produce lint, which may plug the oiling system. So don't use them regardless of how handy they are.

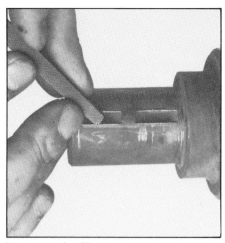

Next use the file as shown here to put a small chamfer around the edges of the slots to provide a lead-in for the keys.

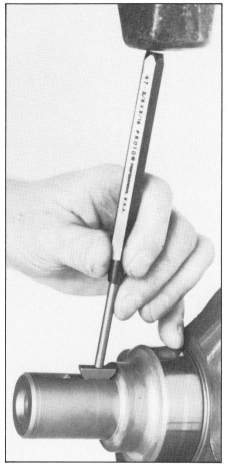

Drive in the crank keys using at least a 5/16-inch diameter punch.

Even though the keyway slot was chamfered, fitting the key may still cause a burr (arrow) to be thrown up.

Any burrs produced as a result of installing the keys must be removed now.

Clean or check the cleanliness of the oil holes before installing the crank. Remember, any dirt here can only go one way—through the bearings.

Lower the crank into position on oiled main bearing shells.

In readiness for laying the crank into the block, smear the neoprene oil seal with oil and liberally oil the rest of the bearings. Rope seals should be installed *after* a trial installation of the crank.

The crank is now ready to be lowered into the block. Before you do, though, make sure the bearing shells in the block are oiled very well. Also, a little oil — just enough to provide initial lubrication — should go onto the neoprene rear-main-bearing oil seal.

Install Rope Seals Later — If you have the very early rope-type seal, a slightly different procedure should be adopted. Because rope seals are tight on the crank when they are first assembled, run through a trial installation of the crank without the rope seal to see that the crankshaft turns freely. Follow the procedure in the next two sections with just one change: leave out the rope seal. Then remove the crankshaft and insert the rope seal so one end is flush with the block face. Then, working progressively from this end, tap the seal into its groove with a large-diameter socket or the handle of a hammer or anything which will not concentrate the load too sharply on one point. Working your way around the seal, get it fitting as snugly as possible. When you are sure it is fully seated in its groove, use a razor blade to trim the other end level with the block, starting from the inside and working out. The same procedure

should then be applied to the rear-main-bearing cap. Prior to final installation of the crank, generously lubricate the seal and allow time for the oil to soak into the rope.

Putting in the Crank — At this point, lower the crank in place and turn it a few revolutions to distribute the oil on it to the crankshaft main bearing surfaces. Next you will need to check the crankshaft end float. To do this, lever the crankshaft towards the rear end of the block as shown in the photo. Using a feeler gauge or gauges, establish just how much clearance there is between the thrust bearing face of the rear-main-bearing insert. This should be between 0.002 and 0.007 inch. You will rarely find one out of this tolerance under normal circumstances. If it is looser than this, investigate why. If the clutch was incorrectly adjusted it could be that the thrust bearing flange has worn badly. If the clearance is over 0.020 inch the crank should be *replaced*. Alternately, you may have had some material ground off the thrust flange or the bearings themselves may be too narrow or too wide. Whichever it is, check it out.

Now pick up your rear-main-

bearing cap, check to see that you have in fact lightly oiled the seal on it and do likewise to the main bearing itself. It doesn't need to be dripping with oil. At this point it only needs to have a smear on it because the crank journal is already well oiled. Using some paper towels, wipe off all the excess oil from the mating surfaces of the rear main cap and the matching block surfaces. It really needs to be wiped off well here, otherwise the sealer you will be using will not stick as well as it should. On the dried-off mating surfaces, use sealer in the areas shown in the photo. The important part in the block is right up in the corner. This is the most likely place for an oil leak if you don't get the sealer in well enough. On the other hand, do not use so much sealer that it will ooze out everywhere and clog things up. The amount shown in the photos should be considered the very most you should use. Position the main bearing cap in the block, then tap it into place with a plastic or rubber mallet until it is seated into the notch in the block. Check that your main bearing bolts have been thoroughly cleaned, oil the threads, and screw them in. Torque these bolts up to 75 pounds-feet with a torque wrench.

Oil the journals and give the crank a few turns to distribute the oil.

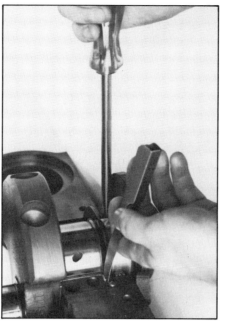

Using a large screwdriver, lever the crankshaft towards the back of the engine. Insert a feeler gauge between the crankshaft thrust flange and the bearing thrust face to determine the end float. Between 0.002-and 0.007-inch is acceptable. Make a note of clearance you measure for later reference.

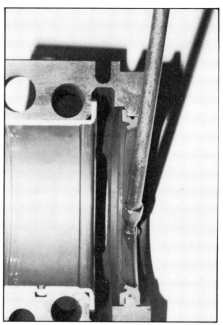

Put a *drop or two* of oil on the neoprene oil seal and smear it around the lip of the seal with a finger. Avoid excess!

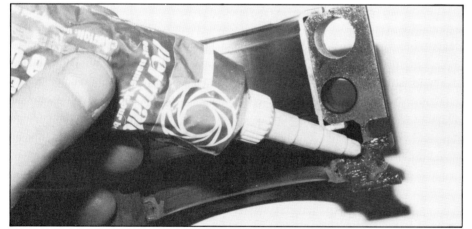

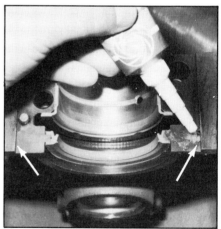

Spread silicone sealer on both sides of the cap in the area shown here. Apply sealer to the block in the area shown and the equivalent area the other side of the bearing. The most important parts are the corners (arrows). Put a bead of sealer here about 1/16- to 3/32-inch thick. The rest of the area need only be covered with a generous smear.

Smear oil on the bearing, place the cap on the block and, using a rawhide or plastic mallet, tap it into position.

Put in the main-bearing bolts. As can be seen here, the bolts are spotlessly clean.

Torque the rear main-bearing bolts to 70 lbs.-ft., then check to see that the crank spins freely.

CHECKING END PLAY

Now is the time to make a final check on end play in the crankshaft. The same technique is used as before. First of all, tap the crankshaft towards the front of the engine and then, using a screwdriver, lever it towards the back of the engine and check the gap between the bearing surface on the bearing insert and the thrust flange on the crank as shown in the photo. Again, anything between 0.002 and 0.007 inch is acceptable. You should have, within 0.002 inch, the same end clearance you had when you checked it previously, with only one bearing half in. If it is more than 0.002 inch or so different, but still within the tolerance, do not worry. Although

it means that one thrust bearing is taking the majority of the load, this is a bearing which does not have a tendency to wear out. Half the bearing can cope just as well as two halves for probably 100,000 miles.

Next install the center main-bearing cap and torque the bolts to 75 pounds-feet. On 4-bolt blocks, the short bolts on each 4-bolt cap should be torqued to 65 pounds-feet. Again check to see if the crank turns easily. If there is any distortion of either the crank or block it will show up as an appreciable tightening of the crankshaft, sometimes only at one point during turning. On the other hand, you could have dirt or particles under one or another of the bearings. If the crank gets tight

or hard to turn, check to find out why. Otherwise, the machining you paid for will have been wasted.

Assuming all is well, go ahead and install the other bearings, and after torquing up each one, check the crank for freedom of rotation. Use plenty of oil on each of the bearings during this assembly process. Remember, it may be some time before you actually install your engine, so plenty of oil at this stage will at least ensure the bearings won't be dry at a future date.

Crankshaft Stiffness—Seal drag with the neoprene seal is almost undectable so the crank should turn easily. If you want to put a number on it, the maximum torque to turn the crank over when *all the caps are on*

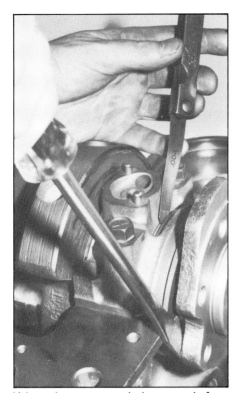

Using the same technique as before, check the end float on the cap half of the bearing. It should be between 0.002- and 0.007-inch and within 0.002-inch of the clearance you measured on the bearing in the block.

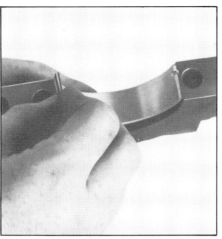

Wipe the main bearings and caps clean and install the bearings into the main caps.

and the neoprene seal is in place should be no more than 1 pound-foot when the bearings are lubricated with normal engine oil. This figure also applies to a rope seal crank *without* the rope seal installed. The drag caused by a new rope seal on a crank can be as much as 15-25 pounds-feet. This amount of stiffness hides any stiffness in the crank bearing so you can see why a "trial" crank fitting prior to installing the rope seal is essential.

If your block uses a rope seal and the trial installation works OK, remove the main caps and install the rope seal as detailed on page 92.

PISTON/ROD ASSEMBLY

If the rebuild involved new pistons or rods, now is the time to install the pistons on the rods. If you are using the original items, then pistons should be on the rods, so what I am about to say won't apply. As you might expect, rods and pistons have to be assembled a certain way. Check the accompanying photographs and make sure you assemble them correctly.

On flat-top pistons, the front of the piston may be indicated by a notch or an arrow or some similar marking. The reason these pistons have to go in a particular way, is that the wrist pins are offset between 40 and 90 thousandths. If the pistons go in back to front, the offset would be the wrong way and as a result, the pistons would rattle a great deal in the bores. Most aftermarket, non-original pop-up pistons have no pin offset. The pin is right in the middle of the piston. This

Oil the bearings in the cap and locate each cap at its correct numbered station in the block. Also note that the bearing tangs (arrows) go to the same side.

On two-bolt main-bearing-cap engines, after all the caps have been installed, go around and torque them *all* to 75 pounds-feet.

type of piston must also go onto the rod a particular way. Though the front of the piston isn't marked, it must be mounted so that the pop-up section is toward the outside of the engine. If this isn't done, the raised section of the piston will not fit into the chamber, nor will the valve relief be situated the right way. Many types of flattop pistons have valve reliefs for mounting the piston in either the right or left bank, so this isn't a problem. With pop-up pistons, make sure you always mount them with the pop-up section towards the outside of the bank of cylinders.

Some Chevrolet pistons around the early '60s in the fuel-injected 283's had pop-up pistons with offset pins. With this type piston, you must have pistons to suit both the left and right banks of cylinders. So if you are installing this sort of piston, make sure you use them in the correct bank. If you buy a set of these pistons from your local Chevy dealer, you will find notches indicating the front of the piston. Installing them the correct way will put the pop-ups all toward the outside of the engine.

Fitting Pistons to Rods—Now for the technique: You can take the simplest way out, but it will cost money. Take your pistons to your machine shop and have them assemble the pistons to the rods. Most shops will use the *press* method. They simply mount the piston, its wrist pin and rod on an adapter in a hydraulic press, lightly lubricate the wrist pin and press it into place.

Or, the shop may use the *heat* method, whereby heat from a torch is applied to the rod wrist-pin bore. Heating the rod wrist-pin bore or rod *eye* can create enough expansion to allow the wrist pin to pass through with finger pressure. I think I may have made it sound overly easy. If you wish to do the job yourself, here are a few hints that will help. Pay attention or you will find yourself with the wrist pin halfway through the rod and firmly fixed so you can

On four-bolt main-bearing-cap engines, torque up the inner (longer) bolts to 75 pounds-feet and the outer (shorter) bolts to 65 pounds-feet.

At this stage your small-block Chevy should look like this.

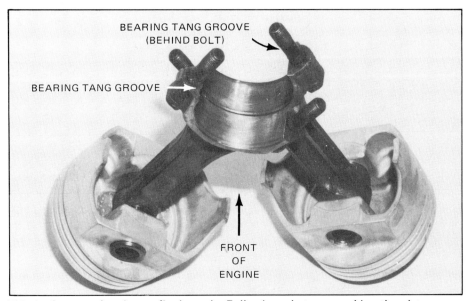
This is the way the pistons fit the rods. Following whatever marking the pistons may have so the front of the pistons are toward the engine front.

96

Before thinking about fitting pistons to rods, establish which is the front of the piston. Some, like this TRW item, may be marked with an arrow. Others, like original equipment pistons, may have a notch at the edge of the piston crown to denote the front.

Here an LPG torch is being used to heat the con rod wrist pin diameter. Note the orderly placing of the pistons and wrist pins in the background.

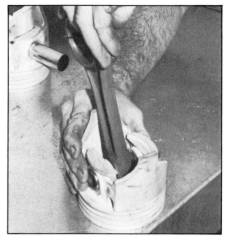

With the rod suitably heated, place your fingers to stop the wrist pin going too far through, then with the thumb, quickly push the pin through and here is how you finish up.

Even if your tear-down inspection indicated accurate rods, this final checkout on a rod/piston aligning fixture is a good idea as it will detect any error in the whole assembly and catch it before it's too late. Charge for such a check is minimal.

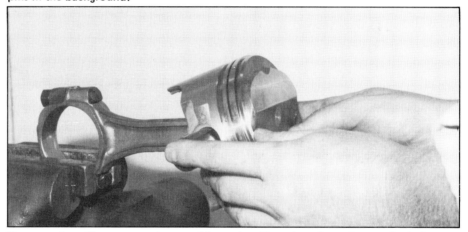

If you are installing pop-up pistons with no pin offset, then the easiest method of assembling them correctly is to hold the rod with the bearing tang slots *upwards*. Having heated the rod eye, put the piston on with the pop-up *upward*.

neither move it one way nor the other. This means going to your machine shop and having it pressed the rest of the way. This will cost, and that's what you were *trying* to avoid.

Piston Temperature—First make sure your pistons are not cold. If you are building the engine in the middle of winter, you may find the wrist pins tight in the pistons them-selves. If this is the case, warm the pistons by allowing them to "soak" at 70°F or a warmer room temperature until the wrist pin passes freely—very freely—through the piston. In cooler climates you may even have to put them in hot water for a few minutes. Secondly, while you are doing this, keep the piston pins themselves as cold as possible. There is really no need to put them in the freezer as some do—just make sure that they are not warm. Otherwise, you'll find the job that much more difficult. To avoid a cloud of oil smoke, and to reduce the heat transfer rate, wipe any oil from the pins.

A piston and ring set from TRW. Before installation, check out the ring gaps.

Next, line up your rods and pistons so you can place them immediately in position and slip the pin through. You have a very short time to do this, because the heat transfers from the rod to the pin very quickly—in about two seconds or so the pin will not slide in the rod. Because of this, it is essential that you know exactly which way the rod is going to go relative to the piston, and that you slip the pin through the piston and rod quickly and firmly *but prevent it from going too far to the other side by placing your finger over the pin bore of the piston.* When you push the pin through, *push hard enough for it to make an impression on your finger.* This means it will have come out of the piston-pin bore by about 1/16–3/32 inch. This is just the amount required to leave the rod centered when the ends of the wrist pin are even with the piston-pin bosses.

Heating the Rod Wrist-Pin Bore— Now for the heating of the pin bore of the rod itself. You do not need to elevate this to a great temperature. If you lightly polish the end of the rod so you can see shiny metal, you will find heating the rod until it just turns dark blue will be hot enough to get the job done. Avoid overheating because it may affect rod strength.

As a last precaution before installation, have the rod and piston

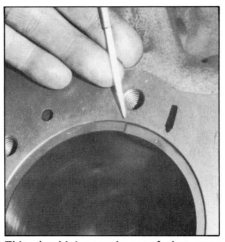

This should be ample proof that some rings come from the factory totally ungapped. These rings are actually overlapping by a few thousandths. Any attempt to install or run these rings would have destroyed the bore surface instantly.

Ring-gap check is a tedious operation but it is important. I number each cylinder to cut down the chance of mixing up the ring sets for each bore.

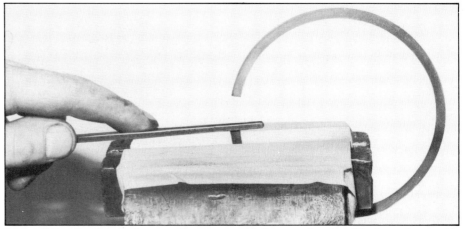

When filing the ring to increase its gap, especially a moly ring, file from the outside in, otherwise you stand a chance of chipping the moly facing of the ring. Only file the edge which is secured in the vise. Note the card for protection of the ring. Don't over-tighten the vise or you will damage the ring.

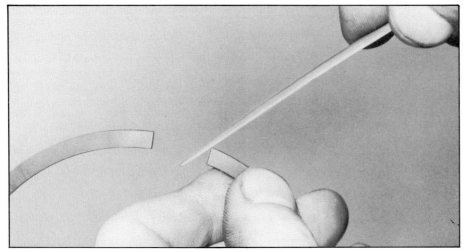

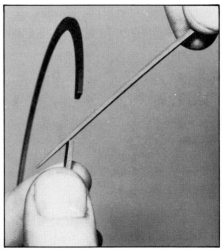

Once the rings have been correctly gapped, any possible burrs must be removed by taking off the sharp corners. The smallest visible chamfer on each corner will do the job.

assemblies checked on a rod-aligning fixture. Any good machine shop should have one, and most of these will check the rod/piston accuracy as an assembly.

PISTONS & RINGS

Moving along to the piston-and-ring assembly, first group the rings into sets for each piston. Working from cylinders one to eight, check the ring end gaps of each ring set in the cylinder they will be used. Gaps should be 0.012−0.020 inch for the top ring and 0.018−0.025 inch for the second compression ring. For the oil-control rings this should be 0.015− 0.055 inch. Some special ring sets may require different end gaps from those just quoted, so as a final check, follow the instructions supplied with the rings.

Even though it's tedious, don't skip checking ring-end gaps. Some ring sets come without any end gap whatsoever. These rings, when fitted into a bore, may be close to butting, and in some cases actually overlap. So, it is necessary on such ring sets to achieve the correct end gap from scratch rather than correct or finally set one that's already there.

Many ring sets are pre-gapped and, if so, it's usually stated on the box. Sealed Power and TRW supply pre-gapped rings. However, if you are fitting rings to bores which, for some reason or another, are larger than nominal or nominal oversize, consider using ungapped rings so you can hand fit them to achieve the correct gap. Good examples of ungapped or over-size rings are the Sealed Power or TRW plus-0.035 rings for 0.030-in. oversize bores.

Once you've checked or achieved the correct ring gaps, using a very fine needle file or die-maker's file, put a very small chamfer on all the edges of the ring ends. Especially important is the edge which runs against the bore. A sharp edge here can score the cylinder bore. This chamfer need only be 0.005-inch wide. In other words, if it's visible, the chamfer is big enough.

While gapping the rings, keep them numbered so they go back in the correct cylinder when fitted to their respective pistons.

With the rail-support ring in place, thread the *top* rail in position—then the *bottom.*

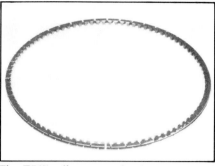

The TRW rail-support ring is constructed so it is almost impossible to get the ends overlapped during assembly.

Now for a very important step if your engine is to survive the first five minutes. Check to see that the ends of the rail support ring are NOT overlapping. The ends must butt up and the colors should show just that, as indicated by the arrows.

The easiest way to do this is to lay out a piece of plain paper and number it 1 through 8, leaving enough space so that you can put a ring set down around each number.

Another way to do it is to use wire twist tags and put a label on and twist the tag to hold the label to the rings. Avoid using sticky tape to label them to their respective cylinders. If you do, some of the gum from the tape may adhere to the ring. Under the hot conditions in the engine, this gum can collect deposits and cause a ring to stick.

Generally speaking, the gaps for most ring sets will be within limits. What you are checking for are the ones that may be out of tolerance. They can cause a problem, especially if they are too small. Too small a ring gap could lead to the ends of the ring butting when they expand due to temperature and this will lead to a piston seizure and severe cylinder-wall damage.

With small engines it is always a good idea to use a ring expander to put the rings on the pistons because this cuts down the chances of breakage. However, with the

Chevy's relatively big bore, the rings have more compliance and need for a ring expander is less— but still desirable. In the absence of a ring expander, you can install the rings by opening them up at the gap with your thumbs. If you have delicate thumbs you will wish you had a ring expander! The next job is to install the rings on the pistons. When doing this be sure to assemble the numbered rings to the piston for that bore.

Oil-Control Rings—The biggest chance of making a mistake usually occurs when installing the oil-control rings. These multi-piece rings can easily be incorrectly assembled. Although there may be many variations in outward appearance, most oil-control rings are basically similar. However, there is bound to be an exception to the rule, so when you install piston rings, take the instructions out of the box and read them carefully!

If required, install the oil-control-ring expander first. There may be instances where an expander is supplied, but not needed because bore wear may not be enough to require its use. The expander—a wavy ring—backs up the entire ring and rail-support ring assembly. It is there to increase pressure against the wall of a bore with more than average wear. This expander is not required for many types of rings, so refer to the instructions to determine if it is needed.

The next step is to install the *rail-support ring*. This formed flexible piece holds the two rings at the top and bottom of the groove. This is where mistakes are most likely to happen. Look at the rail-support ring. The ends are usually painted. In many instances each end is a different color, such as red and green. The idea of painting these ends is so you can easily spot them and see they butt against each other correctly. The ends of this support ring must face against each other. It is easy to assemble them so they overlap one or maybe two notches. When overlapped, they force the rings out to the bore without any ability to spring inward. This means the rings will cause the piston to be very tight in the bore. Also they will not do their job.

Some Sealed Power rail-support rings are made foolproof by the fitting of plastic cubes on the end of the ring which makes it almost impossible for them to be assembled overlapped. The TRW rail-support ring is also a relatively foolproof design which is difficult to assemble overlapped.

Positioning the Gaps—If you have never assembled any of these multi-piece oil-control rings before, you will find it frustrating. As fast as you are trying to insert one ring in its proper place, another one pops out. From the point of view of oil control, the position of the gaps doesn't really matter. From the assembly aspect, positioning the gaps in a certain place

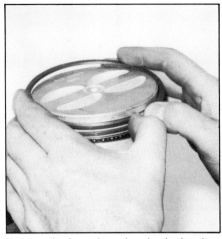

Due to the large bore involved, the rings have enough compliance to be installed without the aid of a ring expander, but if you have one it's much better to use it. Be sure you put the rings on the right way. The uppermost side is usually denoted by a dot or the word TOP.

will make life much easier. Check the manufacturer's instructions, and if there is nothing to the contrary, put them in as follows.

First, lightly hold the piston by the connecting rod in a vise so you are looking down the length of the wrist pin. Assemble the rail-support ring in the oil-ring groove of the piston so the gap faces you. Position the first rail in the upper groove of the rail-support ring so one end is 90 degrees to the right of the gap in the rail-support ring. Feed the ring into position on the rail-support ring, working your way toward the gap in the rail-support ring. This will mean you will have the gap covered after you have fed in about 100 degrees of the ring. Here, position the gap 90 degrees to the left of the gap in the rail-support ring. Feed the ring into position, again working towards the gap in the rail-support ring. Do it this way and you should have very little trouble with rings jumping out of position.

Make sure the ends of the rail-support rings are butting correctly. If they are colored, see that the colors are showing in the correct manner.

Compression Rings—Your next move is to install the second of the two compression rings, the one in the

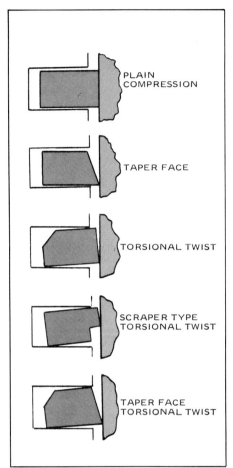

At one time plain compression rings were used for almost every automotive piston-ring requirement. Advancing technology has lead to the production of a variety of rings for different purposes. Basically the modern twist ring has a smaller contact area for a quicker break in and a superior gas seal under the higher cylinder pressures in modern engines.

middle groove of the piston. Depending on the type of ring that you have, it will have TOP or some other indication of which side should go uppermost marked on it. Or, it will have nothing at all. If it has nothing marked on it, it is probably a plain ring and it may not make any difference which way it goes into the second groove. However, plain rings, which were once common, are now seldom used. More than likely, all compression rings, whether second or first (the one that goes in the top groove), will have TOP, some number, letter, mark or machining indicating the top ring face. This must go upwards on the piston. Put

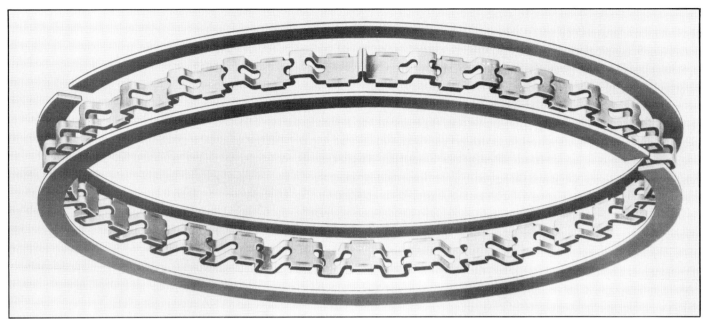

This view shows the approximate positions of the ring gaps relative to each other on a rail-type oil-control ring. The most important thing is to make sure the abutment of the rail support ring ends is correct as shown. Drawing courtesy of Sealed Power Corporation.

the second ring in position and check that it is free in the groove. Then do the same with the top ring. Again, this will have to be installed a certain way. Check with the instructions as to which way it should be. Some rings have the ring face narrowed down, i.e., they have a small chamfer or step on the inside.

With some rings the step or angle goes up, and with others it goes down. Do not assume which side the ring should have uppermost. Always check, because if you install a ring the wrong way up, the engine can become a super oil pumper.

INSTALLING RODS/PISTONS

To install the rod-and-piston assemblies into the block, you must have a ring compressor. If you haven't a ring compressor, I recommend buying one. Or, though it will only suit one bore size, I thoroughly recommend the *taper sleeve* piston assembly. It's available from most good speed shops. Without a ring compressor of some sort, you may break a ring or two.

Lubricating the Parts — Now select the rod assembly you are going to install, remove the rod cap, check that the rod journal is clean, then put a clean bearing half in place in the rod cap and generously oil the bearing surface. Next oil the ring grooves and rings. The simplest, most effective way to do this is to use a coffee can of engine oil so you can dip the ring belt of the piston into the oil. This makes sure the piston rings are well lubricated. If they don't have this initial lubrication, one or more rings may stick in their grooves. Rings that become stuck often do not perform as they should.

Protecting the Journal — Before actually installing the piston and rod assembly into the block, there are two things you should do. First, turn the crankshaft so the journal of the particular bore you are working on is at *bottom-dead-center* (BDC). This means the piston will be low down in the bore when installed. The second thing is, be sure to fit the sleeves over the rod bolts to protect the journal from accidental damage by the rod bolts while you are installing the assembly. Just before installing the piston, check the bore for cleanliness. If necessary, wipe it out and give it a light oiling. The best way is to use kitchen paper towels. Plan to use as much as two rolls during assembly of a complete engine.

Piston Installation — Before placing the piston in the bore, stagger the ring gaps and make sure that the front of the piston — the notched side or the side indicated by the arrow — is toward the front of the block. In the case of pop-up pistons the dome must be towards the outside. If you are using a taper ring installation tool, then the job of getting the piston/ring/rod assembly into the block is easy. Lightly oil the bore of the tool, place it over the bore, and gently slide the piston assembly into the bore. A few light taps with the handle of a hammer is all it takes. If you are using a conventional ring compressor, compress the rings, then gently place the piston into the bore until the bottom edge of the ring compressor rests against the gasket surface of the block. Tap the edge of the ring compressor to make sure the compressor is fully contacting the block all around the bore. Gently tap the top of the piston as you hold the ring compressor firmly against the block. The only snag you will probably find is the oil-control ring rails tend to pop out easily from under the ring compressor just prior to entering the bore. This can be a nuisance and of course, these rings are easy to bend. Therefore, be watchful of this and *do not force the piston into the bore*. Otherwise

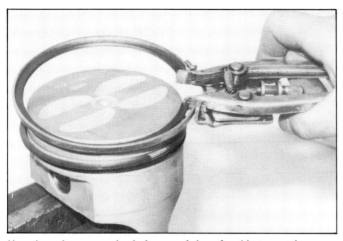

Here is a ring expander being used. I prefer this to putting on rings without because it's a lot easier on my thumbs. If you are inexperienced at putting rings on pistons, a ring expander is a good way to avoid breakages.

With the right numbered rod/piston/ring set going in the correct cylinder, put a cleaned bearing shell in position with the bearing tang in the tang groove in the rod.

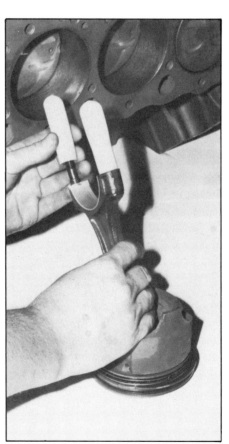

Liberally oil the ring grooves before installing the piston/rod assembly. Then oil the bearing.

Put the sleeves over the rod bolts to protect the crank rod journals during assembly.

With excess oil removed, position the piston in the bore. The rod journal for this cylinder must be at bottom center.

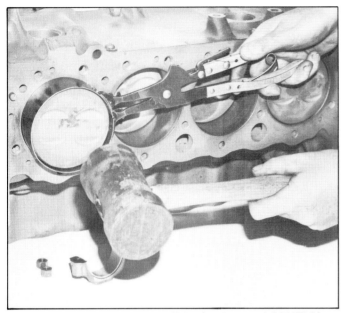

Using your ring compressor, pull in the rings and GENTLY tap the piston into the bore. Take care with that oil ring or you will have problems. If the oil ring rails don't want to go in, maybe you forgot to chamfer the bore as I mentioned previously.

When installing the piston and ring assembly check that the ring compressor is against the block face. If a ring comes out from under the compressor, as shown here, it will hang up on the top of the bore.

If you are using pop-up pistons, put them in with the dome to the outside.

Here's where the bolt sleeves come into their own, just as they engage the journal. Now is the time to make sure you have enough oil on the crank rod journal and the rod bearing.

With its bearing shell in place and oiled, place the rod cap in position. Like the main bearing caps, the rod caps go back with the tang groove on the same side of the split.

you will simply ruin an oil-ring assembly. If a ring or rail pops out from under the compressor, loosen the compressor and put it back so the rings are all compressed again. Don't get short-tempered or in a hurry now. Take your time. If someone is hurrying you, stop work on the engine and come back when you can work on it deliberately and with care.

Use a wooden or rubber-ended hammer handle to tap the piston down the bore. While doing this, guide the rod bearing onto the journal. When it is positioned on the journal, remove the rubber sleeves covering the rod-bolt threads. Check the rod cap for cleanliness and install its bearing shell. Oil the bearing, then making sure the bearing tangs on the cap and on the rod are on the same side, put the rod-bearing cap onto the connecting-rod bolts. Follow this by the two securing nuts, and then as a final operation, torque these to 35 pounds-feet for the 11/32-inch bolts and 45 pounds-feet for the 3/8-inch bolts.

Once the rod and piston assembly is installed, turn the crank over a few times to make sure there isn't any obvious binding. Repeat the procedure with the other 7 piston and rod assemblies. As you install each one, check for freedom of rotation.

You can expect the engine to get stiffer and stiffer as you install each piston and rod assembly. Generally speaking, you should be able to turn the engine over with no more than 35 to 40 pounds-feet of torque as measured with the torque wrench when all the pistons are in. Rope-seal engines may be 15 to 25 pounds-feet higher.

CAM & CAM DRIVE

Moving up to the front of the engine you can tackle the assembly of the lower parts of the valve train. Back-tracking for a moment, I pointed out earlier that several types of gears are available. These, in the order of reliability, are the truck roller chain and gears along with the wide steel gears. The nar-

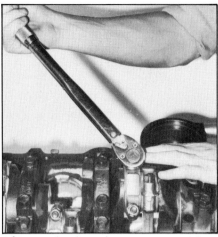

After putting in each rod and cap with its securing nuts, torque the nuts to 30—35 pounds-feet for the 11/32-inch diameter bolts and 40—45 pounds-feet for the 3/8-inch bolts. When all rods are in, go back over and retorque them all once more.

row steel gears and chain are second. The wide chain with the nylon gear comes third and the narrow chain with the narrow nylon gear finishes in last place. With the narrow chain and gears you end up at best with a setup that wears out chains relatively quickly. At worst, in the case of the nylon gear and narrow chain you have one which will wear out chain *and* gears quickly. This is why it is best to use the wide steel ones, especially in warm climates or for heavy-duty use. They will be there and in good working order for a much greater length of time. They will also stay quieter for more miles. Another point in favor of the wide steel gears—generally they are also the cheapest.

Installing the Crank Gear—If you have the gears and chain of your choice, the first step is to put the crank gear on the crank. Now whatever sort you are using it is important to install it without undue force. Normally it should be a light to medium drive fit. The first thing you should do is to check that there are no raised edges or burrs on the crank key to prevent the gear from going onto the crank. The next thing you should do is to lightly lubricate the crankshaft "nose." Then position the gear on the crank nose with the chamfered

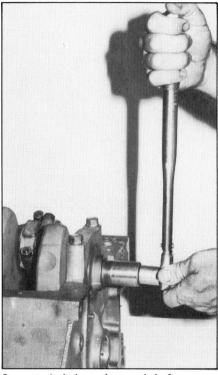

Screw a bolt into the crankshaft nose or into one of the flywheel/flex-plate securing bolts. With a torque wrench, measure the turning torque required to turn the engine over. 35—40 pounds-feet is the maximum you should see on a lip seal-type engine with all piston and rod assemblies installed.

Which Size Bolts are in your rods? The quick and easy way to tell is 11/32-inch bolts have 1/2-inch Across Flats (A F) nuts and 3/8-inch bolts have 9/16 A F nuts.

edge of its bore toward the block. Using a piece of steel tubing or an aluminum or brass punch, gently tap the gear in place. If you use a little heat on the gear prior to installation it will go on easier. Be sure to tap it around its circumference, spreading the load evenly. Do not use undue force, otherwise you can destroy, distort or crack the gear. Using a tube of suitably large diameter as a driver is best because this offers the least chance of any damage to the gear.

CAM INSTALLATION

Having mounted the crank gear, bolt the cam gear to the camshaft. The cam gear will have to come off again in a moment so put one bolt in finger-tight. You are doing this

With the piston and rod installation done, one of the major hurdles is over. Your small block now starts to look like an assembly of working parts.

The crank gear must be put on the crank with the chamfer toward the block.

The correct way to install the crank gear is to use a large piece of thick-wall tube to distribute the impact evenly.

Using a brass or soft alloy punch is permissable so long as you know just how hard you can hit it without risk of damage.

This type of sprocket is powdered metal. To avoid possible damage, use a sleeve-type punch for installation.

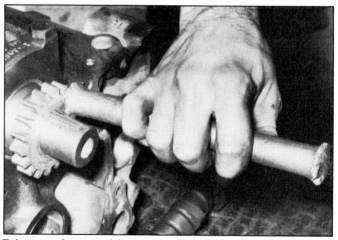

Take care that you drive against the gear center and not on the teeth.

to ease installation.

Ensuring Cam Life — Next, lubricate the cam lobes with a good molybdenum-disulfide grease or other good quality engine-building lubricant such as GM Engine Oil Supplement (EOS). This is important. The greatest danger to the cam in terms of extreme wear occurs during the first five minutes of running when the new engine is turned over. Attention to this lubrication is important! A few drops of oil on the journals is a good idea, but not so much that it will run onto the lobes and wash off the lubricant you have just applied to the lobes.

Timing the Camshaft — The next step is to turn the engine until the number 1 piston is on top-dead-center. Look at the crank gear and you'll see the dot on it pointing towards the top of the engine. Install the camshaft, taking care not to damage the cam bearings. Turn the cam and cam gear until its dot lines up with the dot on the crankshaft gear. Then, taking care not to move the camshaft, remove the camshaft gear by undoing the bolt. Wrap your timing chain around the gear, keeping the gear in the approximate position that it will be installed, that is the dot pointing toward the small gear. Hold the gear close to the engine and place the chain over the crank gear. Now juggle the chain around so the two dots are aligned as you bring the cam gear into alignment with the camshaft. Once you have all the holes lined up, push the gear on, screw in the bolts and finger-tighten them. Now make a final check: Turn the crank backwards from TDC — that's counter-clockwise when viewed from the front — then rotate it in its correct clockwise rotational direction back to TDC on number 1. *At this point, the dots on the crank and cam gear must be in line.* If they are not, remove the gear, move the chain around the appropriate way and reinstall the cam gear. Do this until you have it right. If you don't get this right, your cam timing will be out and your engine will not run. Once the dots are aligned satisfactorily, tighten the cam bolts to 20 pounds-feet.

Before installing the cam, cover the lobes with molybdenum grease or GM Engine Oil Supplement to prevent damage during breaking in. If you have a mechanical cam, note any stamped numbers or paint-color codes on it. You will need to identify the cam so the lash can be determined from the chart.

Putting the camshaft in the block is much easier if you mount the gear to the cam temporarily with one finger-tight bolt. Use the gear as a handle to get the cam into the bearings. Be gentle, as the sharp edges of the lobes can gouge the cam bearings.

OIL-PUMP INSTALLATION

Now turn your attention to the next item on the agenda, the oil pump. As far as the oil pump is concerned, you will either be installing a new one or a good used one. The oil pump is one thing you definitely cannot take chances on. If it isn't good, then the engine will not last that long,

With the engine at TDC, on number 1 cylinder, the cam should be turned so the dots are aligned as indicated by the black arrow heads.

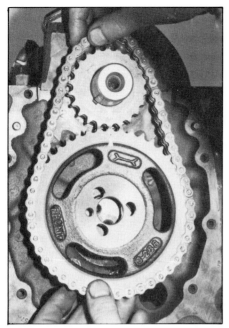

Remove the cam gear *without* turning the cam. Wrap the chain around the cam gear. Realign the dots as you engage the chain with the crank gear.

With the cam gear fully home and number 1 still at TDC, the cam gear dot should be aligned with the crank gear dot and the centers of the camshaft and crankshaft. Tighten the bolts to 20 pounds-feet. Note the position of the cam sprocket dowel. If when the dots are aligned, the dowel is opposite the position shown here you have a sprocket marked 180° out. This is rare but does happen.

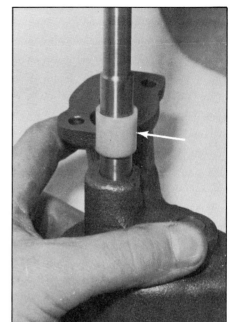

Sleeve (arrow) must be a tight enough fit to hold the distributor drive shaft in place while the engine is upside-down during assembly.

PUMP PICK-UP PIPE INSTALLATION TOOL

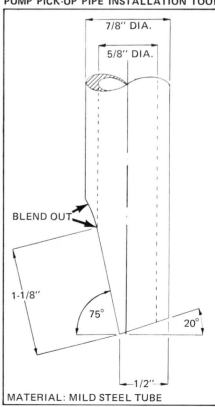

Dimensions shown are for a standard pump. If you are installing a high-volume pump make this tool out of tube 13/16-inch bore x 1-inch outside diameter. All other dimensions required are as shown.

no matter how well you build the rest of it. Installing the oil pump with its driveshaft is easy. Check that the mounting pad on the main-bearing cap is clean. Position the pump on the main-bearing cap dowels, insert the washerless securing bolt and tighten it to 60 to 70 pounds-feet. One point you should check if you are using a used pump, is that the sleeve which keeps the oil-pump driveshaft extension on the short drive coming from the pump is tight enough to hold the driveshaft while the engine is upside down. If it is not, this will drop out the other side and you will have a hard time installing it unless you remove the pump and do it all over again. If the sleeve is not tight enough to hold the drive shaft, replace it. 1955, 1956 and 1957 engines have a longer driveshaft to the

pump and a pump which sits farther from the block face because early pans were deeper. If you are using an early deep pan, you must use the deep-reach pump with its longer drive shaft.

If you were putting an adapted big block pump on your small-block Chevy, here's a word of advice. When these pumps come in the box, the oil pick-up pipe is separate. You will have to mount the pick-up so it ends up in approximately the position your original pickup was, then position the pump on the block and check whether the pan will go on OK. If you have the pickup mounted slightly too high, it will foul the pan so you should make necessary changes to make sure it clears without the gaskets in place. This gives you the correct clearance when the pan gaskets are in place.

107

The oil pump locates on two dowel pins and one bolt secures it. Check that the mating surfaces of the pump and block are clean; install the securing bolt and tighten to 60–70 pounds-feet torque.

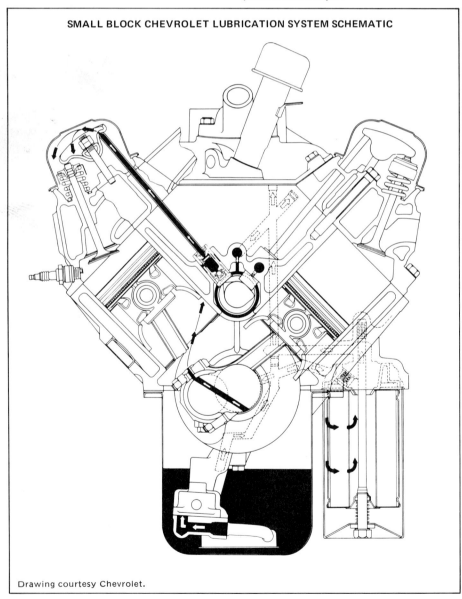

SMALL BLOCK CHEVROLET LUBRICATION SYSTEM SCHEMATIC

Drawing courtesy Chevrolet.

FRONT COVER & PAN

Installing the front cover and pan seems simple, and it is, so long as you follow a few basic rules. Ignore these and your engine will leak oil. First, inspect the oil seal in the front cover. Unless this is perfect, and I mean *perfect*, discard it. You can check to see how worn it is by comparing the lip seal in the front cover with the new one which you will inevitably have in your new gasket set. As I have said, unless it's perfect, replace it. It is easily driven out from the inside by using a wide-blade screwdriver and mallet. When replacing the new seal, be sure to set it square and ease it in, tapping it gently around the edges until it's seated home. Your best plan is to use a rubber mallet for this as anything resembling a hard mallet will merely damage the seal and generate the oil leak that you are trying so desperately to avoid. Another viable method, and frankly the one I favor most, is to use a couple of large thick metal plates to sandwich the seal and cover. Place this in a vice and squeeze the seal into place.

Now take a look at the holes in both the front cover and the pan. Most of the time, you will find

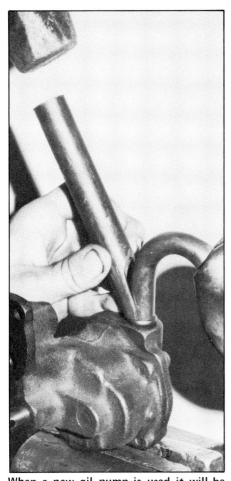

When a new oil pump is used it will be necessary to put the oil pickup pipe in the pump. This is best done with the tool shown here and in the drawing. Be sure to put the pickup pipe in the same position on the pump as the one on the pump you are discarding. If you don't do this, the pan may not fit properly or the pickup may not be deep enough in the oil.

that these holes have sunk, due to tightening up the bolts. The sunken area around these holes needs to be removed or even slightly reversed. The easiest way to do this is to use the ball end of a hammer and tap them out, or get a 1/2-inch or 5/8-inch-diameter ball bearing, rest it in the bolt hole and tap this with a hammer until it indents the hole in the reverse fashion.

Heed a word of warning here: if you miss your intended target with the hammer, you may damage the surface that you are trying to get a perfect seal on, so be careful and take your time fixing these bolt holes.

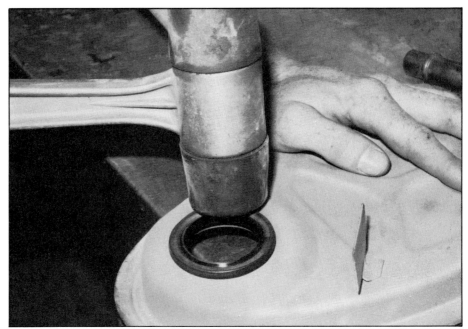

If the seal on the timing-chain cover is anything but perfect, replace it. For the two minutes it takes it is well worth the reduced chance of oil leaks. Be sure to tap the seal in evenly with a rawhide or rubber mallet.

Now give the gasket surface on both the pan and the front cover the once-over to make sure there are no old gasket particles stuck to them. These surfaces need to be spotlessly clean to prevent leaks.

INSTALLING THE FRONT COVER

Smear the front-cover-gasket face on the block with sealer. An even coating of sufficient quantity to just stick the gasket in place will do. It doesn't need so much that tightening the gasket cover causes sealer to ooze out everywhere.

Now place the gasket on the two locating dowels and press it onto the block. Follow up by smearing more sealer onto the face of the gasket and position the front cover onto the dowels and push it up against the block. Locate star washers on the ten front-cover bolts. If you have a degreed timing tag of the sort that bolts on, rather than the type that is fixed to the front cover, position this now. Locate two screws through the holes in the timing tag and tighten them finger-tight. Then position the rest of the screws

and tighten those finger-tight. Now using a torque wrench, tighten all the bolts progressively to 7 to 9 pounds-feet. Don't go any higher than this, otherwise you will end up with a stripped thread or two.

INSTALLING THE PAN

Turn your attention now to the rear-main-bearing cap. Look at the groove into which the rear-main-bearing-cap-to-pan rubber seal fits. If you follow this groove down to where it meets the block, you will find some of the sealer that you put in the corners of the main-bearing-register has squeezed out into this rubber seal locating groove. In all probability it has hardened. What you must do now is scrape this out because the rubber seal has a tongue which goes in at this point. If you don't scrape out the excess sealer, you will distort the seal when the pan goes on and you will have a leak. The photo on page 111, shows the exact position I am describing.

Which Pan-to-Front-Cover Seal?—Most gasket kits contain two front-cover-to-pan seals; a thin one and a thick one. The thick seal is the latest

Make a fine bead of sealer on the front cover gasket area and *around* the securing bolt holes.

Locate the gasket on the dowels and press it down onto the sealer.

Smear sealer onto the gasket face. Don't use so much it comes oozing out in great globs when the front cover is put on.

type. It was an effort to cure sealing of a dubious quality given by the earlier, thinner seal. The question is, which seal do you use? The thick seal is used in conjunction with a later-type pan which has a revised area in the region of the seal to accommodate its greater thickness. Here is a simple test to determine which seal your front-cover-pan combination should take. Place the two pan gaskets in position on the block and position the pan in the correct place. Now, using a 6 to 10 thou feeler gauge, see if you can push the feeler gauge between the front cover lip and the pan lip. If it is the later type, the feeler gauge will go through without bending. In other words you can see directly into the crankcase through the very thin gap between the front cover and the pan. If you have the earlier type, the lip of the pan actually sits down into the groove of the front cover and you will find it impossible to pass the feeler gauge through as it will have to do a double bend to go into the crankcase area. This type uses the thin seal. Select the

Locate the front cover on the dowels and press it into place.

If applicable, install the ignition timing tag (arrow). Next, install the ten 1/4 x 20 x 1/2 bolts together with the star washers. Tighten only enough to hold the cover in place.

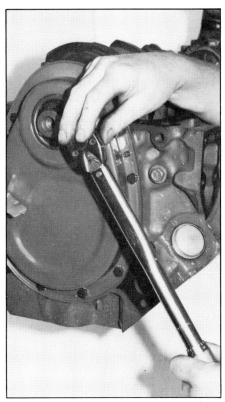

Go around at least two times and tighten the front cover bolts to 7—9 pounds-feet. This feels like it is not tight enough, but resist the temptation to tighten them any farther as you will start to strip threads.

Before installing any gaskets, check that the groove in the rear main cap is clean right to the bottom of the well it forms with the block register. If there is any solidified sealer from installing the main bearing cap, *thoroughly* clean it out. Otherwise the rear seal will not do its job.

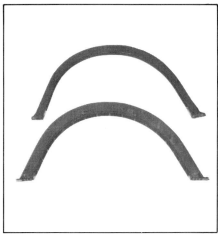

Your gasket kit will contain two front-cover-to-pan seals, thin one at top is for early pans, lower one is for late pans.

relevant seal from your gasket kit and place it to one side, ready for use. Remove the pan and gaskets.

Using silicone sealer, lay a thin bead on the block along the position where the gaskets will lay. Do so circling each bolt hole. The amount of sealer applied here should not be excessive. Too much sealer will be squeezed out and into the crank case to be picked up by the pump. It will certainly start to block the screen in the oil pick-up, so avoid using too much. When you have applied the sealer to the block, position the pan gaskets and apply a similar bead of sealer to these.

You are now at the most crucial part of producing an oil-tight engine. If you look at the front seal, you will notice that the foot part of it at either end has a square cut-off which is meant to locate on the square tab on the end of the pan gasket. To produce an oil-tight seal here, put a generous amount of sealer into the corner where the pan gasket meets the cover gasket,

and press the cover gasket into position on this. Wipe off the sealer which has squeezed out and anything which may be in excess of what is required. Then reapply some of this sealer on the top of the joint in each corner where the pan gasket meets the front cover gasket.

At the rear of the engine, the same technique should be applied to the rear-main-bearing-to-pan seal. First of all apply the gasket sealer onto the pan-gasket corners. Press the rubber sealing strip tongues down into the portion where the groove goes into the block main bearing register. This should leave the tabs sitting on the pan gasket. Apply some sealer on top of each side of this and you are now ready to position the pan. Lower this on gently and try to avoid moving the gaskets as you do so. Once the pan is in position, locate the four 5/16-inch bolts that are positioned at each end of each rubber seal. Screw these down finger-tight. Then, using star washers, install the remaining fourteen 1/4-inch bolts. Using your torque wrench, tighten the four 5/16-inch bolts in each corner to 12 pounds-feet then work your way round the other bolts, progressively tightening them to 9 pounds-feet. As the gasket settles down, you will find previously tightened bolts become looser and you will need to go round all the pan bolts at least

four times to ensure they all tighten down evenly at either 9 pounds-feet for the 1/4-inch bolts or 12 pounds-feet for the 5/16-inch ones.

Remove the drain plug from the pan, check to see that the sealing washer is in good condition, then reinstall it and torque it to 20 pounds-feet.

CRANKSHAFT TORSIONAL VIBRATION DAMPER

You can now install your new or reconditioned *crankshaft torsional vibration damper*, often incorrectly referred to as a harmonic balancer. Three methods are commonly used for installation: the *puller* method, the *heating* method and the *mallet* method.

The puller method uses a special tool which screws into the crankshaft nose and pulls the damper on and is most certainly the preferred way to do it. However, most but not all crankshafts are threaded at this point, so the puller method can only be applied to those that are.

A viable alternative is the heating method. Heat the damper at and around the seal diameter. A propane torch should be used for this, preferably not a very large one. Continue heating the balancer until a drop of oil put on the seal diameter smokes. Be careful not to overheat the damper, otherwise the rubber in it will be affected by the heat and the whole thing

This is the test to determine which pan/front-cover-seal you should use. If a 0.006- to 0.010-inch feeler gauge will slip past the front cover, under the lip of the pan and into the crankcase area, then you need the thick seal. If your pan won't pass this test, use the thin seal. This test must be performed with the block-to-pan gaskets in place.

Lay a bead of sealer along the block-to-pan gasket face, press the gasket in position, then lay a similar bead of sealer on the top surface of the gasket. The same applies here as at other joints—do not use too much sealer.

These two positions are the most critical points if the engine is not to leak oil. Put a blob of sealer on at these points.

Install the front and rear seals, making sure all gasket tabs fit in the corresponding seal grooves and push the seals into place. Be sure you use the front seal with the correct thickness for your pan, as I previously described.

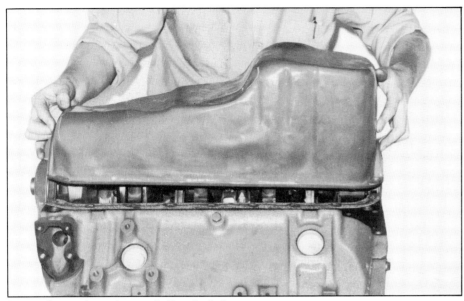
Lower the pan into place and align the holes.

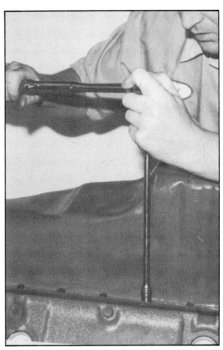
To get the pan to settle evenly, you will need to go around the bolts three or four times with the torque wrench. Tighten the 1/4-inch bolts to 7—9 pounds-feet and the four 5/16-inch bolts to 12 pounds-feet. Although the large bolts will go much tighter without stripping the threads, any tighter will cause the gasket and seal to squeeze out and you will have the one thing you are trying to avoid—an oil leak!

could come apart. Continue to apply drops of oil until the temperature of the seal diameter has dropped, so that the oil does not quite smoke. Now wipe off the excess oil and position the damper on the crank. Using a soft mallet, drive the damper on. This has to be done quickly before the heat transfers and you lose the advantage of the expansion of the damper.

The mallet method is the one I favor least but it will probably be used the most by one-time engine builders. For this you'll need a lead or copper mallet. Make sure the bore of the damper is perfectly clean, smear it with a drop of oil or Moly grease, position it on the crankshaft so it is aligned with the keyway, then drive it on. Try not to strike the damper in the immediate vicinity of the hole as you may cause a burr to be raised on the edge of the hole. If you do happen to strike it there, file this burr off as it will prevent the pulley from locating properly on this hole. If you have a piece of steel plate 1/4 in. or more thick to interpose between the damper and the mallet so much the better. The easiest way to hold such a plate in place is to drill a 3/8-in. hole in it and secure it to the damper so that it covers the center hole. Do not use a steel hammer on this damper as it could

cause it to crack. Never strike the damper outside the rubber bonding ring. If you loosen the bonding between the center and the outer ring, forget about debating the possible effects of a damper explosion, because you will witness one first-hand yours

Now for the crankshaft pulley. If you have raised a burr on the edge of the center hole in the damper, take a file and remove this burr so the pulley will locate properly. Now position the pulley and the three 3/8-inch bolts securing it. Some engines will also have a center bolt which screws into the crankshaft. If this is the case, add this bolt with its washer, and tighten the bolt to 60 lbs.-ft.

Crankshaft Damper Sizes—Be sure to fit the right size damper to the crank. Though many variations exist there are basically three different sizes. Truck engines usually use the large thick ones, as do high-performance passenger cars, while most intermediate-performance passenger cars use the middle-size one. Low-performance models use the small one. The exception here is the 400 damper. This one-of-a-kind unit has a counterbalance weight in it. Be sure you replace a 400 damper with a 400 damper or the engine will be out of balance.

Change of Ignition Timing Marks—Another point to watch is that emission-control engines from about 1970 on have the TDC mark (0 degrees) 9 degrees different on the damper with a corresponding difference in the timing-cover-tab degree marker. Be sure to use the correct combination of damper and degree-marker tab on the front cover.

An easy way to check this, and you should check it at this stage, is to turn the engine over so number 1 piston is at TDC. You can eyeball this close enough. Now look down at your degree tag and see that the line on the front damper is close to the 0 mark. An error of 2 or 3 degrees can be expected because that's about as close as you can eyeball the piston at TDC. However, if it's around 6 or 7 or even 10 degrees off, you'll know you have the wrong tag for the damper you have, so change it.

Before installation, lubricate the oil-seal diameter with a few drops of oil smeared over its surface.

Beat the crankshaft vibration damper on with a copper or lead mallet. A steel ham-hammer can ONLY BE USED IF A 1/4-INCH OR THICKER STEEL PLATE is placed on the damper to spread the impact of direct hammer blows.

To make sure the pulley locates properly, check that there are no burrs as a result of installing the crankshaft damper. Any burrs should be removed with a file.

Front pulley has a short locating extension which goes into the crankshaft vibration damper.

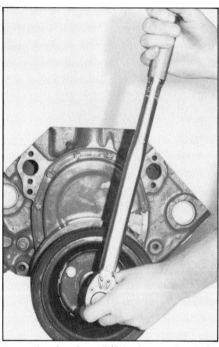

Screw in the three 3/8-inch securing bolts and torque them to 25 pounds-feet. If so equipped, install the 7/16-inch bolt securing the vibration damper together with the washer and torque it to 60 pounds-feet.

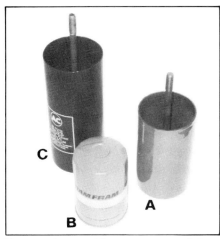

Your engine could use any one of these three filter units. For truck and passenger cars up to 1968 A was used. It was superceded by the spin-on type B in 1968 which is used for all passenger car and light-truck applications. Type C was used from 1968 on for trucks of 1½ tons and up.

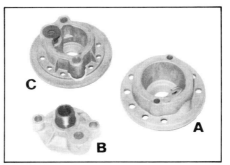

Each filter type shown in the photo at left has its own corresponding pressure-release-valve housing. The housings labeled A, B, and C here go with the respective units labeled A, B, and C at left. The years and type vehicles used still apply. Types B and C are both secured with 5/16-inch-diameter bolts as all blocks from 1968 on were tapped with 5/16-inch threads. If your truck engine is equipped with type C you can convert to type B and use the currently available long canister spin and filter.

Position the pressure-release-valve housing in the block. As long as the threaded extension is available to screw the filter onto, the position of the release valve can go toward the pan or toward the outside of the engine.

Screw in the bolts without washers and torque 5/16-inch bolts to 12—14 pounds-feet and 1/4-inch bolts to 9—10 pounds-feet.

With a spin-on filter, oil the sealing ring and screw the filter to the pressure-relief-valve housing. If you are using the canister type, you must put a filter cartridge into the canister. The box that the filter cartridge came in also contains a rubber sealing ring. This sealing ring goes between the block and the top edge of the canister. Position it in the block first and install the canister with its filter. Tighten the securing bolt to 20 pounds-feet.

OIL FILTER

The next move is to install the oil-filter pressure-release-valve housing. The type you have depends upon the type of block but all '68 and later are interchangeable. Whatever the situation, your block will be equipped with one of the three shown in the above photo. Two types fit 1968 and later blocks and one type fits pre-68 blocks. The pre-68 type is secured by two 1/4-inch bolts. This housing was used with a short canister oil filter on both trucks and cars. After 1968, most vehicles, including the light-duty trucks,

used a spin-on oil filter. This used a type B pressure-release-valve housing. Trucks, 1 1/2 tons capacity filter with pressure-release-valve housing type C. Confusion should not be a problem here. Unless you had to get a replacement you should be using the one the engine came with. If used, check to see that it is clean. Washing in carburetor cleaner is OK but don't leave it in too long because any plastic parts will be affected by the cleaner. A safer cleaner is kerosene and a stiff brush. The Chevy II used a spin-on filter between 1964 and 1967 to provide

installation clearance.

In the photos I show an oil filter being installed now. If you have exhaust headers, put the filter on after the engine and headers are in place. This will simplify installation of the headers. To install a spin-on filter, smear oil on the rubber seal and screw it on hand-tight. With canister filters, locate the rubber sealing ring in the block. Install the correct cartridge in the canister, then locate it on the block and tighten the securing bolt to 20 pounds-feet.

These are the three basic damper sizes you are likely to come across. The lightest is on the left, middle-weight in the center and heaviest (because of greater thickness) on the right.

Even expert small-block Chevy builders have been fooled on this one. Until 1970 the position of the 0° TDC mark on the crankshaft damper remained unchanged relative to the keyway slot. In 1970 the TDC mark was moved 8° to 9° on the damper which meant that the tag on the cover had to be in a correspondingly different position. The photo shows the difference between the two tags. Make sure you use the right tag for the damper you have and that it indicates TDC when number 1 piston is at TDC. DO THIS BEFORE YOU INSTALL THE HEADS.

Piston is at the top of its stroke and the ignition timing tag reads the correct zero degrees. MAKE SURE YOURS DOES.

INSTALLING THE LIFTERS

Summon all your strength—or get a friend to help—and turn the engine over so it is sitting on the pan. Clean off any debris that may have become stuck to the the block faces. Next, position the head gaskets on the dowel pins.

So far the only part of the valve train you have installed is the camshaft timing gears and chain. Now you are going to start on the reciprocating parts of the valve train in detail. The first items to be installed will be the valve lifters (tappets). If you wish to avoid trouble, there are a few hard and fast rules to observe. First, if you installed a new or reground camshaft, you *must install new lifters*. Even lifters which may have gone as little

as 50 miles are now junk so far as you are concerned. Try to prove this little rule wrong and you will wipe out both cam and lifters. Do I make myself clear? You must not try to save money on these parts. When I say, "Buy new ones," that's what you *must* do. If you are reinstalling the cam you removed from the engine because you figured it was OK, then you must use the lifters *in the same order they originally ran on the cam*. If you really didn't keep track of where each lifter came from as you disassembled your engine, throw them all in the trash barrel. If the lifters were not good when you removed them, then you should replace the lifters and the cam too. The reason is you can run into problems with old followers on a new camshaft. To sum

up then, the rule is: *All the lifters on the same lobes as when the engine was stripped down, or all new lifters on a new or reground cam*. Nothing in between will really do. You will only be inviting trouble if you try otherwise. Before you install the lifters in the block, smear a little molybdenum-disulfide grease on each lifter face and a drop of oil on its outside diameter, then put it in its bore.

FUEL PUMP PUSHROD

Clean and lightly oil the fuel pump pushrod then install it in the block. Smear the block gasket face with sealer, position the gasket and lightly smear the gasket face. Place the fuel pump spacer plate in position and secure it with two one-quarter-inch

Grease the faces of the lifters with moly grease, smear the outside diameter with oil and put them in the lifter bores. If you are reusing lifters because they were in good condition, they *must* go back on the same cam lobe they were running on prior to the strip down.

Spin-on filters do not need to be tightened to a million pounds-feet or so. Handtight (one hand, that it) will do the job. Remember, the first filter is only on for 500 miles, after initial break-in it will have to be replaced. In use, the rubber seal grows, causing the filter to become tighter. It's nice to be able to remove the filter after breaking in without having to resort to special tools.

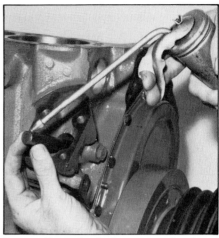

Smear oil on the fuel-pump pushrod and insert it into the block.

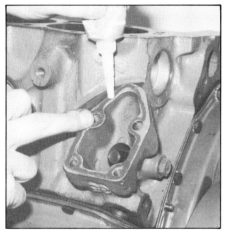

Smear sealer on the block, position the gasket and smear it with sealer in readiness to mount the fuel-pump-spacer plate.

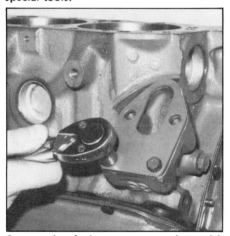

Secure the fuel-pump-spacer plate with two 1/4-inch bolts. Do not over-tighten these bolts; 7—9 pounds-feet will do.

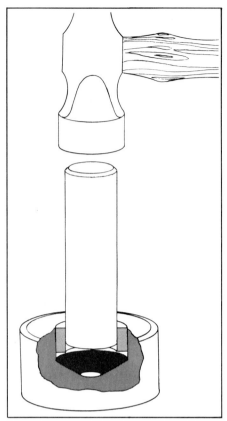

Hydraulic removal of the pilot bearing. Fill the pilot bearing with grease. Drive a 19/32-inch (0.593-inch) diameter bar into the pilot-bearing bore. The hammer impact causes high pressure in the grease which forces the bearing out. Because this method relies on non-compressibility of the grease, you must exclude as much air as possible when packing grease into the pilot bearing.

A common failing is to forget the pilot bearing (arrow) then wonder why you have so many weird transmission noises. Most engines use a pilot bearing with a bore of 0.593-inch, 1.094-inch diameter. 1961 and earlier Power Glide cranks used with a manual transmission use a 0.593-inch bore by 1.065-inch O.D. pilot bearing. Turbo Glide cranks with a manual transmission use an easily recognizable large bearing with the same 0.593-inch bore and a 1.709-inch O.D. Pilot bearings are a drive fit into the crank. If you want to get a worn one out, the drawing shows how.

An old transmission input shaft makes an ideal pilot-bearing-installation tool. If you don't possess one of these, a brass punch and some extra care, or better yet, a large socket which bears only on the outside of the bearing, will do the job.

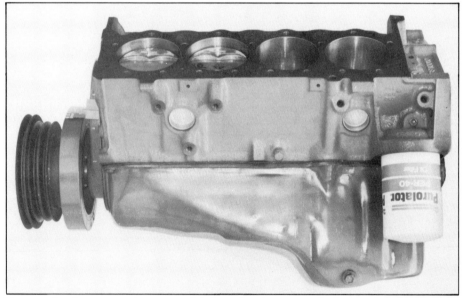

Your engine is now at the stage of being what is commonly known in the trade as a "short engine."

coarse-thread bolts. *If you know* that your fuel pump isn't going to hinder installing the engine mounting bolt, bolt on the fuel pump with the two 3/8-inch bolts that secure it to the block.

PILOT BEARING

Last, check to see if you have a pilot bearing (bushing) in the flywheel end of the crankshaft. If you haven't, and you are using a manual transmission, install one for the type of crankshaft you have. You won't need a pilot bearing in the crank if your car has an automatic transmission. Because the pilot bushings have a large radius adjacent to the bore, there is little chance of accidental damage during installation, but I know of cases where it has happened. There are two ways of putting the bearing into the crank—if you have an old gearbox input shaft you can use this as a punch, together with a mallet to drive the bushing in. If an input shaft is not available, select a socket a little smaller than the diameter of the bushing face and drive the bushing in by hitting the socket with a *soft-face mallet*.

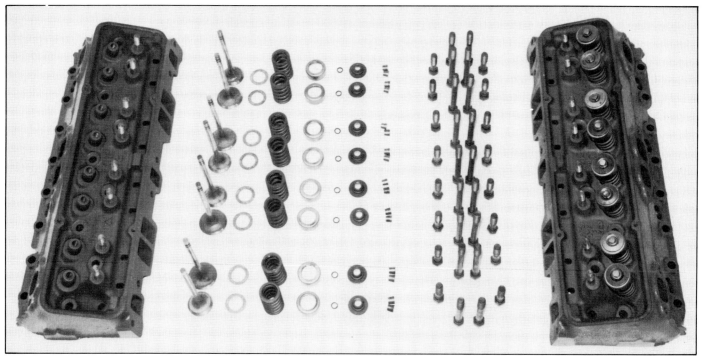

To the right of the four rows of head bolts is a fully assembled head. To the left are all the components to assemble a head. Check the cylinder head parts list to make sure you have all the parts.

CYLINDER-HEAD ASSEMBLY

This is simple enough and should present no problems if you have had the parts overhauled correctly. As you might expect, your first job is to make sure the heads are clean, especially in the valve-guide area. Using engine oil, lightly lubricate the stems of the valves and install them one at a time with the correct spacers, springs, umbrellas, retainers, oil seals and keys (keepers). Incidentally, that list is in the correct order; don't install the oil seal incorrectly as is often done. The oil seal must not be put onto the stem ahead of the retainers.

The correct technique is to install the oil seal *after* umbrella and retainers and *before* the valve keepers (keys). If that doesn't seem to make sense, let me explain. The umbrella keeps oil outside the spring area. However, a certain amount of oil will collect on top of the retainer and this tends to run down the valve stem towards the guide unless it is prevented from doing so. The oil seal makes an oil-tight joint between the retainer and the valve stem. If the oil seal is put

CYLINDER HEADS			
ITEM	NOTES	NUMBER	CHECK
Head castings		2	
Inlet valves	to suit head castings	8	
Exhaust valves	to suit head castings	8	
Pushrod guide plates (if applicable)		8	
Screw-in rocker studs (if applicable)		16	
Spring shims (if applicable)	for use with used springs only	16	
Valve springs with dampers		16	
Umbrellas		16	
Valve spring retainers		16	
Keepers		32	
Oil seals		16	
Cylinder head retaining bolts, short	7/16"—14 UNC x 1-5/8" long	16	
Cylinder head retaining bolts, intermediate	7/16"—14 UNC x 3" long	4	
Cylinder head retaining bolts, long	7/16"—14 UNC x 3-5/8" long	14	

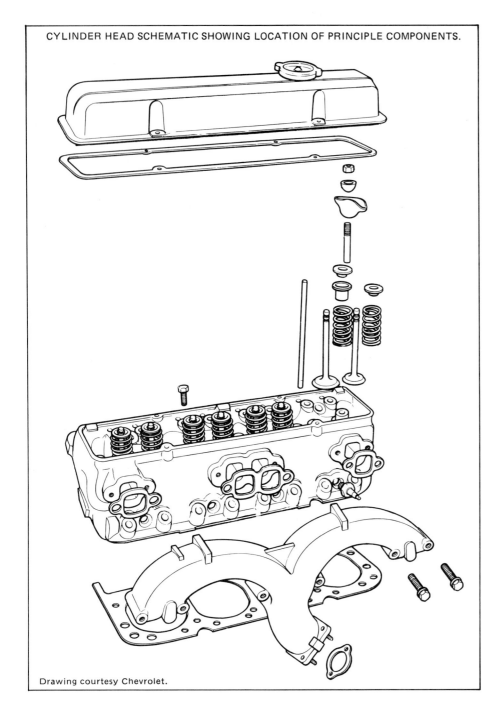

CYLINDER HEAD SCHEMATIC SHOWING LOCATION OF PRINCIPLE COMPONENTS.

Drawing courtesy Chevrolet.

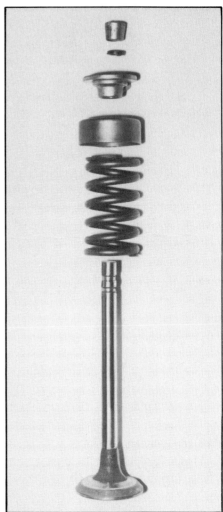

From bottom to top this is the order of valve/spring and retainer assembly. If you are using valve-spring inserts (not shown here because this is a new spring) these go directly under the valve spring on the head.

on before the retainer, installing the retainer will push the seal down the stem of the valve where it will float up and down the stem doing nothing. OK, you now know how it's done, but just to make sure I've shown the final assembly sequence in the photos on page 121.

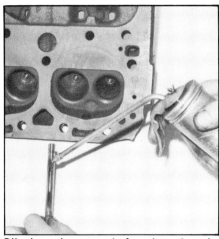

Oil the valve stem before inserting the valve into its guide. Remember the valves should have been numbered after the valve-to-seat-grinding operation. Check to see you are assembling the valves in the correct order.

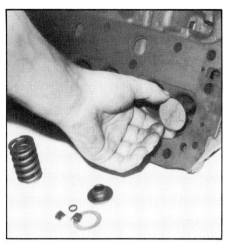

Insert the valve into the guide. If it is difficult, check to see if there is a burr on the keeper grooves. If there is, remove it with a fine file. Wipe the valve stem clean, re-oil it, and insert the valve in the guide.

Place the valve-spring insert over the valve guide. Some valve-spring inserts have to be installed a certain way up. Look to see if there is any indication on yours. If it does not say which way up, it does not matter which way you put them on.

Place the spring and damper in position.

Position the umbrella on the spring.

Place the valve-spring retainer on top of the umbrella.

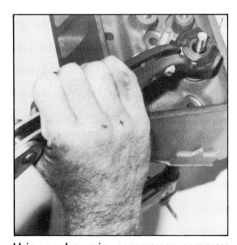

Using a valve-spring compressor, compress the valve spring until the top edge of the retainer is about level with the lower edge of the keeper groove.

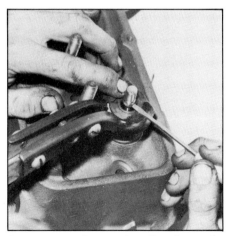

Smear some oil onto the oil seal to make it slide easily, then slide it over the valve stem, down to the bottom of the keeper groove.

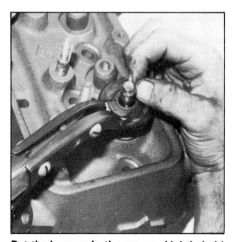

Put the keepers in the groove. Lightly hold the keepers in place on their top corners or stick them in place with thick grease, then release the valve-spring compressor. That's one valve fully assembled into the head. Now repeat the procedure for the other 15.

CYLINDER-HEAD INSTALLATION

Dowel Pins—If your block's head gasket surfaces were refinished for any reason, it will not have these dowel pins. The dowel pins you need are 5/16-inch diameter by 1/2-inch long, available from your GM dealer or many hardware stores. Using a brass mallet or a punch, drive the dowel pins into the block with the rounded end outward. Continue driving them in until the end of the dowel is 1/4 inch above the block face.

Head Gaskets—Although I mentioned it briefly before, I will mention it again because this is the last time you will be able to do anything about it without a major teardown and that is the question of which type of head gasket you should use. I like the composition head gaskets, such as those produced by Fel-Pro, because they are less sensitive to any errors due to warpage of either block or head. Steel-shim gaskets available from GM dealers do a fine job on a new engine but they may not seal if the surface is not flat within 0.003-inch, as discussed on page 69. If for some reason, you are using the Chevrolet steel-shim gaskets, then it will be necessary to smear some gasket sealer around all the water holes on both sides of the gasket before installing it. With the composition gaskets, no such treatment is necessary.

Head Installation—Install your newly reconditioned cylinder heads in place on the dowels. Look at the cylinder-head-retaining bolts to make sure all the threads are clear. Coat the first 1/4 inch of thread with silicone sealer to stop water coming up the threads. To start with, just gently screw all of the bolts in, but don't tighten them.

Now using a torque wrench, work from the center outward as shown in

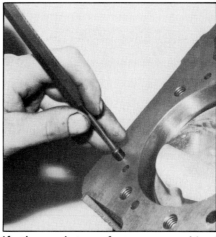

If the gasket surface was machined (decked) then it will be necessary to install new head and gasket locating dowels. These should be driven in with a 1/4-inch-diameter or larger punch.

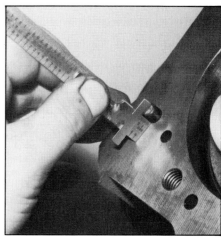

Dowels should be driven in until they are 1/4 inch above the deck of the block.

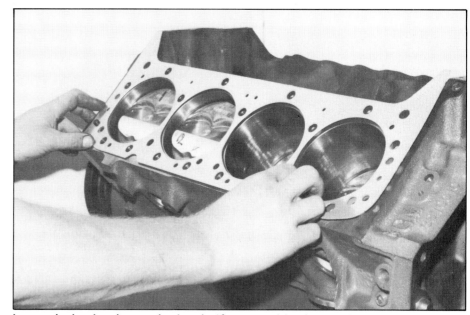

Locate the head gasket on the dowels. If a composition head gasket is used as I'm doing here, *no* gasket sealer should be used. If a steel-shim head gasket is used, smear sealer around every hole on both sides, except the bore holes.

drawing 7-2, page 124, and torque the cylinder-head bolts to 35 pounds-feet. Having gone around them once, reset the torque wrench to 60 to 70 pounds-feet and, in the same order, go around and re-torque all the head bolts in sequence twice more. With the heads in place, your engine is beginning to look finished. At this stage, all the heavy stuff has been bolted on. Next you are going to deal with the upper part of the valve train.

Don't use bolts with dirty threads in the head or anywhere else for that matter as all the torque will be taken up overcoming thread friction instead of clamping down the head. Bolt on left is an example of what should be used.

Lower the head carefully in place on the dowels. Gripping the head as shown here with fingers in the exhaust ports in an easy way to hold it.

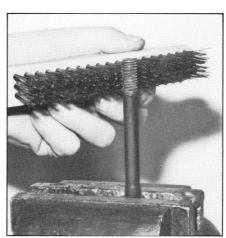

Cleaning the bolt threads can be a tedious job, but whether it's done with a wire brush on a grinder head or by hand power, it *must* be done throughly.

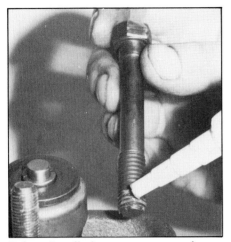

Before installation, put some sealer on the head bolt threads to stop water coming up at this point.

Put the long head bolts to the center, short to the outside. The two intermediate length bolts go at the position arrowed and in the equivalent position at the other end of the head.

Run all the head bolts down until they seat but do not tighten with the speed handle.

In the order shown in the drawing, torque the bolts first to 35 pounds-feet, then go around twice at 60–70 pounds-feet.

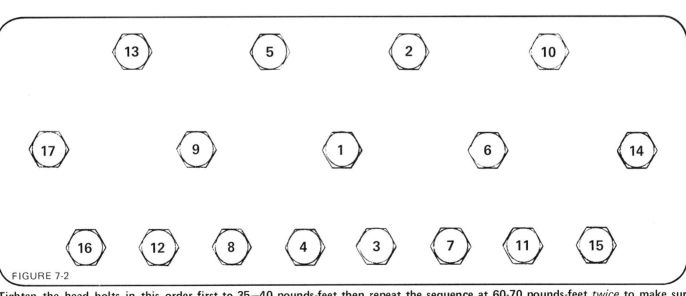

FIGURE 7-2

Tighten the head bolts in this order first to 35–40 pounds-feet then repeat the sequence at 60-70 pounds-feet *twice* to make sure they have all pulled down evenly. Often as the last bolts are tightened they relieve some of the pressure on those tightened first. The object of the second time around at full torque is to make sure the bolts are fully tightened.

This is how your engine should now look. The next stage is the rest of the valve train.

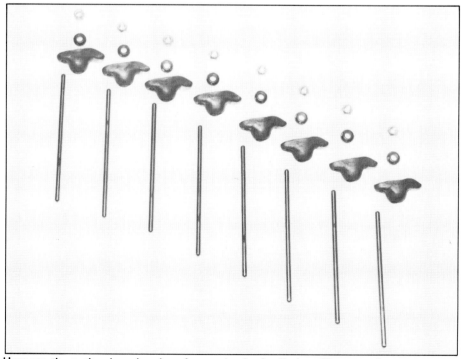

Here are the pushrods and rockers for one bank of cylinders. These are the next parts to be built into your small-block Chevy.

Put the pushrods through the guide slots, then locate the rockers in position.

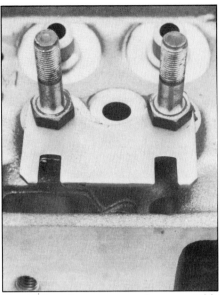

On high-performance engines a guide plate held in position by screw-in rocker studs is used.

Place the rocker in position on the stud, then apply moly grease or GM Engine Oil Supplement (EOS) to the ball seats and put these on the studs also.

VALVE TRAIN			
ITEM	NOTES	NUMBER	CHECK
Pushrods		16	
Rockers		16	
Ball seats		16	
Rocker clearance adjusting nuts		16	

Rocker and Pushrods—Slip the previously numbered pushrods the original way up through their guide slots or plates in the head down onto the seat in the lifters. Put a smear of moly grease on the rocker end of the pushrod. If the rockers are on the studs, remove them and check that they are OK and the balls are not scored. You should have done this during the reconditioning phase of the rebuild. However, make one last check because this is where you have to decide once and for all whether you can run with these rockers or whether you need new ones. The rule with rockers is this: *The engine will run when they are worn, but there will be a lot more valve noise than with good ones.*

Place each rocker on its stud, smear the spherical ball with moly grease, install it on the stud, then put on the adjusting nut. Remember, if you are using rockers which were used before, they must all go back in the same pairs; the ball seat together with its rocker. You cannot use one ball seat with a rocker from another position. This is why I told you to wire these pieces together when I explained the strip-down procedure. If you are installing new ones, all you need do is just assemble them with a dab of moly grease on each of the rocker balls and they will seat in during the break-in period.

Install the lash-adjusting locknuts with the chamfer *up*. Screw these down until the end of the stud just comes through the nut.

The assembly is now looking like an engine, but don't be fooled—you still have a long way to go.

SETTING VALVE CLEARANCE WITH HYDRAULIC LIFTERS

Now comes the time to set the correct valve clearance (lash) into the valve actuating system. This is often called *setting the tappets*. I'll talk about the hydraulic ones first.

Finding TDC With #1 Cylinder Firing—Rotate the engine clockwise as viewed from the front until it is on top dead center with the number 1 cylinder firing. This is easy to check because the lifters on number 6 will be rocking, that is, the inlet will be just opening and the exhaust just closing. Because you have not installed the intake manifold yet, it is easy to watch the lifters and see when the position is achieved. Don't look at the rocker arms because they are not adjusted and won't tell you anything. TDC will be when the pointer on the front cover aligns with the mark on the crankshaft vibration damper, assuming this was checked earlier as required.

Adjusting the Clearance—With the crankshaft positioned at TDC you will be ready to adjust both valves of number 1 cylinder. To do this, use a box wrench to turn the adjusting nut on its stud until excessive clearance is taken up so the pushrod will barely rotate between your fingers. In other words, the slack is just taken out of the system. But you haven't adjusted it so far that you have taken any of the spring-loading action out of the hydraulic lifters. At this point turn the adjusting nut one-half turn farther. This puts the pushrod tip about 0.025 inch into the spring-loaded action of the hydraulic lifter—about a third of the lifter travel. Do this on both valves for number 1 cylinder.

Adjustment Sequence—Now turn the engine over one-quarter turn clockwise as viewed from the front so the lifters are rocking on number 5 cylinder. This should give you top dead center on number 8. As a secondary measure, check that the piston of the cylinder you are working on is at TDC. You can verify this by looking down the spark plug hole. Repeat the procedure that was just carried out on number 1 cylinder, turning the rocker-adjusting nut until the slack is just taken up and then one-half turn farther on both valves.

Continue in the order shown in the chart below.

VALVE ADJUSTMENT ORDER FOR HYDRAULIC LIFTERS

Adjust rocker lash on the cylinder number listed in the left column when the intake and exhaust on the cylinder listed in the right column is just "rocking." For example, adjust the rocker lash on cylinder 1 when the intake and exhaust of cylinder 6 is just rocking.

1	6
8	5
4	7
3	2
6	1
5	8
7	4
2	3

SETTING VALVE CLEARANCE WITH MECHANICAL LIFTERS

If you have solid (mechanical) lifters, the technique is slightly different. In principle you can apply the same order of doing things as with the

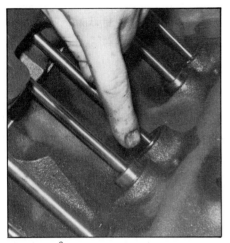

About 45° of crankshaft rotation before you reach TDC on the firing stroke of number 1 cylinder, you will see the exhaust lifter on number 6 cylinder in approximately this position. Continue to turn the crankshaft and number 6 exhaust lifter will start to go down.

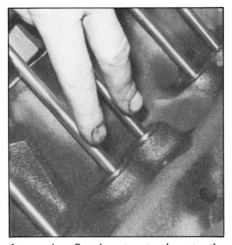

As number 6 exhaust gets close to the bottom of its travel, number 6 inlet will just start to lift. This means number 6 cylinder is close to TDC and about to start its inlet stroke. This also means number 1 cylinder is close to TDC on its firing stroke. Look at the front damper and position the damper line against the zero degree mark on the timing tag. You are now ready to start adjusting your hydraulic lifters.

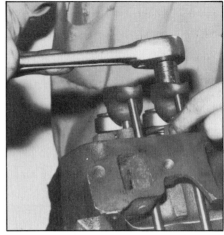

Once the TDC and firing position have been found, you can adjust the valves on number 1 cylinder. With the pushrod between your thumb and forefinger, twist it back and forth as you tighten the rocker-arm locknut. Continue to do so until you feel the pushrod just start to bind as you turn it.

Once you feel the pushrod binding, turn the adjusting nut a half-turn farther.

VALVE ADJUSTMENT ORDER FOR MECHANICAL LIFTERS

Adjust this valve	With this valve fully open
1 intake	6 intake
3 exhaust	2 exhaust
8 intake	5 intake
6 exhaust	1 exhaust
4 intake	7 intake
5 exhaust	8 exhaust
3 intake	2 intake
7 exhaust	4 exhaust
6 intake	1 intake
2 exhaust	3 exhaust
5 intake	8 intake
1 exhaust	6 exhaust
7 intake	4 intake
8 exhaust	5 exhaust
2 intake	3 intake
4 exhaust	7 exhaust

hydraulic lifters. However, with some long-duration cams this could give you incorrect settings. If you are using a long-duration high-performance cam, you may end up turning the engine over a greater number of times than necessary, and running into a great deal of frustration.

Technique—Here is how to set the valve clearance or *lash* as it is often called. The order in which valves should be adjusted follows my explanation of *how* they should be adjusted.

When you have identified which valve you will adjust, select the correct feeler-gauge thickness. Insert this between the valve tip and rocker and then slowly tighten the rocker-adjusting nut, holding the pushrod and rotating it between your finger and thumb. Continue to tighten the adjusting nut slowly until you find the pushrod just beginning to bind because the slack has been taken out of the valve train. At this point the valve clearance is adjusted.

Keeping Mechanical Valve Trains Quiet—Mechanical (solid-lifter) valve trains are noisier than hydraulic

ones. This can be minimized by very careful valve-clearance adjustment. If you are using worn rockers you may find obtaining the correct clearance difficult to achieve and as a result the valve train will be noisy. If you are using worn rockers, try this trick. Trim the feeler gauge or use one narrower than the valve stem. This will mean you are likely to get a more accurate valve-clearance adjustment. A wide feeler gauge

VALVE LASH SETTINGS FOR MECHANICAL CAMSHAFTS			
CAMSHAFT IDENTIFICATION	CLEARANCE INLET (inch)	EXHAUST (inch)	USE
Green stripe, turns brown with age. Casting number 3736097.	0.012	0.018	Corvettes up to 1964
Pink or white stripe. Pink stripe turns a red/brown with age and white turns off-white.	0.030	0.030	327 fuel-injection Corvettes and 327 with aluminum high-rise manifolds with Holley carburetor
3972178. Number usually stamped on back face of number 5 cam bearing.	0.024	0.026	1970–71 Z-28

If you have equipped your engine with new hydraulic lifters that are not yet filled with oil you can check the remaining amount of lifter travel by pressing down on the pushrod end of the rocker. If about this amount of daylight is showing (arrow), you've got it right.

Take time setting the lash on the rockers when using solid lifters. This will ensure maximum operating efficiency. The engine builder here is using a GO/NO-GO type feeler gauge to get in the right ball park quickly.

bridges the wear gap on the tip of the rocker and gives a larger valve lash setting than is called for.

Once you have gone through the valve settings with a mechanical cam, I recommend you repeat the entire procedure. Check all of the valves again in the same sequence as before just to make double-sure you have it right. It is much easier to do this now than after you've installed the engine.

COMPLETION OF VALVE TRAIN

When you have finished adjusting all the rockers, turn the engine to top dead center with number 1 cylinder firing. Number 6 rockers will just be opening and closing (rocking) on the intake and the exhaust. This is important. The reason you are doing this is to make installing the distributor an easier job later on. You know the distributor must be installed so it is sending the spark down number 1 wire at this point. This will give you a pretty close setting so you can start the engine to get the timing absolutely correct with a timing light.

Rocker Covers—Having set the engine at TDC on number 1, you can now put the rocker covers on—temporarily.

If you have had to replace your rocker covers for any reason, be sure you have the right ones. Very early rocker covers had mounting holes which were staggered. This applied up until about mid-1959. Subsequent rocker covers had the mounting holes in line. In other words, if you drew a line between all the mounting holes, it would form a rectangle.

Another point to watch is that some rocker covers have no breather or filler-cap hole. These are the earlier engines up to 1967. On such engines, the oil filler was on the manifold.

Your first job is to give the rocker covers the same treatment at the mounting holes as you did with the front cover and pan, etc. Take a ball-ended hammer and peen the holes so they are flat or even slightly raised to the outside of the cover. Spread a thin bead of silicone or similar gasket sealer on the rocker cover only.

When you put in the rocker-cover-securing screws, be sure you use the little plates that go underneath them. These distribute the load. Without them, the screws will pull the rocker cover gasket surface out of shape and your engine will

VALVE COVER ASSEMBLY			
ITEM	NOTES	NUMBER	CHECK
Valve covers		2	
Valve cover securing screws	1/4" x 20 UNC x 1/2" long	8	
Valve cover screw load distribution plates		8	
Oil breather grommet (if applicable)		1	
PCV grommet (if applicable)		1	
Oil filler cap (if applicable)		1	

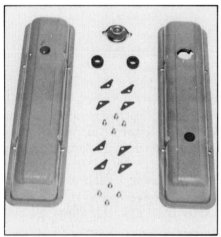

Typical parts for valve cover assembly.

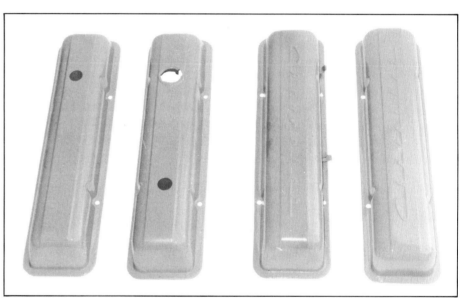

Pre '68 or thereabouts engines had oil fillers in the manifold and used the pair of rocker covers on the right, with no holes. 1968 and later engines with manifolds having no filler had provision for the oil-filler cap as well as a crankcase breather and a PCV hole. The two covers at left illustrate the later styles.

Before installing the rocker covers, use a ball-pein hammer to flatten the area around the holes.

Clean the gasket area of any oil, then apply a bead of sealer to the rocker cover surface *only*.

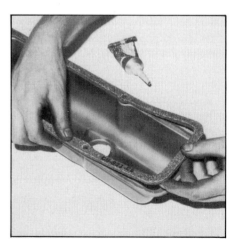

Press the rocker cover gasket in position, making sure the holes line up. The sealer will stick the gasket to the cover. This will allow the easy removal of the rocker cover for ignition-timing purposes.

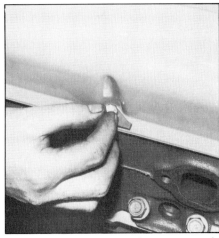

After positioning the rocker covers, add the securing bolts with the special washers underneath. Don't tighten them down fully as you will have to remove them later.

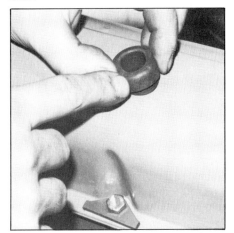

Press the rubber seals for the crankcase vent and PCV valve into place. A drop of oil smeared onto the rubber will make this considerably easier.

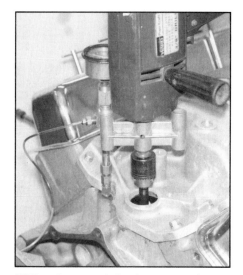

B&B makes a tool that is connected to an electric drill to drive the oil pump and pre-prime the oil system. Doing so lubricates the valve train. An oil pressure gauge connected to the oil pressure/idiot light switch take-off at the back of the block will indicate when pressure is achieved.

If for any reason you replace the rocker covers on post '68 engines, you should be aware of the fact that the cover with the oil filler hole could use one of two types of filler caps. If it's a plain hole, the plastic cap at left will be needed. If it's a hole with two cutouts, the half-turn screwdown cap on the right is required.

This is where your engine should be now. The next step is adding the manifold. With that done the end is in sight. It keeps looking better each step of the way, doesn't it?

leak for sure. You have now buttoned up the valve train and reached another milestone in the assembly of your engine.

PRE-PRIMING THE OILING SYSTEM

Waiting for oil pressure to come up when the engine is installed and is cranked for the first time can be nerve-racking. What if the engine fires and starts running immediately and oil pressure is a little late coming up? This can mean that bearings, bores, etc. have only the lubricant applied during the rebuild. Generally speaking, this is of little problem, but if you want to give your engine the best, it is possible to pre-prime the oiling system. This can be done with the tool shown in the nearby photo or you can make a tool up by cutting the upper half of the body from a distributor leaving only the shaft. The gear will also have to be removed. With the tool or modified distributor shaft, the oil pump can be driven independently of engine operation so as to prime the entire oiling system.

At this point, you need to check that the sump plug is properly tightened and then put in the requisite amount of oil.

These are basically the parts you will be assembling next, but there is a big variation between early and late engines, so refer to the parts list.

INTAKE MANIFOLD

Preventing oil leaks from the bottom of the intake manifold can be a difficult job on a small block Chevy. The combination of downward pressure and hot oil seems to squeeze the rubber seals out of place and this creates an oil leak. If the sealing medium can be prevented from moving, the manifold-to-block joint will remain oil-tight. There are two methods which eliminate manifold oil leaks.

The first method uses rubber seals at the end of the manifold; the second method uses silicone sealer instead of rubber seals. Let's deal with the first method.

Select the correct rubber seal from your gasket set for each end of the valley. You will find your gasket set contains four different ones. Two will have rubber flaps on the side to locate them on the block. The second pair will have little rubber pegs which locate the seals into holes drilled in the block face at

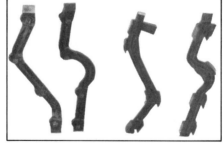

Your gasket set contains two types of manifold valley seals. Flap type on the right is for pre '68 engines, and the peg type (left) is for 1968 and later engines. If the block has holes drilled in the seal surface, use the peg-type seal.

either end of the valley. The later type of seal (phased-in between '68-'71) locates in the holes and this is the type you are most likely to have. Having selected the right seals from the kit, place them where you can immediately lay your hand on them. Now using 3M® Weatherstrip Adhesive, coat the block where the rubber valley seal goes. A fairly generous amount should be applied here to *an oil-free surface*. The

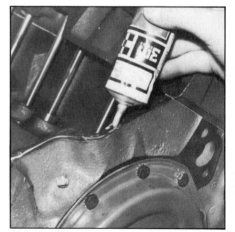

The back and front horizontal sealing faces are prime points for oil leaks. One of the principal reasons for a leak is that the seals tend to squeeze out slowly because of the downward pressure caused by tightening the manifold. To avoid this, wipe the seal face completely free of oil and apply 3M® Weather-Strip Adhesive or similar, and stick the seal in place.

idea is to stick these seals in place so they can't move. As soon as you have applied the sealer, position the seals on the block and press

INTAKE MANIFOLD ASSEMBLY			
ITEM	NOTES	NUMBER	CHECK
Intake manifold		1	
Oil filler cap (if applicable)	only on intake manifolds to 1968	1	
Intake manifold securing bolts	3/8"–16 UNC x 1-1/4" long	12	
Thermostat housing		1	
Thermostat/distributor advance valve (if applicable)	emission engines only	1	
Thermostat housing plug (if applicable)		1	
Thermostat	check for correct temperature rating	1	
Manifold temp/vacuum advance switch (if applicable)	emission engines only	1	
Automatic choke heat stove		1	
Automatic choke bimetal strip assembly		1	
Automatic choke operating rod		1	
Carburetor		1	
Distributor clamp		1	
Distributor clamp securing bolt	3/8"–16 UNC x 1" long	1	
Coil mounting bracket (if applicable)		1	
Accelerator cable bracket (if applicable)		1	
Coil mounting bracket securing bolts (if applicable)	also secures carburetor throttle-cable bracket 5/16"–18 UNC x 1" long	2	
Power brake vacuum fitting (if applicable)	usually incorporates trans. vacuum and accessory vacuum	1	
P.C.V. valve		1	

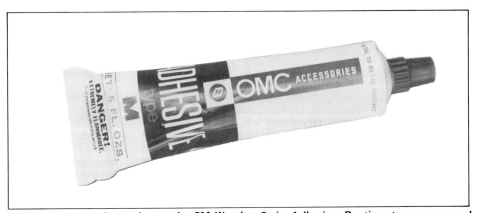

Here is just one alternative to the 3M Weather-Strip Adhesive. Boating stores are a good source for this.

The corners are the most important place to get right. Make doubly sure all four ends of the seals are securely glued down.

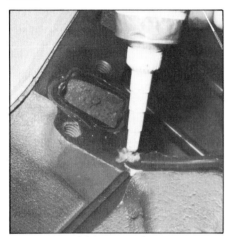

Once the seal is firmly glued in position, put a blob of silicone sealer in the corners. Be fairly generous, the amount shown here is what is needed.

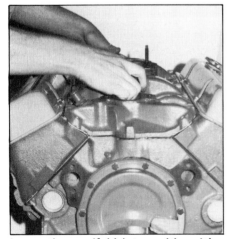

Lower the manifold into position. It's a lot easier when two people do it. Try to get the bolt holes aligned first time, as too much shifting around will dislocate the gasket as we did on the cover photo.

Using silicone sealer, run a thin bead around the square water holes. There is one at each end of the manifold face on each cylinder head.

Position the required manifold gasket on the head, making sure tabs on each end of the gasket engage with the slot in the rubber valley seal. Excess silicone sealer which may be displaced here, should be wiped over the top of the tag on the gasket. If there is any doubt about the gasket's ability to seal in these corners, put on another dab of silicone sealer.

them down so they adhere to the block. While the 3M® adhesive is setting, put a thin smear of silicone sealer around the four water-jacket holes on the manifold-gasket faces. Your best plan is to refer to the photos and you will know exactly which holes I am referring. to. Now place your manifold gaskets onto the heads, making sure the tags locate properly in the square cut-outs in the end of the valley seals. This is the important point because this is where leaks are most likely to occur. Having positioned the manifold gaskets, put a blob of sealer

Early engines with a road-draft breather vent can be converted to one or two later setups. The PCV plug that fits in this hole, plus the PCV valve from engines between 1963 and 1967 can be used as a direct replacement. An alternative if you have to replace rocker covers, is to plug the hole with a 1-1/4-inch freeze plug as shown and use later rocker covers with provision for crankcase ventilation and PCV valve.

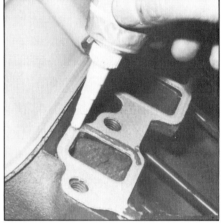

Before lowering the manifold in place, put a thin bead of sealer on the gasket around the square water holes.

on those four corners. Lastly, go around the four water-jacket holes on the gasket with a thin bead of sealer. You are now ready to lower the manifold in place. Do so carefully, trying not to disturb the gaskets as you lower it. If you have to slide the manifold around to locate it you may disturb the positioning of the gaskets and you'll have to reposition the gaskets to avoid any possibility of a leak. Once you have lowered the manifold in place, insert the bolts and tighten them progressively, as described on page 135.

Be sure to use the correct 1-1/4''-long manifold bolts for those here and their opposite numbers for the other side of the manifold. If they are too long, they will bear on the pushrods. Progressively working from the center outward, tighten the manifold bolts to 20 lbs.-ft. Make about six round trips to get them fully tightened down.

Some gasket companies, notably Fel-Pro, have improved the sealing capability of their gaskets, especially their blue, teflon-coated manifold gasket. However, many gasket kits contain a cork valley seal gasket that is adhesive coated and sticks to the block. These work very well, but they lack the compressibility to properly seal when the gap between the block and manifold is reduced due to head and/or block milling. If using this type of gasket, check the installed gap between block and manifold. Do not attempt to crush this gasket more than about 0.030-0.040 inch as the pressure it exerts may cause a leak in one of the other manifold gaskets.

Silicone Sealer—This is the method I favor most. First, go around the square holes on the head with sealer and position the manifold gaskets, without having put any rubber seals at the ends of the valley. Position the manifold gaskets on both heads, then place a 1/4-inch diameter bead of silicone sealer from the tabs of the gasket right across the block to the tab on the opposite side. What you are doing is forming a gasket of silicone sealer. Wait at least 5 minutes (10 in cooler weather) until a skin has formed on the surface of the silicone sealer. When this has happened, lower the manifold carefully into place.

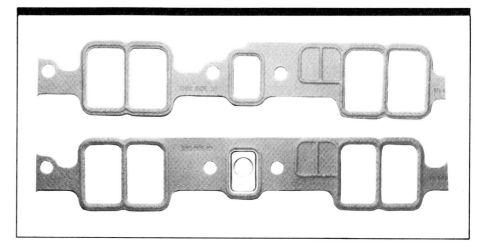

1955-72: All cars and trucks take the open port heat-riser gasket. That's the top one of this photo.

1973: All 302-350-400 cars and light trucks take restricted left side (viewed from driver's seat) and open on right. 350 heavy duty, that's 3/4 ton capacity and up, take open left and right.

1974: 350-400 car and truck applications with two-barrel carburetor use restricted left, open right, 350-400 car and truck applications with four-barrel carburetor use restricted both sides, but heavy-duty 350 with four-barrel carburetor uses open both sides.

1975: All 262-350-400 light truck and cars use restricted gasket on left, open on right. 350 heavy-duty applications with two-barrel carburetor use open both sides. 350-400 heavy duty with four-barrel carburetor use restricted both sides.

1976: All 262-350-400 four-barrel carburetor applications use open gaskets both sides. 305-350 with two-barrel carburetor and 350-400 with four-barrel carburetor to California emission standards and 350 trucks with four-barrel carburetor use restricted left, open right. 350 heavy-duty with two-barrel carburetor uses open both sides. 350-400 heavy-duty with four-barrel carburetor use restricted both sides.

1977: All cars and light trucks use restricted gasket on left side. 350 heavy-duty trucks with two-barrel carburetor use open gaskets both sides. 305-350-400 heavy-duty trucks with four-barrel carburetor use restricted both sides.

Make sure there is no oil where the silicone is sealing. Otherwise it will not stick and eventually leak. Again, you must position your manifold carefully, lowering it so you don't have to slide it around to position it. Doing so may create a leak.

Manifold Bolts—Now install the manifold bolts and working from the center outward, tighten the bolts down to 20 lbs.-ft. Make sure you are using the correct length bolts. All bolts used in the manifold are 1-1/4-inch. If you should use longer bolts, some of them will bear on the pushrods and lock them in place. You will realize this when you have a bent, rattling pushrod. The holes where this may happen are near the center of the engine. Check that you have the right length bolts for the job.

Incidentally, tightening those 9/16 across flats manifold bolts can be a pain because some can only be turned one flat at a time due to the proximity of the casting. If you want to simplify the job, get some "Mr. Gasket" manifold bolts with the "mini hex" head that take a 7/16 across flats wrench.

This distributor has just been pulled out of a high-mileage small-block Chevy and it's looking as if it has seen much better days.

Remove the rotor cap by undoing the two screws securing it.

Under the rotor cap is the centrifugal advance/retard mechanism. Rust often forms at the pivots at the point indicated by the pen, and under the weights.

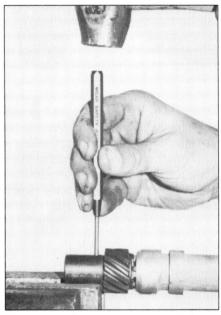

To remove the gear, use a punch just a little smaller than the roll pin and tap out the roll pin. Don't clamp the gear, just rest it on a slightly open set of brass jaws as shown here. An alternative is to place it on a block of wood. Whatever way you choose, the object is to ensure damage-free removal of the gear.

Once you have the manifold in place, there will be a host of items which can be installed, usually associated with some aspect of the intake manifold. However, you will put these on at a later stage.

DISTRIBUTORS

Turning now to the ignition, consider the distributor. Let's face it, this is a vital part of the engine. The standard Chevy distributor is basically of sound design. The only reason it will wear out in any places that are a little inconvenient to recondition is through sheer neglect. However, it's best to give it a complete teardown and rebuild before you install it.

Distributor Types — The most common type of distributor is the conventional single-point contact breaker type, followed by the HEI (High Energy Ignition) electronic ignition. There are also some Corvette distributors with dual points but you may never see one of these unless you own a Corvette. The overhaul of a dual-point distributor will basically follow that of the single-point unit which I will now explain.

CONTACT-BREAKER DISTRIBUTORS

First, remove the distributor cap and place it to one side. Under this you will find the rotor. Remove this by undoing the two securing screws and lift it off. Under the rotor is the mechanical advance/retard mechanism. This is where uncared-for Chevy distributors usually suffer. Condensation causes corrosion here and this mechanism can stick. Usually the weights will jam on their pivots due to rust forming at the pivots. You are going to withdraw the whole shaft assembly. Don't bother to remove the springs and weights at this point.

Check the Bearings — Use a punch to knock out the pin holding the spiral gear onto the end of the shaft. Remove the gear from the shaft. Just before you withdraw the shaft, check to see if there is any excessive side play (wiggle) in it. If there is, this indicates the distributor bearings have worn, in which case you have one of the alternatives from which to

choose. You can go to your local parts store and exchange your unit for a rebuilt one, or you can go down to the wrecking yard and find one with less wear, or buy a new housing from the Chevy store. Those worn bearings cause the sparks to occur at times different than you want them to, which is known as *spark scatter*. This will cost you power and economy.

Removing the Base Plate — Once you have checked that the bearings have no excessive clearance in them, pull the shaft out. This will allow you to get at the contact-breaker-plate

After taking off the drive gear, withdraw the shaft assembly.

To remove the condenser (capacitor), undo the screw indicated by my finger and the screw securing the wires to the contact-breaker set. Screwdriver is just descending upon the breaker screw.

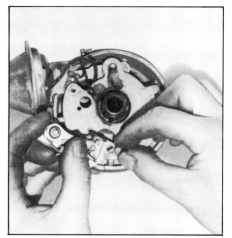

Undo the screws holding the contact-breaker set in place and remove the contact-breaker set.

Using a fine pointed-screwdriver or a scriber, remove the thin wavy snap ring holding the base plate in position.

Now the base plate is off, you have access to the screws securing the vacuum can mounting to the distributor body.

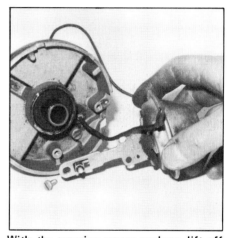

With the securing screws undone, lift off the vacuum can.

parts. With a screwdriver, remove the points from the baseplate. Now return to the distributor housing which has the vacuum advance and retard "can" still connected to the baseplate. There are two ways to remove the vacuum advance can. One is to swing the baseplate around to uncover the one screw farthest from the diaphragm, undo that screw and release the baseplate. This is difficult, but OK if you just need to change the vacuum can. The easier way on a complete stripdown is to remove the baseplate first by removing the circlip at the top of the shaft bearings and then simply lift off the contact-breaker baseplate and remove the vacuum can. Now push the wire from the underside of the

distributor body through its hole so you can remove it completely from the distributor housing.

Turn your attention to the grease well surrounding the top bearing of the distributor housing. Using a fine-point scriber or a small screwdriver, remove the felt pad and the plastic grease-retaining cap. Having done this, scrape out all the excess grease from the grease well. It has probably been there so long that it will have hardened. Scrape out as much as possible, then wash the distributor body in solvent. Lacquer thinner will do a good job if nothing else is available. Once you have the distributor body spotlessly clean, lay it to one side ready to accept the reconditioned components when the time comes for

reassembly.

First remove the springs, take off the weights and pull the center shaft out and give the whole thing a thorough cleaning, wire-brushing off any stubborn deposits and rust that may be present. Wash everything in solvent.

Look at all of your distributor components. Chances are most of them will be in perfectly good order, except they may be slightly marked from corrosion. Wire-brushing all the parts should fix this. Your distributor contact-breaker mounting plate may be another thing altogether.

Rewiring the Base Plate—The grounding wire on the base plate tends to suffer from engine heat. The insulation on it will, in most

Now is your chance to get that piece of wire out of your way by pushing it and the grommet through the base of the distributor body. You will need this wire again if it is in good condition so don't throw it away.

Remove the felt washer and hook out the plastic cap covering the grease well. This is a delicate item and may have become stuck to the grease, so take care not to damage it.

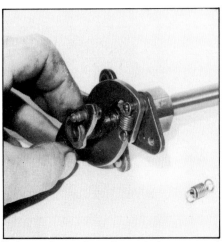

Release the springs from their posts and strip the centrifugal advance/retard assembly. Clean all the parts thoroughly.

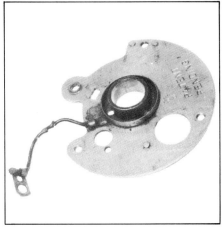

Heat and fatigue have taken their toll. See how the insulation on the base-plate grounding wire has cracked. Eventually the wire itself may break. This will lead to high contact-breaker resistance due to poor grounding. The least-expensive cure is to replace the wire rather than the base plate.

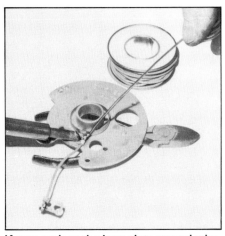

If you replace the base-plate ground wire, use multistrand, not single-strand wire. A single-strand wire will fatigue and break in a few weeks. Pay careful attention to producing a good solder joint and make sure the insulator clamp tab grips the wire tightly.

cases if the distributor has seen lengthy service, be cracked. If this wire should break, your contact breaker electrical resistance can increase due to bad grounding. The cheapest way to rectify this is to replace the old piece of wire with a new piece soldered in place. These joints are subject to vibration. Make sure you do a very good solder joint otherwise it will fail. Also make sure the clip which holds the insulation just prior to the joint on the plate and the terminal is doing the job. If it isn't gripping the

insulation firmly at this point, the solder joint may fatigue and break. If you do a good job it will last a lifetime.

Assembling Your Distributor—The starting point is the centrifugal advance/retard mechanism. Using a moly grease or something similar, lubricate the posts on which the advance/retard weights pivot, the underside of the weights and the center bearing of the distributor. Look at the photos and you will see which points I mean. Don't overdo

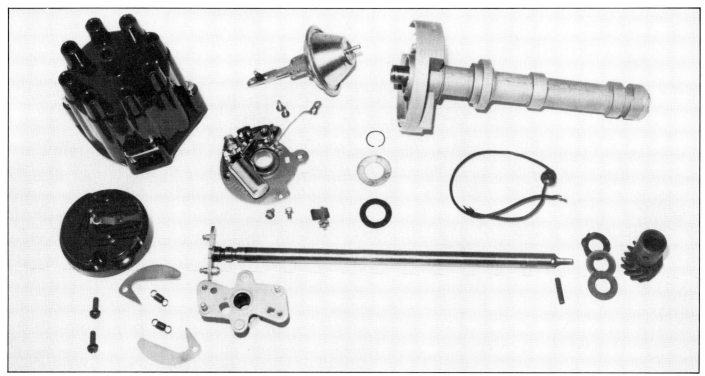

These are all the parts you should have before starting to rebuild a contact-breaker-type distributor.

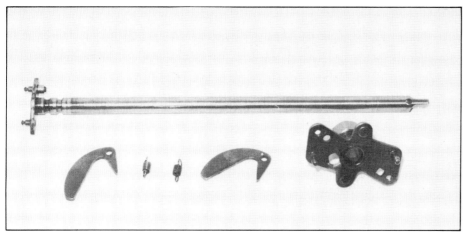

The first components to assemble are those of the centrifugal advance/retard mechanism.

the grease on the weights. The centrifugal force will cause it to fly off; it just needs enough on there to keep it moving freely under all conditions, but not so much that the excess will gum up the works. A smear is really all that's needed. More generous lubrication can be applied to the center bearing.

Advance Stops--Now check that the rubber sleeve on the advance/retard stop peg is in reasonable condition and in one piece. The photo on page 140 shows the sleeve I mean. If the rubber sleeve is not

there, you can easily have too much centrifugal advance, even though your initial advance may be set right. If this sleeve is missing and you tend to drive your engine hard, you could run into detonation problems. This, as I said earlier, is one of the contributory factors to spun bearings in rod journals. So if that sleeve is not there, replace it.

Distributor-Body-Bearing Lubrication—Now turn your attention to the distributor body. You must give it a thorough cleaning. If the top and bottom bearings were in good

139

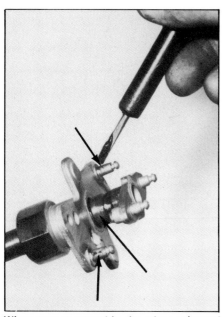

When you re-assemble the advance/retard mechanism, use distributor grease such as Borg Warner CL70, GM Cranking Motor and Distributor Lubricant 196095 or moly grease where indicated. Only a smear is required on the weight pivot posts.

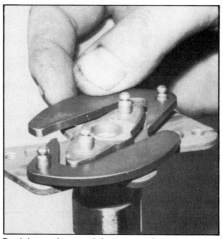

Position the weights on the posts as shown, and make sure that they can swing freely.

Install the springs.

Make sure this sleeve, as well as the one on the vacuum-advance module, is in place and intact. An over-advance situation can occur if it's not there!

Fill the grease well with lubricant and just to make sure, put some in the bearing bores.

order then it's OK for further use. When it has been thoroughly cleaned out, fill the grease wells with moly grease or a similar distributor lubricant. If you look down the bore of the distributor bearing you will see at the top end there is a hole connecting the bearing with the well which is supposed to contain the grease. Be sure that you fill this well with grease or the shaft and distributor housing will wear quickly from lack of lubrication. The bottom one is not so important because it gets oil-mist lubrication from the engine. When you have filled the top well with grease, install the plastic cap that keeps the grease in

place. Then install the felt washer on top of the plastic cap.

Vacuum Advance/Retard—Now it's time to install the vacuum advance/retard can, after you have checked that it is working. The way to do this is by making sure that the small-diameter tube coming out of the diaphragm case which connects to the distributor is clean. Suck on this to see if there is any leak. You will have to suck pretty hard on it and then stick your tongue over the end of the hole to see that it seals. This particular test isn't totally foolproof as you probably wouldn't detect the beginnings of a leak. However, it does

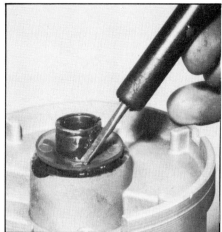
Put the plastic seal in place.

Remove the excess grease with a paper towel but make sure you have a smear of grease left on the diameter arrowed to lubricate the vacuum advance/retard action of the base plate.

Place the felt washer in position on the plastic cap.

Secure the vacuum can at the position shown here with one of the securing screws. Check the other advance/retard sleeve (arrow). If it's not there, vacuum advance may be too great. If buying a new, non-GM replacement, chances are the cam comes without a sleeve.

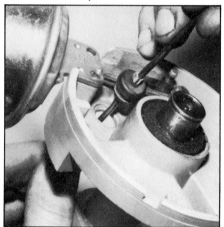
Feed the contact breaker wire through the distributor body.

give you some idea of whether it is usable. After the engine is broken-in, you should have a professional tune-up job done on it. Should the diaphragm have been slightly leaky when it was installed, it sure will be leaky by the time the engine is broken-in and the tune-up man should find that out for you.

Base Plate—Your next move is to install the contact-breaker base plate. First of all take the coil wire and push this through the base of the distributor body and seat the grommet snugly in its hole. Lightly lubricate the center bearing of the contact breaker base plate with distributor grease. A smear here is

adequate. Position the contact breaker base plate onto the distributor body but don't bother to seat it just yet. Take the wire coming from the base plate and position the terminal under the screw nearest the vacuum can on the vacuum-can mounting plate. The tag will have a hole which must engage with the peg on the vacuum-can mounting plate, otherwise your distributor cap will not seat properly. Tighten this screw, securing the tag and then turn the base plate so the relevant hole in it locates with the vacuum-advance mechanism peg. Once the base plate is seated install the wavy snap-ring to hold it in position.

Position the base plate and locate the ground wire under this screw, making sure the small peg on the vacuum-can mounting plate is located in the hole in the tag. Notice at this stage that contact-breaker base plate is not in its final installed position. It is raised and turned clockwise so that this second vacuum-can-securing screw can be tightened.

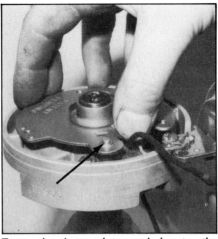

Turn the base plate and locate the vacuum-can peg (arrow) in the hole in the base plate.

Press the base plate down into position and install the snap ring.

Smear some grease on the bearing surfaces of the distributor shaft and slide it in place.

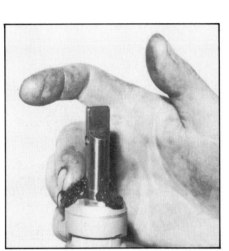

Apply a liberal quantity of grease to the lower bearing.

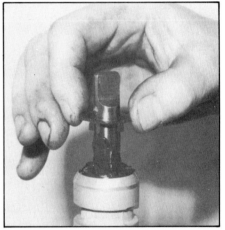

Add the eared thrust plate with the ears toward the distributor body.

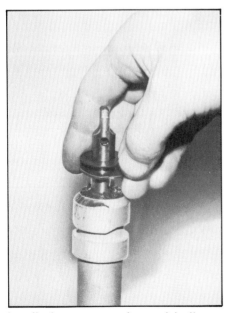

Install the spacer washers originally removed.

Shaft and Drive Gear—Grease the distributor shaft where it contacts the bearings, and slide it into the housing. Then turn the distributor upside-down and install the spacing washers. Position the drive gear on the shaft and drive in the roll pin that holds the gear. Do this on a surface which is suitably soft to cushion the blows so you do not damage the gear while you are installing the pin. Normally the pins go in without a great deal of force but you may get a stubborn one. If you damage the distributor gear you will also damage the camshaft gear if you install the distributor and this will mean a lot of work later on, so be careful.

Put a few drops of oil on the felt pad which lubricates the distributor cam and reinstall this felt pad by snapping its plastic holder back into place on the contact breaker plate. **Condenser & Contact-Breaker**— After you have the gear installed you

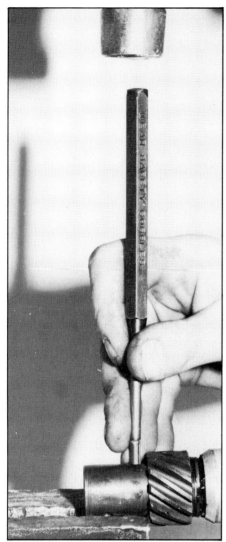

Position the drive gear on the shaft and install the roll pin. Do this on a surface that will ensure no damage to the gear.

Insert the nylon clip holding the cam lubricating pad into its hole in the contact-breaker base plate. Apply two or three drops of engine oil to the felt pad.

Mount the contact-breaker set on the base plate and tighten the screws.

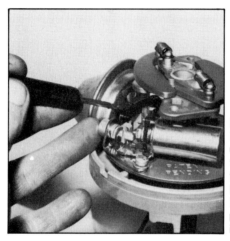

Some contact-breaker sets, such as the Borg-Warner type shown here, do not use a screw to secure the contact-breaker wire. Instead, the wire is clipped between the contact breaker spring and the nylon block positioning the end of the spring. Notice that the condenser is an integral part of the contact set, requiring no wiring connections.

can put in a new contact-breaker (points) set. The latest kind has the condenser attached. This is probably the best type to use as it also has the contact-breaker assembly supported by a *bridge spring*. This cuts down the likelihood of point bounce, making the distributor that much more effective at RPM over 4500. By adjusting the dwell screw, set the points gap to 0.018 inch when the cam follower is on the top of a lobe. Take the wire that comes through the underside of the distributor body and install it on the points terminal. Some of the very latest types of points do not have a screw to locate this. What you have to do is locate the tag underneath the contact breaker spring. The spring load then holds it in place. Many points sets still use a screw in this position to hold the wire, in which case undo the screw, position the terminal and tighten the screw.

Rotor caps. The darker of the two is the E-type, so called because of the E stamped on the arm. These work best with wire-wound ignition cables. The other rotor cap has an arm 0.050-inch longer. It is not as good as the E-type cap for radio supression, but it is less likely to produce a misfire if carbon-string ignition cables are used. The long-arm rotor is generally only available as a specially produced high-performance item.

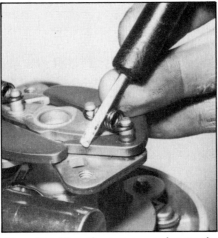

When installing the rotor cap, locate the square peg on its underside in the square hole shown here.

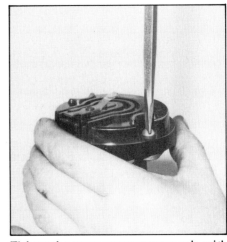

Tighten the rotor-cap screws securely with lockwashers underneath.

Set the distributor dwell approximately correct before installation. Position the heel of the cam follower on one of the cam lobe peaks. Adjust the socket screw until an 0.018-inch feeler gauge is a snug fit between the contact-breaker points.

Put on a new distributor cap and this unit is ready to go back into business as good as new.

Rotor Cap—Here you have two choices: short arm and long arm. The short-arm ones, known as *resistive* or *E-type rotors*, are better for radio suppression. If you have carbon-string resistive plug wires that aren't in perfect order you could get a poor spark with the E-type rotor, so beware of this. If in doubt, use the long-arm rotor or wire-wound plug wires. Borg Warner makes ignition-cable kits of this kind for the small-block Chevy.

Look at the rotor. You will see the the square peg on the underside of the rotor arm engages in a square hole, and the round peg with a round hole. Install the rotor. Though you can only put it on this one way, people break it by tightening the cap before making sure the rotor is properly seated.

Secure the rotor in position with

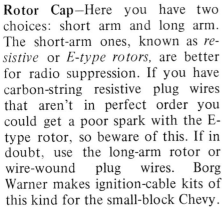

its screws, and make sure they are suitably tight with lockwashers underneath. If this comes undone while the engine is running, your ignition is gone!

The last job to make your distributor like new is to add a new distributor cap. The best ones have brass-type inserts in the towers. At this stage you have a distributor ready to put in your engine.

HEI DISTRIBUTOR

This may be found on a few 1974 vehicles and virtually all vehicles from 1975 on. This differs greatly from the contact-breaker-

type distributor because it uses a magnetic pickup to trigger the spark. While designing a new distributor, GM incorporated a few other useful ideas such as making the coil integral with the distributor cap—but still replaceable. Also the high-voltage plug-wire connectors on the cap are the same as spark plug ends. This means one type of connector is used for both ends of the plug wires.

Cap Replacement—Due to its design there are a few problems with this distributor. Its biggest enemy is dirt and lack of lubrication, so most of the work you will need to do

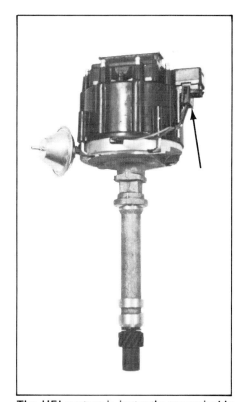

The HEI system is instantly recognizable by its bulky appearance, top-mounted coil, and spark-plug-type connectors. Except for the need to pull out the coil connectors (arrow) the cap is removed the same as on a conventional distributor.

If you need to replace a coil, remove the cap covering the coil by undoing the screws, then loosen the four screws holding the magnetic core.

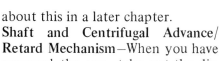

Undo the corner screws and lift out the coil.

Next, carefully pull out wiring connectors.

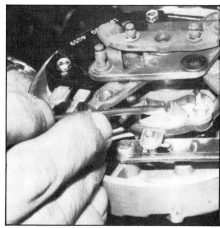

The close approach of the rotating triangular segment with the stationary one triggers the spark. These segments should clear each other. If they touch, the bearings are probably worn, necessitating a replacement body. Because loads are less than with a contact set, worn bearings are not a great problem.

will be cleaning, lubricating and checking for wear. Starting at the top of the distributor, remove the cap and inspect the posts inside the cap. If they are badly pitted, a new cap may be needed, so I have shown how the cap is removed from the coil. It is possible, but unlikely, you may need a new coil, so the same shots show how the coil is removed from the cap! However, I don't advise replacement yet for one simple reason. Because the HEI system delivers a much higher voltage than the contact-breaker-type system it is able to compensate for more corrosion on the posts and still produce a good spark. Your best bet is to let a professional tune up man with all the proper test equipment tell you whether or not you need one after you have installed your rebuilt engine in your car. I talk

about this in a later chapter.

Shaft and Centrifugal Advance/ Retard Mechanism—When you have removed the cap, take out the distributor shaft by removing the gear as on a conventional distributor, then clean and inspect the shaft. If it's worn then so are the bearings in the distributor body. This will mean a new shaft and bearing or bearings.

Once the shaft is out, remove the centrifugal weights and springs and inspect the pivot posts and weights. Even on a vehicle that has seen normal service, these parts and the holes in the weights can wear.

There is no fix except to replace the worn parts. An HEI mechanical overhaul kit contains the shaft and centrifugal advance/retard mechanism as an assembly. With these overhaul kits, and distributors from mid-1976 on, the weights turn on nylon bushings at the pivot posts, thus reducing wear at these points. To reduce wear on those distributors *without* the nylon bushing give the posts a smear of distributor grease. Apart from cleaning and reassembling, the only other thing you need to do now is to refill the grease well under the segmented pickup ring in the body.

Centrifugal advance pivots on early HEI distributor wear rapidly as seen here. The shaft-removal procedure is the same as for the contact-breaker distributor.

Not only do pivots wear, but also the holes in the weights. The cure is to replace the worn advance/retard and shaft assembly with a new one.

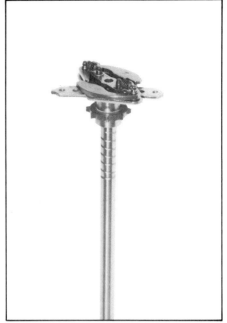

This assembly usually cures most mechanical ailments the HEI distributor may have. It is available as a unit from your local Chevy dealer.

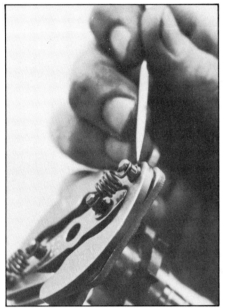

Mechanical overhaul kits plus HEI distributors from mid-1976 on, have nylon bearings on the advance/retard weight posts. This appears to eliminate most of the wear problems on the earlier versions.

The vacuum can is removed by undoing the two securing screws, pressing down the post connected to the lever arm (arrow) and then sliding it out. If the coil checked out okay but the unit did not deliver a spark, it could be the module next to it has gone out. Replacements should be available from your nearest auto parts store.

To recharge the grease well, undo the three small hex bolts holding the segment ring, then lift off the small induction coil (arrow). Under the coil you will see the grease-well cover. Remove this and recharge the well as on a conventional distributor.

DISTRIBUTOR INSTALLATION

I will now describe distributor installation and ignition timing for the engine at this point, although it is better to do it while the engine is in the car. It's not easier to do it in the car, but makes sense to do so because you may bump the engine against the firewall and break the distributor while installing the engine. Avoid this by installing the distributor after the engine is in. The same generally goes for the spark plugs. However, you may have one of those difficult vehicles which has hard spark plug accessibility. V-8 Monza's up to about '78 had a spark plug right in line with the steering shaft. In such cases put the relevant plug in before installing the engine and take care not to break it. So when you get to the stage where you have the engine in and you are ready to time the ignition, turn back to this particular part. Also, the accompanying photos and the illustration show where each wire goes. Again this is difficult, if not impossible, to show while the engine is in the car, so I have done it at this stage to simplify things.

SETTING IGNITION TIMING

Now that you understand why I did some things out of sequence, let's proceed, one step at a time. If you did as I previously suggested, your engine is now set at TDC on number 1. With both valves on number 1 closed and

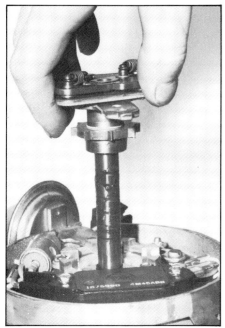

Before installing a new HEI shaft, smear it with the same type of grease as used in the well.

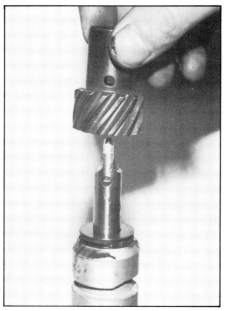

Install the shaft, grease the lower bearing, position the eared thrust plate, spacer washer and gear, then drive in the roll pin to secure the assembly. Take care to avoid damaging the gear as you do this.

Setting Ignition Timing: At this point you should have the engine with number 1 piston at TDC on its firing stroke. From here, turn the engine backward (counter-clockwise, viewed from the front of the engine) about 1/4 turn. Now rotate the crank forward (clockwise) until the mark on the crankshaft vibration damper is aligned with the advance figure on the timing tag that you want for static timing. In the example here, the timing will be set at 8° BTCD.

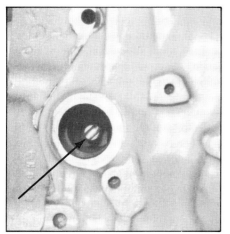

Setting Ignition Timing: Using a long screwdriver, turn the oil pump drive shaft (arrow) until the slot aligns with number 5 cylinder intake pushrod.

Setting Ignition Timing: Here the screwdriver indicates aligning the oil-pump shaft slot with number 5 cylinder intake pushrod.

number 6 cylinder valves rocking, this means number 1 cylinder is in firing position. Now turn the engine backward (CCW viewed from the front) about 15 degrees then turn it forward (CW viewed from the front) until you have the required static-timing figure on the front cover degree tab showing next to the mark on the crank vibration damper. Depending upon the year and type of engine you have, this can be anything between 12 degrees to 0

degrees BTDC. At this stage, if you are not sure what the timing should be to get the engine running reasonably, turn the engine so the mark on the damper is opposite 8 degrees BTDC on the front-cover tab. On 1972 and later models there should be a label in the engine compartment which lists the correct static ignition timing.
Positioning the Oil-Pump Shaft— The next operation will be to set the oil-pump-shaft slot in the correct

position to receive the tang on the end of the distributor shaft. Look down the hole in the inlet manifold into which the distributor fits, and using a long screwdriver, turn the oil-pump shaft until the slot lines up with number 5 intake rocker as shown in the photo.
Positioning Rotor Cap for #1 Cylinders— Next, as shown on page 148, mark the number 1 plug-wire post on the distributor cap and install the cap on the distributor body. Using

147

Setting Ignition Timing: Mark the number 1 cylinder post. This is recognizable as the one directly above the right edge of the sliding window. Many engines come from the factory using the post immediately left of the one shown here as number 1. If you decide to use this one as number 1, the same procedure still applies.

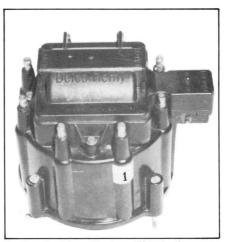

Setting Ignition Timing: This is the number 1 position for the HEI distributor.

Before installing the distributor, position this paper gasket on the distributor body against the gasket face. Use sealer to hold it in position. Do not put sealer on the face that goes against the block.

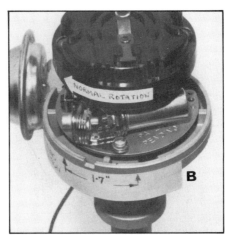

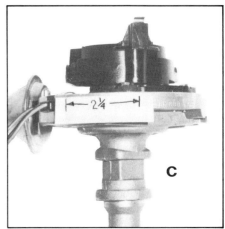

Setting the Ignition Timing: Transfer the position of the number 1 post from the cap to the body of the distributor by installing the cap and marking down from it to the distributor body. This firing position is shown in photo A. On the distributor body measure 1-11/16-inch back from the firing position and set the leading edge of the rotor arm directly over the 1-11/16-inch retarded mark shown in photo B. Because the HEI body is larger in diameter the dimension to position the rotor to is 2-1/4 inches back from the firing line as shown in photo C.

a sharp scribe or something similar, transfer the position of the number 1 post from the cap to the distributor body. Do this as accurately as possible. What you are trying to do is to get the center position of the number 1 post accurately marked on the distributor body so you can locate the position the rotor will be in with the distributor cap off. Once you have transferred this mark to the body, take the distributor cap off. Now turn the rotor so its leading edge is directly above the mark you just made on the distributor body. This is the approximate position

it will be in at the point of firing. I say approximate because its exact firing position will depend upon the centrifugal and vacuum advance at the time. Using a tape measure, mark a line on the contact breaker-type distributor body 1.7 inches (approximately 1-11/16 inch) back from the number 1 line as shown in the nearby photos. For the HEI this dimension should be 2-1/4 inches. Next, turn the rotor counterclockwise (opposite to its normal rotation) until the leading edge is over the new mark you just made, leaving it as shown in the photo.

Positioning Distributor in Block—
You are now about to install the distributor but first place the paper gasket under the clamping flange with sealer between it and the *clamping flange only*. Hold the distributor body above its location hole with the vacuum-advance can 45 degrees across the engine. Lower the distributor into the hole. As the drive gear on the distributor engages with the cam gear, the rotor will turn clockwise towards the firing position from the 1.7-inch or 2-1/4-inch retarded position you previously set.

Setting Ignition Timing: Hold the distributor in the position shown here and slide it straight down into the block.

Setting Ignition Timing: As the distributor drive gear engages the cam gear, the rotor cap will turn until it is positioned approximately over the firing line mark on the distributor body as shown in conventional ignition at left, and HEI ignition at right.

Setting Ignition Timing: To time the HEI distributor, turn the body until the segments line up as shown here. If the vacuum can is not approximately 45° across the engine, the timing is probably one set of segments off, so correct the situation as necessary.

Setting Ignition Timing: Mount the coil and, if applicable to your particular engine, the throttle-cable bracket.

Setting the Ignition Timing: Connect the wire from the distributor to the negative side of the coil.

As the distributor gets close to its "fully home" position, you should feel the tang end of the distributor shaft engage with the slot in the oil-pump shaft. You will know if it doesn't engage because the distributor body will stop about 3/8-inch above its final position in the block. If it doesn't engage, try jiggling the rotor and distributor a little each way until it does engage. If that doesn't do it try turning the crankshaft back and forth about 1/4 of a turn while applying downward pressure on the distributor. At some point or another in that range, the distributor should drop into engagement with the pump shaft. The position the rotor should end up in is shown in the photo for whichever type you are doing. Install the distributor clamp and bolt but do not tighten the bolt just now.

TIMING THE HEI DISTRIBUTOR

At this point the procedure for the HEI and contact-breaker distributors differ. The procedure for the HEI is simple, if you have followed the steps just outlined. You should find that the triangular segments on the shaft are in line or nearly in line with those on the distributor body.

If they are not aligned, turn the distributor body to line up the closest rotor segments with the closest distributor body segments. This should leave the distributor with the vacuum can about 45 degrees across the engine. Now tighten the distributor clamp just enough to hold the distributor in place. This ignition timing is close enough to get the engine started. An ignition timing light can be used for final setting after the engine is installed and running.

TIMING CONTACT-BREAKER DISTRIBUTORS

This involves a little elementary electrical circuitry to time the ignition. The first thing you must understand is that the spark occurs when the contact-breaker points *OPEN*. You can connect a battery and a light bulb in series with the contact-breaker points. When the points open the light will go out. That's the plan—here's how to do it.

First of all, connect the positive (+) side of a battery to the positive side of the coil. Connect the other side of the battery through a light bulb to the engine, the distributor body, or anything else making electrical contact with the distributor body. This should give you the circuit shown in Figure 7-3. The light bulb should be the right voltage for the battery you are using.

At the front of the engine, check that the mark on the crankshaft damper is still lined up with the number of degrees BTDC you want your static ignition timing to be. Tighten the distributor clamp just enough towards the back of the engine to hold the distributor body. Push the vacuum can around towards the back of the engine a little way, say 1/2 inch. The lamp you have just connected should be on at this point. Now pull the vacuum can *very slowly* towards the front of the engine and watch the lamp. When it goes out, stop rotating the distributor body and tighten the clamp. Your static ignition timing is now set.!

ROUTING IGNITION CABLES

Install the distributor cap so the plug wires can be sorted out so each goes to the appropriate cylinder. With number 1 as shown in the photo, go around the cap clockwise as viewed from the top 1, 8, 4, 3, 6, 5, 7, 2. Figure 7-4 should make it all clear.

So far, all I have described can be done in or out of the car. In many cases it's best done after the engine is installed because the distributor could be bumped while the engine is going in. The choice as to

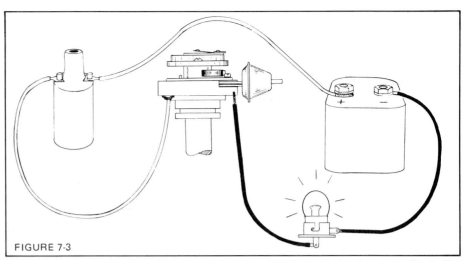

FIGURE 7-3

The wiring for the lamp method of setting static ignition timing is as seen here. The battery used can be either the vehicle battery or a flashlight battery. Prior to setting the timing, set the contact-breaker gap to 0.018-inch with the points fully open.

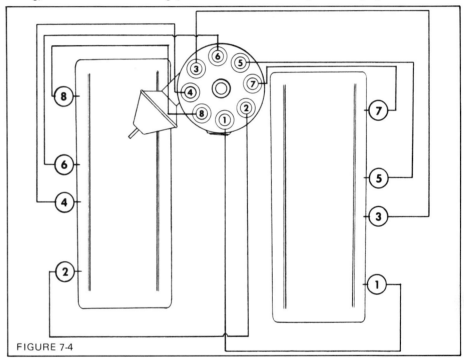

FIGURE 7-4

To wire the distributor cap posts in the correct order to the plug, follow this wiring sequence from number 1 in a clockwise direction. If you have the post marked here as 8 for number 1 (many engines are laid out this way) move each number a position clockwise then wire number to number as shown here.

which way it's done is yours. You pulled the engine out in the beginning so you should have some idea as to how much room exists.

Plug-Wire Clips—After this practice in inserting the distributor and timing the ignition, you can put the finishing touches to the engine. Still working in the ignition area, consider the spark-plug-wire clips. They are essential to avoid burning the plug wires on the exhaust manifolds, but the type of clips you

must use depends on the kind of exhaust manifolds you have. If you have exhaust pipes going down and away from the head. you need clips to bring the wires over the rocker covers. On the other hand, if you have the up-and-down-in-the-center type exhaust manifolds (called *rams horns*), you need clips to take the wires around the back of the engine and up between the exhaust ports. These should be plastic clips or steel ones and should be very wide

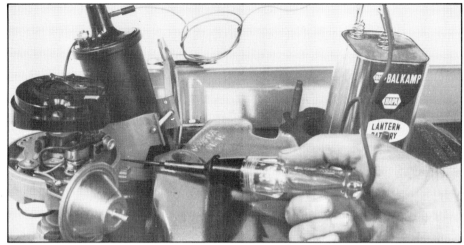

Setting Ignition Timing: This is what the real-life version of the wiring diagram for timing looks like. Here, instead of a plain bulb, a circuit tester is being used and a light in the handle of the circuit tester shows whether the circuit is made or broken. Note the position of the distributor, the vacuum can 45° across the engine and the rotor arm pointing almost straight up the middle of the V. To set the timing, push the vacuum can toward the back of the engine about 1/2-inch, then *slowly* pull it forward. Just as the lamp goes out, stop turning the distributor.

Setting Ignition Timing: The last chore is to tighten the distributor clamp bolt enough to hold the distributor firmly in place.

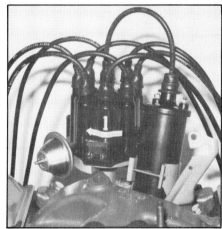

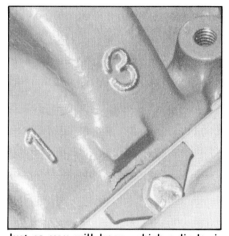

Connecting Plug Leads: Going around in the direction of the arrow, the leads go to cylinder number 1 from the tower mark 1, then 8, 4, 3, 6, 5, 7 and 2.

In case you cannot remember or plain don't know the firing order of a small-block Chevy, it is cast on the manifold.

Just so you will know which cylinder is which, that's cast on the manifold too.

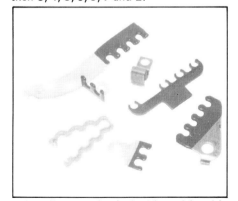

Using clips to make the ignition wiring tidy is not a case of dressing up the engine, but a question of reliability. Cables hanging loose in the engine compartment can get caught up in moving parts or burnt by the hot exhaust. Here are some of the clips your Chevy dealer has in stock to hold your plug cables in place.

If you have "up and down in the center" (rams horn) manifolds, the longer plug cables are clipped to the oil pan with clips like these.

All leads whether short or long will go through these block-mounted clips. These are essential to stop rams horn type exhaust manifolds burning the plug leads.

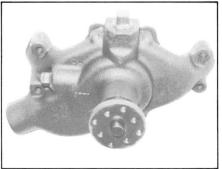

All vehicles through 1969, Corvettes through '71 and light trucks through '73, used this short pump. It has a small shaft and small bearings as compared with later pumps. The pump shaft is 5/8-inch diameter and the pulley mounting flange has two sets of bolt holes: the small pattern is a 1-3/4-inch bolt circle and the large pattern is a 2-1/8-inch bolt circle.

This extended pump was used on most passenger cars from 1969 through '76. It has the large bolt circle pattern on the pulley flange. This big-bearing pump has a 3/4-inch diameter shaft with the nose machined down to 5/8-inch diameter.

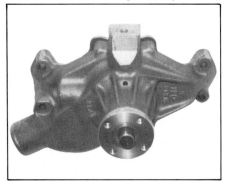

When installed in the Monza, the small-block Chevy uses this pump. It is a large-bearing, large-bolt-circle pattern, large-shaft, short-bodied pump with a special mounting boss.

Heavy trucks one ton and up, Corvettes from 1971 on, light trucks '73 on, and other vehicles from '76 on, except the Monza, use this pump. It has the large-bolt-circle pattern with large bearings and shaft. The body is short with deep ribs to support the bearings.

There are minor length differences between the short pumps, but the biggest length difference is between the short and long pumps as seen here.

or else have a rubber or plastic coating so they won't cut through the insulation. To get the right-length plug wires in the right place, temporarily screw in the spark plugs finger-tight. If you are not installing the distributor for good at this stage, put it in temporarily also. Locate your cable clips and sort out the wire routing to the plugs. Replace the plug wires unless they are in good condition. TVR (Television and Radio suppression) cables over two years old should be replaced. If they are wire-wound cables, then these do not deteriorate electrically and unless damaged by exhaust heat will last until the insulation fails. Hot climatic conditions may also cause the insulation on cables to fail. A sign of this is a dried cracked appearance of the insulation material.

PARTS TO REPLACE

Let's see what else must go back onto the engine.

Water Pump—Generally pumps can wear out at mileages between 40,000 and 200,000 so determining replacement by mileage is not the way to do it. Here are two tests to determine if the pump can be used. The first is to see if there is any slop in the bearings. If not, it's okay. If there is, trade it for a new or quality rebuilt one. Beware of cheap rebuilds. If the bearings are okay look at the holes in the pump body just below where the fan mounts. If these show a trail of rusty water, then the seal has gone so a replacement is necessary. Install the pump using gaskets between the pump and the block. Coat both sides of the gaskets with silicone

sealer. Pump-securing bolts must be the correct length for the pump. Some pump-bolt holes are blind so don't use bolts which could bottom before tightening the pump. This can allow a water leak or cause stripped threads in the block and you don't want either! Refer to the short-block parts list for the correct bolt lengths.

The water pump used depends upon the accessory mounting positions, the pump pulley securing bolt pattern, the pump length and the size of bearings used. For these reasons, it is important to use the correct water pump for the job. If you are rebuilding an engine which came from another vehicle, install the pump and pulleys from your vehicle or new ones just like them.

Oil-pressure Gauge/Switch—If you are not using an oil-pressure gauge,

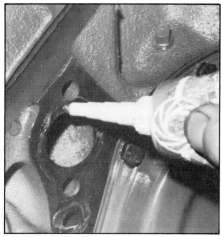

Installing Water Pump: Smear sealer on the water-pump-mounting faces. The right side (as viewed from the driver's seat) has two water holes. Be sure to go around both.

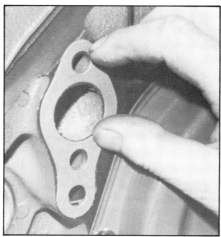

Stick the gasket in place.

The gasket for the left water hole is the same as for the right side, though the left side has only one water hole.

Position the pump and screw in the bolts. Sealer will be required on the threads on the bottom right bolt (when viewed from the front). Check you have the right bolt lengths as ones too long will bottom out in the blind holes.

If there is a trail of rust from these holes, then the water seal has gone. The cure is to buy a new or rebuilt pump. Rebuilt pumps are usually cheaper as your old pump "core" is part of the purchase price.

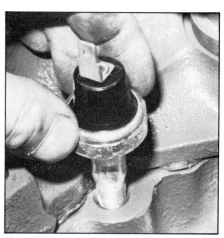

The oil-pressure switch or the take-off for the oil-pressure gauge fits here. To avoid an oil leak without excessive tightening of the fitting, use teflon thread sealer and avoid overtightening.

Exhaust gas recirculating (EGR) valve on emission-control-type engines. It's held in place by a clamp-and-screw arrangement. All passages for transferring exhaust to the inlet are built into the manifold. Vacuum side of the diaphragm (arrow) is connected to a take-off point on the carburetor base plate.

Before putting on the thermostat cover, be sure the thermostat is in working order by placing it in hot to boiling water. If there is any doubt, replace it. Quote the model and year when ordering from your parts man as ones on emission-controlled engines open at higher temperatures. The cover goes on with a gasket coated with sealer (not shown).

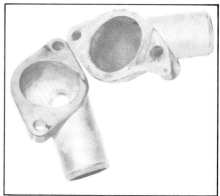

Before putting your thermostat housing back onto your engine, check that the sealing face is not badly eroded as is often the case. If you are handy with a file, all but the worst cases can be remedied. Usually some filing and a silicon sealer are all that's needed but in extreme cases you may need a new thermostat housing as shown on the left.

153

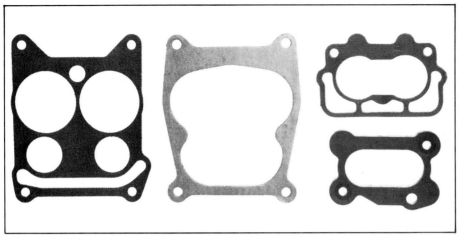

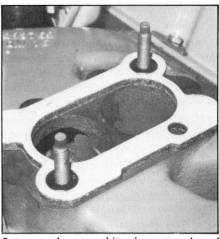

If the carb gasket is changed from a thin to a thick one, the choke rod length must be reset. The 4-barrel gasket at right and the lower 2-barrel gasket are the thick type. Many '69 Chevys use the gasket on the far left. They must be used with a heat shield (3884576) between gasket and carb base. Match the old gasket with the new one to insure they are the same.

Some carburetor kits have two-barrel gaskets with only two holes. Only two studs are necessary, so remove the others from the manifold so the gasket will fit.

install the oil-pressure switch in the back of the block near the distributor. Even if you do use a pressure gauge, it is a good idea to use a fitting which also allows installing the oil-pressure switch so the "idiot light" will function when there is no oil pressure.

EGR Valve—If you are rebuilding a late-model engine with emission equipment, put the exhaust-gas-recirculation (EGR) valve back onto the manifold. This valve is vacuum-operated and a hose will later be connected from this to the carburetor.

Thermostat—Check that the thermostat operates by immersing it in boiling water. It should open about 1/2 inch when the hot water activates it. If it opens correctly, install it in the manifold. If it does not work, install a new one with the *correct temperature rating*. With the thermostat in place install the gasket and thermostat housing. If any corrosion of the housing has taken place use silicone sealer on both sides of the gasket.

Coil—Locate the coil mounting bracket on the manifold and secure it with the two 5/16 UNC bolts. After you install the distributor, connect the points wire to the negative terminal of the coil and tighten the securing nut.

Carburetor—If your carburetor has seen many miles, then the least it could do with is a simple rebuild.

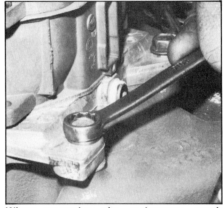

When mounting the carburetor, work around the bolts/nuts and tighten them progressively. Do not over-tighten as this can cause fuel leakage problems with some types of carburetors.

Doing little more than thoroughly cleaning the carburetor can often make all the difference between your engine being an horrendous gas guzzler and the economy thing you had hoped for. Probably the simplest way to overhaul your carburetor is to buy a carburetor overhaul kit. These contain all the gaskets and parts that usually perish under normal useage. Generally these kits cost less than $10 and are a good investment. If your carburetor does need an overhaul, you will find it most helpful to read Holley or Rochester Carburetor books by H. P. Books. Most small-block Chevys have Rochester carburetors; a few of the high-performance engines had Holleys when they left the factory. Although the number

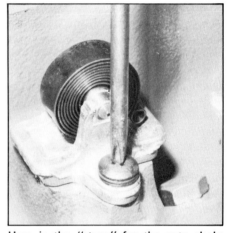

Here is the "stove" for the auto choke mechanism going back on. The coil seen here is a bi-metal strip which uncoils about a quarter of a turn when heated up. On most two-barrel and Holley carburetors, the bi-metal pulls down. On Quadrajets, it pushes up. There are numerous bi-metal elements so be sure you have the correct one.

of makes is limited, the types of carburetor used over the years are not, hence the reason for a whole book on each carburetor.

Once you are sure that your carburetor is ready for another long stint of service, install it on the manifold and tighten the securing nuts. Do not overdo the tightening of the nuts on the carburetor flange as this can lead to distortion of some carburetor bodies and bring about fuel leakage from the float chambers. Under extreme circumstances, it can also bind the throttle shaft, making it stiff to operate.

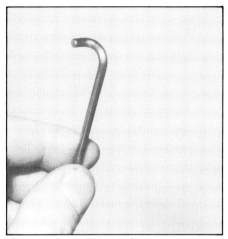

You may need to make up your own choke rod. If you do, be sure to bend the end that hooks into the carburetor linkage slot in a double 90° bend, as seen here. If you don't do this, the rod can drop out of the choke-linkage slot.

Choke should be closed when the bimetal element is in its "cold" position. Check that there is no binding in the choke linkage by moving the choke rod to open the choke.

On most two-barrel applications, the choke butterfly (arrow) should be fully open when the choke actuating rod is pressed *down* onto the bi-metal base. See Figure 7-5 to adjust to the correct rod length.

On the Quadrajet four-barrel carbs, the bi-metal element pushes the choke rod (arrow) *up* to take the choke off. Typical settings are shown in Figure 7-5.

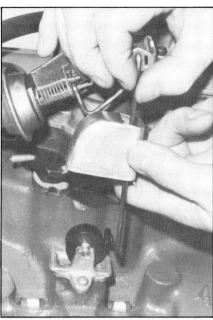

With the rod length correctly set, remove the rod, insert it into the sheet-metal choke-stove cover. Relocate the rod into the choke linkage and bi-metal element, then press the stove cover into place.

You will notice when installing your carburetor that some gasket kits contain a two-barrel carburetor-to-manifold gasket with only two holes, whereas your manifold will more than likely have four studs in it. The very latest manifolds have only two studs or threaded holes and if you have a two-hole gasket, the solution is to remove the two studs in the positions where the gasket has no holes.

Automatic Choke Mechanism—In replacing the automatic choke mechanism, you may run into a few potential pitfalls which I should warn you of. Basically, installing the automatic choke mechanism is the reverse of taking it off. Fitting the bi-metal strip to the manifold is no problem, but from there on you may run into a few problems. Most gasket sets contain a manifold-to-carburetor gasket. If you happen to be overhauling your carburetor, the carburetor kit will also contain such a gasket. Manifold-to-carburetor gaskets can vary from 1/16-inch to 5/16-inch thick. If you change the gasket thickness, you will find your automatic choke will be out of adjustment. Also if you

have fitted a new bi-metal element, the setting required may be slightly different. Combine these two factors and you may have an automatic choke which is only 50% operational. Your fuel consumption may be wildly increased or conversely you may find it difficult to start the engine when it is cold. Once you are aware of this problem, you may be able to solve it by bending your existing choke rod to reset the choke mechanism so it functions correctly. Whether or not you can do this depends on whether a shorter or longer rod is needed. Sometimes the rods have a deliberate bend in them so you can make quite big adjustments to their length to suit requirements.

On the other hand it is often simpler to make up a new choke rod from some 1/16-inch welding rod. Whichever way you choose, here is the basic technique for checking/setting the choke mechanism.

First of all check which way the bi-metal element rotates as it is heated up. The easiest way to do this is to strike a match and let the flame go onto the bi-metal element. It will very soon have enough heat

If it doesn't impede the installation of the engine, then put the fuel pump on. In this photo the plugs were installed to route the cables. They will be removed prior to installing the engine so as to avoid bumping and breaking them.

in it to start it rotating. As soon as it starts rotating, see whether or not it's going the correct way to open the choke as the engine heats up. On two-barrel carburetors the bi-metal element will have its end rotate from a high position down to a low position on the manifold, thus pulling the automatic choke mechanism rod downward. With most four-barrel carburetors except Holleys, the bi-metal operates in the reverse direction. With the cover off the bi-metal element, insert the end of the choke rod in the eye of the bi-metal element. Now open the choke fully by hand and bend the rod to line up with the hole in the choke mechanism lever as shown in the nearby drawings. With the rod held in the fully downward position, the choke butterfly should be

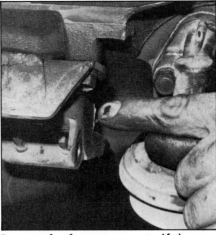

Beware of soft motor mounts. If the ones that came out with the motor looked oil-soaked or flabby, replace them because your new engine will most certainly finish them off.

Your engine may be equipped with a TVS valve. If it is, connect the top outlet to the ported vacuum supply on the carburetor. This can be identified as the vacuum tap that enters the carburetor bore just above the level of the closed throttle butterfly. The center outlet of the TVS valve is routed to the distributor vacuum advance/retard; lower outlet goes to manifold vacuum.

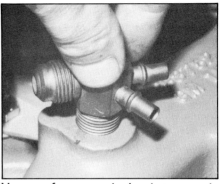

Vacuum for power brakes is commonly tapped from the manifold. As shown, the power brake takeoff may also incorporate the vacuum connections for the automatic transmission and accessories such as heater/air conditioner flap valve.

If you have changed manifolds, check that there are no air leaks because of the absence of components unnecessary to your particular installation. Left over holes as seen here should be plugged with threaded pipe plugs.

NOTE: PERFORM ADJUSTMENTS IN PROPER SEQUENCE.

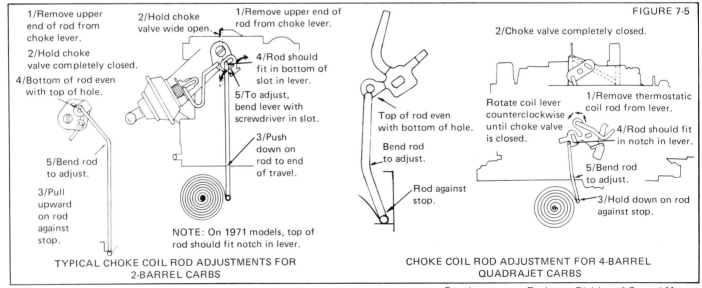

1/Remove upper end of rod from choke lever.
2/Hold choke valve completely closed.
4/Bottom of rod even with top of hole.
5/Bend rod to adjust.
3/Pull upward on rod against stop.

2/Hold choke valve wide open.

1/Remove upper end of rod from choke lever.
4/Rod should fit in bottom of slot in lever.
5/To adjust, bend lever with screwdriver in slot.
3/Push down on rod to end of travel.

NOTE: On 1971 models, top of rod should fit notch in lever.

TYPICAL CHOKE COIL ROD ADJUSTMENTS FOR 2-BARREL CARBS

FIGURE 7-5

2/Choke valve completely closed.

Top of rod even with bottom of hole.
Bend rod to adjust.
Rod against stop.

Rotate coil lever counterclockwise until choke valve is closed.

1/Remove thermostatic coil rod from lever.
4/Rod should fit in notch in lever.
5/Bend rod to adjust.
3/Hold down on rod against stop.

CHOKE COIL ROD ADJUSTMENT FOR 4-BARREL QUADRAJET CARBS

Drawing courtesy Rochester Division of General Motors.

You may have a temperature sensitive vacuum (TSV) valve to switch in the EGR valve only when the engine is at normal operating temperature. The valve will look like this. It usually screws into the thermostat housing. Top port connects to the ported vacuum takeoff on the carburetor and the lower port to the EGR valve.

Carburetor vacuum signals to various parts of the engine are important to get correct operation of emission systems and vacuum spark timing. Vacuum takeoff points shown are for exhaust gas recirculating valve (EGR), 1; PCV valve, 2; vacuum advance/retard on distributor, 3; choke vacuum brake, 4.

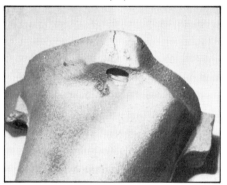

This crack could be repaired but if it's left any longer, welding or brazing may cost more than a sound one at the wrecking yard.

When using exhaust manifold gaskets of this type, metal-faced side goes toward the manifolds.

wide open. If it isn't in the wide-open position, bend the rod to make it shorter. On the other hand, if the choke is wide open and the end of the rod in the eye of the bi-metal strip has not bottomed on the alloy casting, then lengthen the rod until it does. Having the choke not open fully can be just as bad as having the choke open too early. One way you will use a lot of fuel and the other way, you'll have a cold engine stumble. That can be a nasty situation at intersections on the way to work. Once you have the rod length set correctly, unhook it from the choke-lever end, slip the bi-metal element cover over the end of the rod and press it down into position, then install the choke lever to the carburetor.

Fuel Pump Installation—Reinstall the fuel pump if you have the type of engine mount which has a nut welded to one half of it. In such a case you don't need the accessibility you'll get by leaving the fuel pump off.

Carburetor Hose Connections—Once you have a fully functional carb in place, connect the exhaust-gas-recirculation (EGR) hose to the carb, along with the vacuum-advance tube. Check the hose routing in the photo to make sure you have it right.

Installing Cast-Iron Manifolds—If you are using stock cast-iron exhaust manifolds, check to see that they are in good shape. Some types are prone to crack at the exhaust-pipe-flange-stud holes. If the manifolds are very dirty, it may be hard to see these cracks. A good wire brushing helps make cracks visible. To make installing the exhaust manifolds a little easier, I usually put a dab of gasket compound on the manifold and stick the gasket to to. While this stickum will burn off after a few minutes running, it will hold the gasket while the manifold is being installed. If you are using tubular headers do not install them at this point.

FLEX PLATE

With the cast-iron exhaust manifolds on, you are ready to turn your attention to the transmission aspects of your engine. Whether you have a flex plate or a flywheel, what you will now have to do is to bolt either of these items back onto the crankshaft in the same position it came off. With a flex plate, your job is completed once it is bolted in place. The flex-plate-securing bolts should be tightened to 50–60 pounds-feet.

FLYWHEEL/CLUTCH

With a manual transmission you will have to install the clutch and align the clutch plate. You probably noticed during the stripdown that nothing holds the clutch disc in place. This is because it is actually sliding on the spline of the transmission which is still in the car where you left it.

This pressure plate is suffering from having been overheated. Pressure ring is warped concave as can be seen by the gap between the ruler and the friction surface.

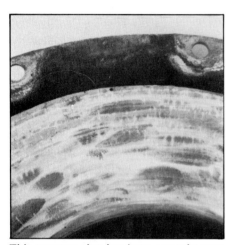

This pressure ring has been severely over-heated as evidenced by the heat-checks and chatter marks. There's no point in trying to save a pressure plate that's this bad.

To line up the clutch plate, position the plate, put on the cover and finger-tighten the securing bolts. Put the clutch aligning tool in the spline and pilot bearing. This is just about to take place in the photo. Having aligned the plate, tighten the clutch cover bolts and remove the tool.

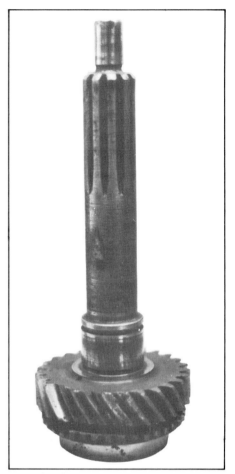

Best clutch-aligning tool is an old transmission input shaft, the same as the one in your car.

Clutch-Disc Alignment—When you try to put the engine back in the car, the clutch disc must align with the pilot bearing or the input shaft will miss the pilot bearing. The trick is to align the clutch disc with the pilot bearing prior to tightening up the bolts around the outside edge of the clutch cover. The way to do this is with a dummy transmission input shaft. Moulded urethane clutch alignment tools are available at most parts houses. As an alternative you can either use a plain shaft which fits the inside diameter of the spline and the inside diameter of the pilot bearing, or you can go down to the wrecking yard and get an old input shaft from a manual transmission, as shown in the photos. This is ideal because it exactly duplicates what is in the car, because that's just what it

was originally. Be sure to get a shaft which has the same number of splines as your transmission-input shaft also, or nothing will fit or work. This is just one more of the hundreds of things you must think about when rebuilding an engine.

CLUTCH ASSEMBLY PROCEDURE

Before you do any assembly, you must determine whether the flywheel and clutch are okay for further use. If the flywheel has been scored by the rivets, it can be refaced. If it has severe heat checks, as shown in the photo, or if any cracks are evident, *replace the flywheel.* The same rigorous inspection should also be applied to the pressure-plate friction surface. Remember, an exploding flywheel is at least as effective at destroying your

car as a hand grenade. If the flywheel is up to standard, install it and torque the bolts to 60-65 lbs-ft. Check the friction surface of the pressure plate for flatness with a straight-edge. A good machinist's rule is okay for this. Using feeler gauges, determine how much error there is across the friction surface. If it is up to 0.010 inch you can reuse the unit as it is. If the friction surface is out of flat by more than 0.010 inch, or scored by rivet heads, get a rebuilt or new unit. On diaphragm clutches the diaphragm can fatigue after prolonged use. If any of the release fingers are out of the regular pattern, the diaphragm is broken. Replace the pressure plate assembly with a rebuilt one.

Check the clutch disc for wear. Most have grooves in them. If these don't show because they are worn

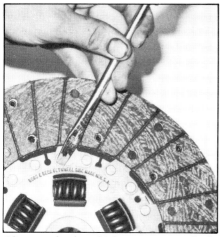

Always check which way around the clutch disc should be installed. As seen here, the FLYWHEEL SIDE is marked.

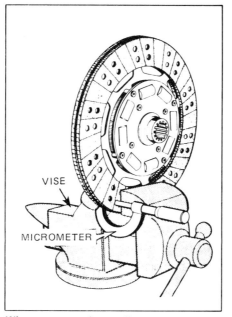

When compressing a disc to measure its thickness, be careful not to damage the facings or get them dirty. Measure as close to the clamping device as you can get so your reading will be accurate. *Drawing courtesy Schiefer*

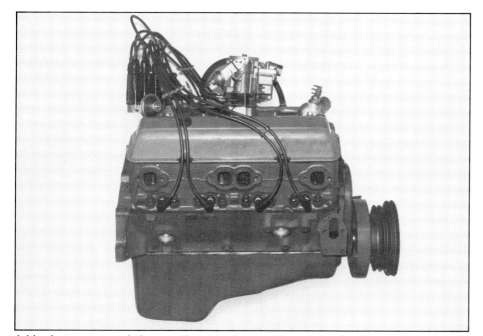

Add whatever transmission you intend using to this and you have an engine ready for installation. Depending upon installation requirements, the exhaust manifolds and fuel pump may be added before or after installation of the engine in the vehicle. Pull the distributor off before installing the engine.

away, you need a new clutch disc. Some clutch discs are not grooved so this method of telling whether it's worn or not won't work. Instead measure the thickness of the disc on the outside edge as shown in the drawing. They generally measure between 0.310 inch and 0.320 inch. At 0.280 inch they are worn out. If the clutch disc appears oily, replace it—no matter how thick it may be. Oil and clutches do not mix so **DON'T handle the clutch plate with oily hands.** Remove any traces of oil from the flywheel and pressure-plate friction surface with a suitable solvent such as lacquer thinner. *Don't use gasoline or kerosene* as these do not dry deposit-free. Break the glaze of the friction surfaces on the flywheel and pressure plate with 120—180 grit emery cloth, then remove all grit particles before installation. Position the clutch disc on the pressure plate the correct way round. One side is stamped Flywheel Side. Hold the pressure plate and disc up to the flywheel. Bolt it up *the same way it came off.* That's the way you marked it at the stripdown. At this stage screw in the bolts finger-tight only. Put the clutch aligning tool through the center of the clutch disc and into the pilot bearing. Tighten the cover bolts progressively to 20 pounds-feet, then to 35 pounds-feet. Finally remove the clutch-aligning tool.

PAINTING

Your last job is partly cosmetic, partly useful, and that is to paint the engine. Do this and you may stop any *small* oil leaks that you otherwise would have had. To get the paint to hold on, you must remove any oil from the surfaces to be painted. Lacquer thinner and paper towels are as good as anything for this. As for the type of paint to use, I always use lacquer because it dries quickly and although not a high-temperature paint, it is quite adequate for engines running at the correct temperature. If you burn off lacquer from anywhere other than around the exhaust ports of the head, then you have trouble because the engine is overheating.

SERVICE MANUALS

Although I have gone into detail on procedures for rebuilding your small-block Chevy, there are many other jobs you may wish to do on your Chevrolet vehicle. Should this be the case, I suggest you acquire a factory-recognized service manual from Helm Inc., P.O. Box 07130, Detroit, MI 48207. Write them for an order blank and prices for the manual/s covering your car.

8
REPLACING THE ENGINE

The 327 CID small block has been the performance enthusiasts' favorite for many years. Its excellent bore/stroke ratio, plus good RPM potential made it the natural choice as the engine for the 1962-67 Corvette.

Putting the engine back is the reverse of pulling it out. When I'm not specific, you should be doing the reverse of what you did for removal. For instance, on smog pump vehicles, it is usually easier to install the smog pump before putting in the engine.

During the first few steps of the installation there are differences between manual and automatic transmissions so work from the appropriate paragraphs. Before installing the engine there are things to do on the transmission.

Manual Transmission—Remove the old throwout bearing from the sleeve of the front bearing retainer. Because your vehicle had done enough miles to need a new engine, chances are it needs a new clutch throwout bearing. A great deal of time is needed to replace one after engine installation, so do it now. Clean the sleeve on which the bearing slides. If the bore of the new throwout bearing has a groove, fill it with moly grease. Smear a thin film of grease on the sleeve and the pilot bearing diameter of the input shaft,

then install the throwout bearing. Check the bearing is free to slide, then remove excess grease from the sleeve so it won't get into the clutch. To ease later engagement of the gearbox spline with the clutch, put the transmission in high gear.

Automatic Transmissions—With the engine out, torque converter weight can cause permanent deformation of the front seal, causing a leak. To replace this seal pull the torque converter from the input shafts and lean it out of the way in its working attitude so the oil inside doesn't spill. Remove and replace the front seal as shown in the photo on page 161. To relocate the unit you have to engage two dogs on the converter shaft and two gearbox input splines. Do this by pushing the converter into place and turn it at at the same time until all three elements have engaged. As each engages the converter will "clonk" back toward the final position an inch behind the bell-housing face.

INSTALLING THE ENGINE

From here, engine installation procedure is similar for manual and

automatic. Start with the engine supported on the hoist and follow the instructions:

1. Tubular headers should be held at the sides of the engine compartment. Cast-iron ones should be installed on the engine. Put a jack under the transmission and remove anything you may have used to support the transmission while you were working on the engine.

2. Lower the engine into the compartment. Avoid catching any pulleys etc., on the cross members. To aid engine installation jack the transmission to the same angle as the engine.

3. With an automatic, rock the engine sideways and push it back to engage the transmission. As they engage, move the engine so the dowels in the block locate in the bell-housing dowel holes, then insert some bolts into accessible bolt holes.

With a manual transmission, mating the gearbox and engine can be more time-consuming than with automatics. Usually the splines on the input shaft and those in the

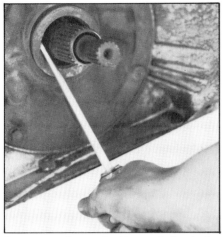

As a precaution against transmission leaks, replace the front seal on an automatic *whether or not it leaked before.* A screwdriver can be used to lever out the old seal. Install the new seal by gently tapping it around the edge so it goes in evenly. Relocate the torque converter after the new seal is installed.

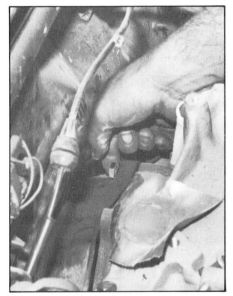

When you have lined up the dowels, screw bolts in the easily accessible top holes to hold the engine and transmission together.

If you have tubular headers, tie them in this position in the engine compartment.

The end bolts in the headers are loosely supporting them as the engine is lowered onto its mounts. The motor-mount bolt on this side goes in from the back.

Lower the engine into the bay. Try not to snag on cross-members and make an attempt to keep the engine at about the same angle as the transmission. This is especially important on manual transmission cars as the transmission input spline will be easier to engage. With a manual transmission you will need a wrench to turn the engine over a small amount to find the position where the splines in the clutch plate and transmission input shaft line up.

clutch disc are misaligned. Position the engine next to the transmission input shaft and try to jiggle it onto the spline. If, after a moment or so you don't succeed, take a wrench and using a bolt on the crank damper, turn the engine a few degrees. Try the spline-engagement operation again. You may have to do this several times before the clutch and gearbox splines are aligned. Once aligned, they will engage and the engine will slide down the spline toward the gearbox. With the trans-

mission on the engine dowels, screw in one or two bolts to hold engine and transmission together.
4. On either transmission, if you have headers, locate them and their gaskets on bolts at each end of the heads so they follow the engine the last few inches into the mounts. Replace the engine mount bolts. Remember the one on the fuel pump side goes in from the back.
5. Remove the engine-lifting chain and reinstall and torque the inlet manifold bolts which held the chain.

Torque to 20 pounds-feet.

6. Jack up the car and support it safely on axle stands. On automatic transmission cars, line up the marks on the converter made at the time of removal with those on the flex plate. You can now put in one of the bolts.

7. Put on the starter motor. This is a lot easier if it is done before putting on the converter shroud or dust shield. Connect the wires as shown in the diagram. The solenoid-energizing wire which is normally purple and is the heavier of the two smaller wires, goes to the S terminal. R will be the remaining small one and the main wire from the battery will be the very heavy cable. It fits the terminal with the large nut. Having done this, on automatic-transmission cars install and connect the battery. Using the starter motor, "inch" the motor

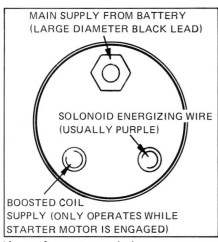

MAIN SUPPLY FROM BATTERY
(LARGE DIAMETER BLACK LEAD)

SOLONOID ENERGIZING WIRE
(USUALLY PURPLE)

BOOSTED COIL
SUPPLY (ONLY OPERATES WHILE
STARTER MOTOR IS ENGAGED)

If you forgot to mark the starter motor wires, this is how they should be rewired.

After you have removed the lifting chain, don't forget to retighten the manifold bolts, otherwise your *manifold* may spring a leak which will take hours to fix. Torque them to 20 pounds-feet.

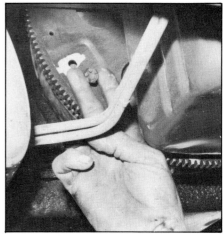

Line up the mark on the converter and flex plate and screw in a bolt.

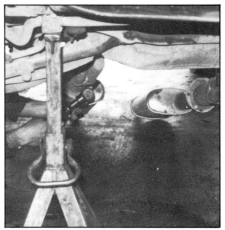

Reinstall the mufflers, then lower the car. Note the sturdy axle stands. Do not rely on a hydraulic floor jack to support an any car you plan to work under!

Before filling the engine with oil, check that the plug in the pan is correctly tightened. You would not be the first to find a gallon of new oil on the floor. Also check that the oil filter is installed.

over a little at a time so you can get successively at each bolt which attaches the transmission converter to the flex plate. Once you have all the transmission bolts in, torque them to 45 pounds-feet, then replace the converter shroud or dust cover.

8. If you are using headers install the remaining header securing bolts and tighten them to 25 pounds-feet. Of course this won't apply if you are using cast-iron manifolds as they will be on the engine already.

9. Install the exhaust system from the exhaust manifold back and lower the car.

10. Reinstall the accessories in the reverse order that you took them off. These will include the power-steering pump, air conditioning and the fan shroud and radiator.

11. If not already done, install the carburetor and connect the fuel lines. I assume you've already reinstalled the fuel pump so it is there to connect to the carburetor. Be sure to use a tubing

wrench on the fuel nuts so you don't wipe off the flats and wreck the nut.

12. Remove the left side rocker cover (as seen from driver's seat). You are now going to time the ignition as described in the previous chapter, so refer back to read how it is done, step by step. I detailed ignition timing while the engine was out because it is easier to show how things are done this way.

13. After installing the distributor and timing the ignition, reinstall the rocker cover and tighten the bolts on both covers to 7 lbs-ft.

14. Check that the drain plug with its nylon washer is tightly installed in the oil pan. Fill the engine with oil to the

prescribed level on the dipstick, including a pint of General Motors Engine Oil Supplement (E.O.S.) in this initial fill.

15. Reconnect water hoses and tubes.

16. Install the PCV valve after you have checked to see that it works. Blow through from the end that sticks out of the rocker cover and it should close. Blow through the other way and it should pass air. Install the coil in its correct position on the manifold and attach the two small wires. Don't connect the wire from the distributor cap to the high-voltage outlet of the coil. With the HEI system, do not connect the plug carrying the wires between the distributor body and the cap.

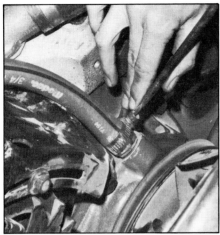
Before reconnecting hoses, make sure they are OK for further service. Nothing will ruin a new engine faster than a split hose which dumps all the water and leads to a severe overheating problem.

If the PCV valve is not working properly, you won't get a good idle so check its functioning as described in the text.

Anti-freeze serves a number of purposes. It inhibits corrosion and raises the boiling point of the coolant, helping to prevent boiling in summer. It also lowers the freezing point for protection against freezing blocks in winter.

Buy a new filter element. Don't run with an old one as this will cut power. If you are looking for the Rolls Royce of filter elements a KLN element is highly efficient and durable.

17. If your car has an automatic transmission, connect the transmission lines to the cooler in the bottom of the radiator. If you forget to do this before you start the engine, you'll have automatic-transmission fluid all over the floor very quickly.

18. Fill the radiator with a mixture of water and anti-freeze. Even if you live in a hot climate, you should still use anti-freeze because most anti-freeze contains a corrosion inhibitor to stop your radiator fouling up so quickly, thus preventing over-heating. Make sure that you have installed the oil-pressure switch, or pressure-gauge connection just behind the distributor. If you haven't, you will have a large quantity of oil all over the back of your engine if you try cranking it. If the oil filter was not installed at an earlier stage, fill it with oil and install it now. With the spark plugs out, crank the engine over to get oil pressure. **DO NOT START IT UNTIL YOU SEE OIL PRESSURE** or the oil-pressure "idiot light" goes out to indicate that there is pressure. The next step is to screw in the spark plugs, torquing them to 20 pounds-feet. If you haven't already done so, install the distributor cap and connect the plug wires, routing them through the wire holders as you did before installing the engine. Again check to see where each of them goes. If you have an HEI, plug the wires from the distributor body into the distributor cap and insert the supply plug from the wiring harness into the socket in the distributor body.

19. Check to see that the choke butterfly is closed. Try to start the engine. If you start with a bone-dry carburetor and the oil pressure came up quickly when you cranked the engine over, the float bowl in the carburetor may not be full due to insufficient cranking. To overcome this, prime the engine by squirting a couple of shots of fuel down the carburetor barrels with a squirt-type oil can. Don't overdo it or flooding will result. If you have followed the ignition-timing sequence exactly and have correct gap at the points (if you are using a points-type distributor), then the engine should fire up almost immediately.

If you have hydraulic lifters, there will be a lot of valve noise until the lifters "pump up" hydraulically to adjust the clearance. This should happen in one or two minutes. If the engine hasn't become quiet after a couple of minutes running, find out which rockers are noisy and readjust them as detailed earlier.

After the engine has warmed up and run awhile, check for oil and water leaks. Once you are sure everything is as it should be, install the air-cleaner base on the carburetor, add a new air-filter element and the lid. Next, with a helper, install the hood in the reverse manner of its removal.

20. As a final thing, before you go out on the road, check again for water leaks and make a final check on the oil level. All that now remains is for the car engine to be broken in correctly and, so that you may get the best from it, to have all its settings done correctly. I will detail this in the next chapter.

9
BREAKING IN

Here is a 1970 350-CID 300-HP small block. Evident in this view is the layout of plug cables with this style of exhaust manifold.

BREAKING-IN

Once you have rebuilt your small-block Chevy and reinstalled it in the car, then comes the job of "breaking-in" the engine. This is straightforward enough: all you really need to do is drive *gently* for 500 miles. Don't assume your oil level is going to stay constant for the first 500 miles. Depending on the type of rings you have, your engine may use some. Keep that oil level on the FULL mark. After 500 miles, change both oil and filter and retorque the head bolts. Because you have gone 500 miles this does not mean you can floor the accelerator pedal and forget how new your engine is. For the next 2000 miles do not deliberately use a lot of output from the engine. After about 2000 miles, change the oil and filter again and you can now treat the engine as fully broken-in. Care during the break-in will definitely extend the life of your engine. I promise you that!

EMISSION STANDARDS

These days we are very conscious of the fact that we are polluting our atmosphere, and emission from cars is a major contribution to this pollution. If we look at the pollution caused by motor vehicles, we find that the biggest offenders are cars whose ignition and carburetion are either not functioning correctly or are out of adjustment. With emission requirements becoming so rigorous, it is getting to the stage where an individual cannot really be expected to set his engine up to get the car to meet emission standards.

REDUCING EMISSIONS & INCREASING PERFORMANCE

Setting up or tuning to meet standards requires sophisticated equipment and usually the cost of getting a professional tune-up is at least recouped in the saving on fuel. A typical tune-up varies between $25 and $50, depending on the amount of work required. If you have rebuilt your engine properly, the amount of setting should be minimal.

You are doing all these things to make the best use of your fuel, to get the best performance and to reduce emissions.

Let's look at a typical tune-up procedure. Here's a situation where

the car should be tuned in one of two ways. First of all, if the car has been built exactly to manufacturer's specifications, a tune-up can be done with just an electronic engine analyzer.

Chassis Dynamometer–Another way of doing things requires using a chassis dynamometer. Here the car is driven just as it would be on the road and the various electrical connections to the engine measure the output of the ignition system to see that the spark is being correctly delivered to the cylinders. For instance, it checks whether voltage is high enough to spark the plugs, whether or not a misfire is occurring, whether the timing is right throughout the rev range, etc. The exhaust is also analyzed to see if the mixture is correct and that the emissions are not excessive and so on. Various corrections can be made if and when a problem is discovered. With this type of equipment you can expect the best results in performance, economy and the meeting of emission standards.

If you have made subtle changes

Although many shops still don't have one, a device of increasing importance is the chassis dynamometer. This allows the car to be "driven" in the shop and also allows measurement of rear-wheel horsepower.

Some chassis dynos have a built-in inertia simulator which allows the operator to get a good idea of the car's acceleration and test driveability during the acceleration phase.

While the driving modes are being gone through on the chassis dyno, equipment like this tells the operator about the emission situation.

to the engine, put in a different camshaft or replaced one type of carburetor with another or a different exhaust system or whatever, then the chassis dynamometer is definitely the way to tune the combination. Only with the aid of proper equipment will you derive the maximum pleasure from driving your newly rebuilt small-block Chevy.

To keep pace with today's complex tuneup requirements, the tuneup shop must use very expensive electronic and mechanical equipment.

Power at the rear wheels plus the road speed, is read out on a dial like this. The more horsepower you have, the better your car will perform.

Electronic engine analyzer investigates and fault-finds various engine functions.

INDEX

A

Alternator 26
  removal 26
  installation 162
Altitude 4, 6
Air conditioning 5, 20, 26
  removal 26
  installation 162
Anti-freeze 163
Automatic choke 155-157, 163
  adjustments 155-157
  bi-metal strip 154, 155
  heat stove 154, 155
Automatic transmission 28, 30, 32, 160

B

Barometric pressure 4
Battery 4, 5, 25, 162
Bearings
  camshaft 39, 40, 48, 78
  main 88, 94
  rod journal 102, 104
  thrust 90, 92, 94
  water pump 152
Block 12, 45, 76, 80, 85, 88
  bearings 79, 88, 94
  boring 12
  disassembly 35
  cleaning 39, 88
  counterweight clearance 13
  decking 54
  identification 14, 15
  reliability 14
  welding 45
Bore
  brush hone 54
  chamfering 55
  diameter 13
  to piston clearance 48, 49
  wear limits 48
  wear measurements 46, 47, 48
Bronze valve guide liner 65, 66
Breaking in 164

C

Camshaft 39, 62
  bearings 39, 40, 48, 78-82
  bearing modification 80
  bearing chart 81
  early 12
  installation 104-106
  lash 127-128
  lift 8
  lubrication 12, 13
  plug 83
  removal 39
  timing 104-106
  types, mechanical 127, 128
  wear 7, 8, 62
  wear measurement 8
CID 12
Carburetor 153-157, 162
Compression
  gauge 3, 6
  high 4, 6
  pressures 4
  ratio 4, 17, 19, 20
  test 4
  wet test 6
Connecting rods 16, 17, 95-99
  aligning 56
  bearings 56, 102, 104
  bolts 56, 104
  bolt sleeves 35, 101-103
  cap facing 57
  crack testing 57
  crush 58
  distortion 55, 56
  faults 55, 56

length 17
  overhauling 56, 57
  rebuilt 57, 58
  resizing 56
  spit holes 17
  types 17
Coil 25, 149, 150, 154
Contact breaker points 137, 142, 143
Crankshaft 15
  bearings 59, 60, 88-94
  cast 15, 16
  damper 31, 62, 111
  forged 15, 16
  grinding machine 60
  identification 15, 16
  installation 90-94
  kits 60
  large journal 16
  pilot bearing 118
  regrind limits 61
  removing 39
  replacement 60
  stroke 13, 14
  wear 9, 10, 59
  wear limits 60, 61
  small journal 15
  stiffness 94
Combustion chamber 18
  shape 18, 20
  volume 18
Cylinder heads 18, 43,
  accessory mounting 20
  assembly 119-121
  cracking 17
  bolts 5, 119, 123, 124
  identification 18, 21
  installing 122
  removing 33
  types 18, 19
  stud removal 70, 71
  valve seat cutting 69
  warped 69

D

Damper 31, 61
  installation 111-114
  removal 31
  repair 62
  sizes 113, 116
Detonation 33, 56
Decarbonizing 5
Dial caliper 8
Dial gauge 8
Distributor 9, 27, 28, 29, 136
  advance stops 139
  condenser 137, 142
  ground lead 137, 138
  installation 146-148
  mechanical advance/retard 137-141
  overhaul 136-145
  removing 32
  shaft & drive gear 142, 143
  vacuum advance/retard 137-141
  base plate 141
  cap 144, 145
  rotor cap 136, 144, 147
Dowels
  engine to transmission 160
  cylinder head to block 122
  oil pump to block 106
Dynamometer, chassis 164, 165

E

Economy 7, 164-166
Electronic engine analyzer 164-166
Electronic ignition 136
Emission control equipment 24, 153, 157, 164
Engine
  assembly 76-159
  identification 14

installation 160-163
  removal 24
End thrust bearing clearance 92
EOS 74, 126, 162
Exhaust
  crossover 35
  gaskets 157
  gas recirculation (EGR) 153
  manifold 28, 157
  system 28, 162

F

Fan 25, 26
Feeler gauges 33, 37, 49
Filter
  air 163
  oil 115, 162
Flywheel 29, 157
  installation 157
  removing 29
Freeze plugs 14, 15
  installation 83-85
  removal 41
  kit 78
Fuel
  lines 27, 162
  pump 27, 117, 118
  pump pushrod 116

G

Gasket
  set 88
  head 19, 69, 122
  intake 133, 134, 135
  pan 109, 110
  rocker cover 130, 131
  timing cover 109, 110
Guide, see valve guide

H

Head gasket 19, 69
  blown 45, 54
  installation 122
  types 69
Headers 160-162
Heat shield 32-34
HEI Ignition 25, 28, 136, 144, 146-149, 162
Hoist 22, 30, 160
Honing
  block 52
  machine 53
  rods 58
Hood 25, 162
Hot tank 39, 40, 43

I

Ignition
  coil 154, 162
  leads 150-152
  timing 113, 130, 147-151, 162
  timing tag 110, 115, 163
Inserts, bearing, see bearings
Inserts, guide 64-68
Inside micrometer 46

J

Journals
  camshaft 13, 82
  connecting rod 56
  main bearing 56, 60, 88-94

K

Keys 90, 91
Knocking 8
  engine noise 9
  symptoms 8
Knurling
  pistons 52
  valve guide 64

tool 65, 68
    effects of 52, 64

L

Leakdown
    test 7
    machine 7
Lifters 39, 49, 62, 116
    hydraulic 63, 127
    mechanical 63, 127-128
    wear 63
    installation 116, 117

M

Machinist 22
Main
    bearings 9, 14, 77, 88-94
    bearing end float 92
    caps 77, 92, 94
    journals 56, 60, 88-94
Manifolds 21, 28, 131-135, 157
    exhaust 28, 157
    four-barrel 155
    gasket 133-135, 157
    heat shield 32, 33
    intake 21, 30, 32, 131, 132
Manual transmission 29, 32, 160, 161
Micrometer 22, 23, 46
Mufflers
    installation 162
    removal 28

N

Nuts, rod bolt 104

O

Oil
    additives 3
    burning 3, 4, 65
    filter 115, 162
    flow diagram 108
    level on early pans 107
    pressure 9, 152, 163
    pressure release valve 115
    pressure sender 152
    pump 63, 64, 106
    pump driveshaft sleeve 107
    pickup pipe 107, 109
    seal, rear main 13, 92, 93
    seal, front cover 108, 109
    seal, valve 35, 119
    early 115
    Chevy II 15, 114
Oil gallery
    plugs 40-42, 76-78
    cleaning 76-78
Overheating 38, 163

P

Pan 107-111
    gasket 109, 110
    installation 108-111
PCV valve 130-134, 157, 162
Performance 3, 7, 164
Pickup pipe 107, 109
Pistons
    assembly 95-99
    cleaning 51
    clearance 48
    collapse 38, 51

compression 4, 17, 20
compression height 17
    domed 20, 97, 103
    installation in engine 101
    installation on rods 96
    overheating 38
    removal from engine 36
    removal from rods 55, 56
    reringing 51
    ring groove cleaning tool 50, 51
    wear pattern 37, 56
Powerglide 118
Power steering 26
Pulley, installation 114
Pushrod 75, 126
    ends 75
    guide plate 126
    straightness 75
Pump, see fuel, oil or water pump

R

Radiator
    removal 26
    installation 162
Rear main oil seal 13, 92, 93
Reboring 51
Reamer
    valve guide 67, 69
    tapered 78
Ridge reaming 37, 46, 52, 53
Rings 6
    belt 49
    broken 38, 51, 52
    compressor 99-101
    expander 99, 102
    gaps 51, 98, 100
    installing 99-101
    oil control 99
    second 99, 101
    top 99, 100
    types 99
    wear 49-52
Ring grooves
    checking 50
    cleaning 51, 52
    clearance 50
Rocker arm 32-35, 75, 126
    adjustments 127-129
    ball pivot 75
    replacement 70
    studs 70-72, 75, 126
    covers 129-131, 162

S

Seals
    front cover 108, 109
    intake manifold 132
    rope 92
    rear main bearing 13, 92, 93
    pan 109, 110
    valve stem 119-121
    water pump 152, 153
Shaft
    distributor/oil pump 106, 107
Snap gauge 46
Spark plug 163
    cables 150
    cable clips 150-152
    cable routing 150
    firing order 150
    fouling 4, 65

Sprocket 37, 104, 105
Starter motor 4, 161, 162
    wiring diagram 162
    installing 161
    removing 29, 30
Stroke, see crankshaft stroke

T

Thermostat 5, 15
    housing 153
    testing 154
    installing 153
Timing chains 104
Timing gears 37, 61, 104
    nylon 37, 61
    steel 61
    truck 61, 62, 105
Tools
    cam bearing driver 40
    crank damper removal 31
    heat shield rivet removal 33, 34
    basic requirements 22, 23
Torch LPG 97, 111
Torque
    converter 28, 161
    wrench setting 76-162
Tune-up 10, 11, 164-166
Turboglide 118

V

Vacuum
    advance/retard 136-141
    brake takeoff 156
    can diaphragm testing 140
    manifold 132-135
    ported 157
Valve
    exhaust 35, 36, 73
    guide 35, 65-68
    guide oil seals 35, 119-121
    installation 119-121
    intake 35, 36, 73
    margin 35
    leakage 6
    oversize stem 71
    reconditioning 73
    removal 35, 119
    seats, angle cut 69, 70
    seat, dial gauge 70
    seat grinding 69, 70, 73
    seats, induction hardened 19
    springs 74, 119-121
    spring compressor 11, 22, 23, 36
    spring keepers 119-121
    spring inserts 74, 120
    spring retainers 119-121
    spring testing 74
    wear 35

W

Water pump 9, 152, 153
Wrist pin 16, 51, 96, 97
    installing 96
    wear limit 51
Wiring
    coil 25, 149, 150
    HEI 25, 28, 136, 144, 146, 149, 162
    plugs 150
    distributor 137, 138, 150

Notes

Notes

Notes

Notes

Notes

Notes

Notes

Notes

OTHER BOOKS OF INTEREST

1,001 High Performance Tech Tips by Wayne Scraba   1-55788-199-5/$16.95

Auto Math Handbook by John Lawlor   1-55788-020-4/$16.95

Automotive Electrical Handbook by Jim Horner   0-89586-238-7/$16.95

Automotive Paint Handbook by Jim Pfanstiehl   1-55788-034-4/$16.95

Brake Handbook by Fred Puhn   0-89586-232-8/$16.95

Camaro Performance Handbook by David Shelby   1-55788-057-3/$16.95

Camaro Restoration Handbook
by Tom Currao and Ron Sessions   0-89586-375-8/$16.95

Chevrolet Power edited by Rich Voegelin   1-55788-087-5/$19.95

Classic Car Restorer's Handbook by Jim Richardson   1-55788-194-4/$16.95

Holley Carburetors, Manifolds and Fuel Injection (Revised Edition)
by Bill Fisher and Mike Urich   1-55788-052-2/$17.00

How to Make Your Car Handle by Fred Puhn   0-912-65646-8/$16.95

Metal Fabricator's Handbook by Ron Fournier   0-89586-870-9/$16.95

Mustang Performance Handbook by William R. Mathis   1-55788-193-6/$16.95

Mustang Performance Handbook 2 by William R. Mathis   1-55788-202-9/$16.95

Mustang Restoration Handbook by Don Taylor   0-89586-402-9/$16.95

Mustang Weekend Projects 1964½–1967
by Jerry Heasley   1-55788-230-4/$17.00

Paint & Body Handbook (Revised Edition)
by Don Taylor and Larry Hofer   1-55788-082-4/$16.95

Race Car Engineering & Mechanics
by Paul Van Valkenburgh   1-55788-064-6/$16.95

Sheet Metal Handbook by Ron and Sue Fournier   0-89586-757-5/$16.95

Street Rodder's Handbook by Frank Oddo   0-89586-369-3/$16.95

Turbo Hydra-matic 350 by Ron Sessions   0-89586-051-1/$16.95

Turbochargers by Hugh MacInnes   0-89586-135-6/$16.95

Welder's Handbook (Revised Edition)
by Richard Finch   1-55788-264-9/$16.95

Mustang 5.0 Projects by Mark Houlahan   1-55788-275-4/$16.95

The Car Builder's Handbook by Doug McCleary   1-55788-278-9/$16.95

TO ORDER CALL: 1-800-788-6262, ext. 1, Refer to Ad #583b

HPBooks
A member of Penguin Putnam Inc.
200 Madison Avenue
New York, NY 10016

*Prices subject to change